Praise for CHILDREN OF THE JINN

"...half romance, half horror story-- very illuminating, intensely readable...." **Jonathan Raban, author of ARABIA: A JOURNEY THROUGH THE LABYRINTH and many other books**

"What a pleasure to see a new edition of this beautiful book. Margaret Kahn's lyrical portrayal of a multi-ethnic and dynamic Iranian society is unforgettable. Her characters: Persians, Assyrians, Azeri Turks, Northern and Southern Kurds, are beautifully drawn. Her vivid portraits, drawn forty years ago, are as fresh and alive today as they were when first written"

--John Limbert, Former Deputy Assistant Secretary of State for Iran in the State Department's Bureau of Iranian Affairs. Former official at the U.S. Embassy in Tehran, where he was held captive during the Iran hostage crisis

"As a Peace Corps Volunteer who taught English in the girls' high school of Mahabad, a main Kurdish city of northwest Iran, I find her escapades gripping and uncomfortably familiar. Especially recommended for cross-cultural communication, social/cultural anthropology, and international business classes."

--Mary Elaine Hegland, Department of Anthropology, Santa Clara University

"[Kahn] describes her efforts to learn of Kurdish life with sensitivity and humor, within the framework of a more general discussion of human communication between two very different cultures. She expresses concern for the fate of Kurdish nationalism and ethnic identity under the Shah's police state, and under today's revolutionary government as well, but writes most memorably of her personal contacts with the Kurds and her explorations of village and family life. This book is primarily for the general reader interested in exotic places, but deserves to be read seriously also by those interested in understanding diverse cultures and those who wonder about American foreign policy responsibilities in little

known areas." **Elizabeth R. Hayford reviewing for LIBRARY JOURNAL**

"In this absorbing book a young American describes with passion and humor, her search for Kurdistan in the Iran of the Shah and his secret police and her success in gaining the friendship of a number of Kurds and learning their language. Here are vivid portraits of sex-obsessed Turks and Iranians, as well as of ferocious but hospitable Kurds, of feudal chieftains, unveiled, brilliantly dressed women poverty-stricken villagers, harems, wedding customs and the fierce desire of a remarkable people to live, as Kurds, with their own culture, and to have that culture respected." **PUBLISHERS WEEKLY**

"No one has written as graphically or as poignantly of the real tragedy of Iran. Reading "Children of the Jinn" it becomes very easy to see why the country made its break with the paranoid totalitarianism of the Shah only to replace it with the paranoid totalitarianism of the Ayatollah. Margaret Kahn makes one feel the desperate personal and political climate of the place on one's own nerve-ends. She has written a compelling and distressing book." Jonathan Raban **THE SUNDAY LONDON TIMES Book Review Section 15, March 1981**

"...a riveting book about cultural conflict. When at last the doorway to Kurdistan opens for her it also opens delightfully for the reader." **Harriet Waugh writing for SPECTATOR named it as one of her two favorite books of the year 1981.**

"Ms. Kahn's affection for her Kurdish friends and her sympathy for the sturdy but ill-fated Kurdish people stand out in her book. We must be grateful for the introduction she has afforded us." **John S. Kennedy in THE CATHOLIC TRANSCRIPT 1980**

[Margaret Kahn is] "one of few Americans to meet the Kurds on their own terms." **from the preface to THE SECOND SALADIN by Stephen Hunter**

CHILDREN OF THE JINN

CHILDREN OF THE JINN

THE STORY OF MY SEARCH FOR THE KURDS AND THEIR COUNTRY

MARGARET KAHN

Pearlnote Press
Pacific Grove, California

First Edition by Seaview Books Copyright ©1980, Margaret Kahn
Second Edition by Pearlnote Press Copyright ©2020, Margaret Kahn

COVER & PHOTOS © 2020, Margaret Kahn

All Rights Reserved. No part of this book may be reproduced, stored in a retrieval system, or transmitted in any form by an electronic, mechanical, photocopying, recording means or otherwise, or adapted for other media, without prior permission of the author.

ISBN-978-0-578-81188-8

A Note to the 21ˢᵗ Century Reader

When I went to Iran, Kurds were virtually unknown to the American public. I was constantly explaining who they were. Field linguists who happened to be women were not unknown but far less common than they are today. My dissertation committee of all-male faculty members demanded to know how my husband was going to occupy himself while I did fieldwork --something they would never have asked a man.

The internet which is now ubiquitous and filled with detailed information and misinformation about the remotest places on earth did not exist in 1974. Nor did cell phones. Even old-fashioned telephone lines were stretched to their limits when it came to a place like northwest Iran. I made two calls to America during the entire year and the connection was not good.

When I first arrived in Iran in 1974, the last shah who had been put in place by American interests, still ruled. By the time I went back in 1978, the regime was already crumbling. In the beginning there were high hopes for serious change, but those soon faded. The Kurds rose up to assert their rights and were soon crushed.

Just over the border in Iraq, during my stay, the Kurds had fought a revolution egged on by the United States. They were also defeated. As a result Saddam Hussein was emboldened to launch his genocidal Anfal campaign. Chemical weapons rained down on Halabja in 1988. Then came the Gulf War in 1990 when a photograph of Kurds fleeing Saddam's wrath hit the cover of *Time* magazine. Finally Americans seemed to know who the Kurds were. They learned still more about the Kurds when in 2019 after assisting the United States Kurds were again betrayed in an eerie and even more cynical reprise of what I saw in 1975.

In Tehran at that time there were two institutes for scholars, one run by the Americans and one by the British. During my time in Iran, I stayed at both. There I tried to glean any further knowledge about the country where I had come to work and do research. The scholars I met were often quite unforthcoming or spoke in veiled negative terms about their experiences.

When I sat down to write my book, I was determined to write the truth as I had experienced it. That meant being honest about the misunderstandings I encountered and the mistakes I made, something many male scholars I met wouldn't have felt comfortable with. Above all they were conscious of their roles as cultural authorities. I felt I was following more in the footsteps of those explorers of an earlier era – the ones eager to escape their own cultures and to learn more about other ways of doing things.

An attitude of openness is not always easy to maintain and I'm sure there are many ways I failed. But in this account, first published 40 years ago, I tried to render the truth as I saw it at the time. Forty years later I have also resisted the urge to gloss over any of it, no matter how gauche or ignorant it may make me look. Instead I ask the modern reader to put herself or himself or themselves in my shoes, set down without much cultural preparation in a land where you could not find out much of anything in advance. For the modern day reader who might want to understand the roots of our current troubles in the Middle East (and they are legion) reading about what happened to a young scholar who stumbled into the results of an American intervention gone wrong may prove instructive.

My hope then as now is for the stories of my adventures to help to introduce you to the extraordinary group of people I was fortunate enough to meet. Except for a more careful editing of the prose and the addition of more pictures, I have left my account pretty much intact.

Margaret Kahn

2020 Monterey, CA

KURDISTAN—THE MYTH VS. THE REALITY

Centuries ago, Solomon supposedly threw 500 of the magical spirits called jinn out of his kingdom and exiled them to the mountains of the Zagros. These jinn first flew to Europe to select 500 beautiful virgins as their brides and then went to settle in what became known as Kurdistan. This is just one of the myths which tries to explain how such a fair-skinned, light-haired people known for their unlikely combination of ferocity and hospitality came to be living in the mountains that lie astride the borders separating present-day Iran, Iraq, Turkey, and the USSR. Their language is similar to Persian and distantly related to English as well as to the majority of the tongues of Europe. Kurds, shut away in their mountains, did not intermarry with Arabs and Turks as much as Persians did. Maybe that is why some Kurds look Irish or even Swedish. Or perhaps it is the genes of those long-ago European virgins carried off by the jinn.

I went in search of Kurds because, to me, they represented adventure far from home and a righteous cause to believe in. I had an airplane ticket and a job waiting for me in Iran. But Kurdistan, not Iran, was my destination. There were no maps, except those drawn by the Kurds and their friends, that read *Kurdistan*, Land of the Kurds. There were no signs which pointed the way, no tourist bureau and no guides. There were secret police who would quickly and forcefully point you in the opposite direction. But Kurdistan is a real place. It has its boundaries and its cities; it has its language. To find it takes time and searching, like other magical principalities in the mists of mountains, Kurdistan has a way of appearing and disappearing, opening up to an outsider and then, disconcertingly shutting itself in her face.

Many Americans and Iranians have found it difficult to understand why I decided to study Kurdish. There was no money in it, no job teaching the language or literature the way there might have been for French or Arabic. In fact, there has not been much Kurdish literature written. To many Iranians, Turks, and Arabs, Kurdish is not even a real language, but just a rustic dialect spoken by illiterates, beneath the dignity of anyone who would call herself a real scholar.

The Kurds themselves never had any difficulty in understanding my choice of their language. To a people fighting for their lives and control of their land, their own language is a very precious thing. Not all Kurds are fair with European features; some look like Arabs. Not all Kurds wear their traditional trousers or many-colored dresses; some work in the city and attend universities in Western clothes. But until now, nearly all Kurds, educated or uneducated, fair or dark, living in Turkey or Iran or Iraq or the USSR, have spoken Kurdish. Only in the last few decades of modernization have the three governments succeeded in eroding this last and most important sign of Kurdish identity.

Kurdish clothing, jewelry, and handicrafts will come into style in Iran the way American Indian culture came into style in America, when the exotic tribal people are no longer a threat to the dominant culture. The sooner that happens, the more comfortable Iranians will be about people who want to study Kurdish. But I didn't want to wait until that time. It was my hope that somehow that time will never come.

Long before the shahs of Persia came to sit on their peacock throne or build the Ozymandias columns of Persepolis, the Kurds were settled in their mountains. Long before Mohammed was born, Kurds embraced the Zoroastrian faith, recognizing both good and evil gods, building fire temples, celebrating the rites of Newroz, the New Day, on the vernal equinox. When the Arabs came, most of the Kurds, like most of the Middle East, bowed to Islam. The Kurds gave Islam one of its greatest defenders, Saladin (Salah ed-Din Ayyubi), who battled Richard the Lion-Hearted and the Crusaders to regain Jerusalem in 1187. True to the times that he lived in, Saladin fought for the Muslims against the Crusaders, not for the Kurds against the Arabs.

Times changed again and, in the context of the great Islamic empires, the Kurds sought their own identity. Saladin had been theirs, but he had gained them little. Now they wanted relief from the onerous taxation of the Ottomans and recognition of their culture and language before they were overpowered by the ubiquitous Arabic. But only visionaries like the great Kurdish poet Ahmedi Khani asked for these things in those early days. Most Kurdish leaders were holed up in their mountains, like the old Scottish lairds, fighting their Kurdish enemies, looking only to the battle and this year's tribal victory, missing entirely the question of Kurdish unity.

Now, like their jinni ancestors, Kurds have been trapped – not in a bottle, but in their mountains. They have been excluded from many of the advantages of the twentieth century, remaining poor shepherds and farmers, grazing and working a difficult land with the methods and tools of their forefathers. No government has seen fit to improve their lot. Like Solomon with his jinn, these governments are afraid of the Kurds, afraid of what they would do with a fair share of the proceeds from the oil that lies under Kurdistan, afraid of what they would demand if they knew how to read and write and were free to speak their own language and assert their right to be Kurds. Kurds already occupy some of the most inhospitable, inaccessible terrain in the area, but the Iraqis have managed to banish them one step further: to the burning deserts in the south. Iran and Turkey have relied on psychological methods to control the Kurds, and in these countries as well, the Kurds are in constant danger of being banished--not to the mountains this time, but to being non-Kurds, stripped of their language and even of their own clothes.

In the last three decades, the Kurds have been courted and jilted by the British, the Russians, and the Americans. They have allowed themselves to be played as pawns in the great Middle East chess game in the hope of gaining autonomy as Kurds. Each great power promised them freedom when the job was finished. Each time, although they fought bravely and honorably, the Kurds have been abandoned in their struggle. No country, no matter what it promised the Kurds at the moment it decided to use them, has allowed the Kurds to fight for themselves and their dream of their own nation. In the last quarter of the twentieth century, with American and Soviet acceptance of the regimes in Tehran, Baghdad, and Ankara, there was little interest in the Kurds and their claims.

The struggle for Kurdish self-determination keeps shifting-from Turkey in the early twentieth century to Iraq in the 1930s and '40s, to Iran in 1946, again to Iraq through 1975, and now, finally, back to Iran. The Kurds residing in these three countries as well as Syria and the USSR outnumber the combined populations of Denmark, Norway, and Sweden. Yet, because of their history and their tribal divisions, the Kurds have never secured their rights. Each time, just when there seemed to be no hope left, the Kurds have risen, again and again. Each government holds the Kurds in a death grip, but when that grip weakens, even a little, the Kurds are ready to fight. As the Kurds say, *"Kurdistan ya naman"*-Kurdistan or death.

What follows is the story of my search for Kurdistan in Iran of the 1970s, Iran of the shah and his secret police. When I returned for another visit in 1978, Kurdistan was more visible, partly because I knew where to look for it, partly because the shah's power was weakening. Now the shah has toppled and no one knows exactly what will happen in Iran, especially in that unruly northwest corner which is Kurdistan. Again, as so many times in the past, Kurds are fighting for recognition and for their lives.

Table of Contents

A Note to the 21st Century Reader..i
KURDISTAN—THE MYTH VS. THE REALITY.........................iii
TWO VERY DIFFERENT ARRIVALS.......................................1
NEIGHBORLY EXPECTATIONS...16
MAHABAD VS. SAUJ BULAQ..28
RADIO REZAIYEH..40
A LESSON IN TA'AROF..58
AMEER..77
A CONFUSION OF WOMEN..94
A SELF-POSSESSED 15 YEAR OLD.....................................107
AISHA AND THE DOCTOR..123
KURDS FROM IRAQ..143
THE KURDISTAN OF TURKEY...156
A CHARISMATIC SHEIKH...175
PICNIC FOLLIES OR "KEYFA TE".......................................187
THE HEART-WARMING HOSPITALITY OF HAJI ISMAIL..............200
A TALE OF TWO VILLAGES...212
A WOMAN-RUN HOUSEHOLD...226
JOURNEY TO THE SOURCE AND FINALLY A WEDDING.............237
AN INLAND SEA..253
SER CHAVA..274
KURDISTAN REVISITED...284
The Story Continues..292
Glossary...294
Suggested Further Reading...297
Acknowledgements...298

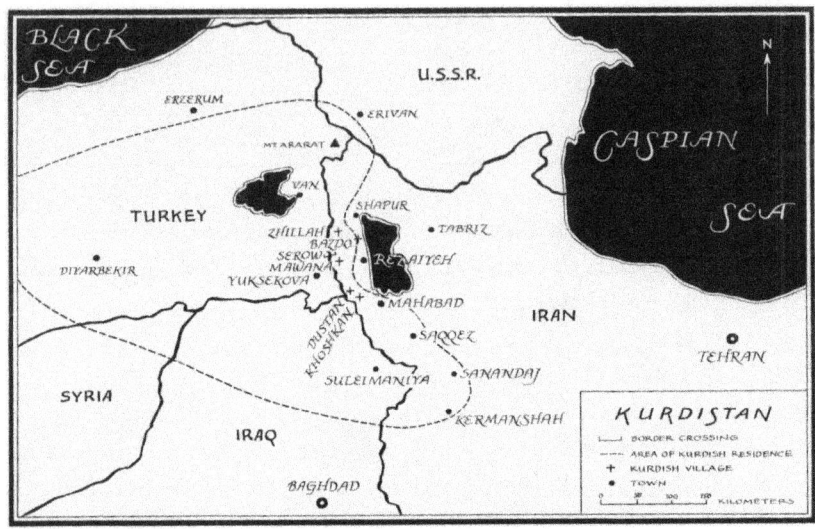

PART ONE

OUTSIDE KURDISTAN

CHAPTER 1

TWO VERY DIFFERENT ARRIVALS

In Iran a woman's clothes, especially her outer clothes, are her refuge, her shelter, a construction that tells the world she is not actually there but safe at home where she belongs. The word for veil in Persian is *chador*, literally a tent, and the difference between being without and with a chador can mean the difference between being molested and being ignored by men on the street. A woman who is shrouded in her chador and is molested anyway has a right to be outraged. She has assumed the appearance of virtue, and in Iran appearances can be far more important than what lies beneath them.

When I first arrived in Tehran airport I was instantly surrounded by a bevy of black-tented ladies, whispering to each other and staring at me, eager for the opportunity to scrutinize a relatively naked foreign woman. Taking a cue from their behavior, I stared back, and was surprised to see the quantities of makeup on their exposed faces and the glimpses of flesh revealed by the constant readjusting necessary to keep a slippery chador around one's body.

Although more and more modern Iranian women are throwing aside their chadors, going to work or school and walking uncovered, albeit uneasily, in the streets, the chador has been the traditional covering of Persian women for centuries. Only many hundreds of miles away to the northwest of Tehran did I find a large group of women who have never worn the chador, women to whom the word still means a tent—a heavy piece of black homespun wool which they must lug up the side of the mountain when the tribe moves to summer quarters. Ironically, these women wear far more modest clothing than the dress that many modern Persian women have on beneath their chadors.

A Kurdish woman's clothes are, by Western standards, something of a fortress—layer upon layer with heavy pantaloons, a slip, several dresses, outer coats, a vest, and one or two scarves. Even on hot summer days Iran always makes me feel exposed. On my second visit, sitting in a bus terminal in Tehran I was sweating in a long-sleeved black turtleneck under a heavy cotton dress. Since the dress came only to my knees I wore long pants underneath. A large scarf hid most of my hair. But people were still staring at me. It is easy in the United States to sneer at the idea of the veil, to say that it might be all right for uninformed women coerced by husbands and fathers into feeling shame. But once you are in Iran enduring the stares, you begin to long for a veil, for anything to make other people's eyes pass over you, for the camouflage to enable you to stare with impunity and not be stared at in return.

As my husband, Jared, and I sat, waiting for our bus to be announced, we saw a Kurdish man walk up to the counter across the room. If he had been an Iranian Turk, an Armenian, an Assyrian, a Jew, or an Arab, we might not have been able to guess his heritage, at least not until he opened his mouth and spoke a distinctive language.

Kurds are another story. They are one of the few remaining national groups who wear their traditional dress. With a mother tongue close to Persian, Kurds are capable of blending in much better than the Turks, who are ridiculed for their accented Persian. But many Kurds do not particularly care to blend in. Jared and I stared in silent appreciation as this Kurdish man strode away from the counter, conspicuous in his baggy blue serge trousers, fitted matching jacket, and turban wound around an embroidered skullcap.

We were a little disappointed when we boarded our bus. There were no Kurds. With a long uncomfortable night ahead of us and the other passengers' eyes directed out the windows, I was free to drift back into my apprehensions. For two years I had dreamed of returning to Kurdistan. Yet when the time came and I found myself conveniently in the Middle East, I hesitated. What about the riots that had been breaking out all over the country since late winter? What about the hatred I had heard Iranians express for the American presence in their country? With all of Iran's incipient violence for an excuse I didn't need to look into any more personal reasons for being afraid. Once the bus began climbing up into the hills, old memories and doubts came crowding into my mind.

Four years earlier I had dragged a somewhat unwilling husband of six months to a small city called Rezaiyeh close to the frontier where Iran meets Iraq and Turkey. Fifteen million people living in and around the mountains of that frontier all speak one dialect or another of Kurdish. I went to study their language, but I told the Iranian government I had come to teach English at a local college. Foreigners have never been encouraged to spend time with volatile minorities like the Kurds, and at the time of my stay another war in a long series of wars had broken out just over the Iraqi border. Certainly it would have been much easier to have studied a more accessible language like Spanish or Arabic or even Chinese—languages that do not require subterfuges to reach the people who speak them.

I looked out the bus window at the dusk falling over the bleak Iranian landscape, green grass broken only occasionally by a wind-bent tree or an outcropping of rocks. What had brought me back to this uneasy mysterious land? Was it the *perries* and the *deevs* (like our fairies and devils) that had woven a spell over me, tempering dread with fascination, depression with delight? When I had left Iran three years before, it had been after a year filled with jagged, vivid memories, a year that until now has stubbornly resisted being captured on paper or even in polite conversation.

"How did you like Iran?" was a reasonable enough question. After our return it came predictably enough from the lips of family, friends, and Iranian acquaintances living in the United States. No one expected more than a polite answer. "We liked it a lot" or "It was a little difficult" would have been acceptable. Most people were taken aback when they saw the grimace of thought as we tried to put our feelings into words. The kaleidoscope of memories—both visual and emotional—was almost too vivid. I longed to speak of my experience living in Iran in flowing generalities, to make sense of this uncomfortable experience, to decide once and for all: Did I love Iran or did I hate it?

Many people have remarked that the pervasive psychological climate in Iran is one of paranoia. At one time or another it is likely that everyone you know will suggest that you or an acquaintance you are beginning to trust is an agent of the secret police. It is almost as unnerving to realize that people might be smiling at you, inviting you to their houses, telling you they're crazy about you, simply because it is the thing to do. In their hearts they may despise you.

Among all the people I met that year in Iran, I had grown to trust the Kurds, and they alone had seemed to trust me. Yet, three years' absence, despite the reassurance of not a single unanswered letter, had shaken my trust. Too Iranized now to accept trust at face value, I wondered why they had trusted me at all. I had shown up in the middle of the Kurdish Revolution, a war in which only Iraqi Kurds were supposed to be fighting but which had rekindled hope for Kurds everywhere. When I returned to America I learned something I had only suspected in Iran—that America had had a far more extensive and sinister involvement in that war than many people had seemed to realize.

When I left Iran the first time, five months after the collapse of the Iraqi Kurdish Revolution, Iranian Kurds were still blaming the shah for double-crossing their Iraqi brothers. Only a few Iraqi Kurds seemed aware of the role the CIA had played in that sellout of Kurdish interests. What if my friends had belatedly decided that I was a spy after all? What kind of welcome would they give me when I returned?

At the time that I had been in Kurdistan I had felt more comfortable with Kurdish men than with any other group of men in the area. Yet in remote mountain villages and little Turkish border towns among strangers there had been frightening confrontations with Kurdish men. Jared was with me now, as he had been then on most of my expeditions; but with all the weapons in a Kurdish village, it would be an easy matter to dispatch one inconvenient American husband.

I stared out the window again for reassurance and saw only faraway pinpricks of light. In underpopulated Iran, the land between cities is often deserted. For centuries the mountains were a haven for brigands. Even now, in the latter part of the twentieth century, 1 wondered who might be hiding there, waiting for our bus to pass by.

Inside the bus, I watched a woman in the front seat re-drape her chador over her head and upper body in preparation for sleep. Again, I felt exposed and shelterless. The villages where we were planning to stay are not that far from the city in kilometers, but those kilometers are often tortuous ones that wind through the mountains on dirt roads. And the villages have no electricity, no telephones. You couldn't step into a booth and dial the police if something bad happened. I knew I was letting my imagination get out of hand, but *deevs* were taking possession of me.

"I'm afraid," I finally managed to whisper out loud to Jared. "Suppose they don't want to see us anymore? Suppose they think we're with the CIA?"

"I'm not sure they won't," Jared answered unreassuringly. "But I trust Haji Ismail. He's our friend."

Haji Ismail. For two years he had been answering my letters in his scrawling, self-taught Persian script. In the hectic lives of old-time Kurdish feudal lords there had been little time for formal schooling. Even with my more educated correspondents, it was sometimes an effort to decipher their letters in Kurdish, because none of them had had any instruction in writing their own language. In many places where Kurds live it is illegal to write Kurdish. But Haji Ismail wrote anyway and sent me regards from a group of women who did not write. They spent their lives in the village, far from any post office. Not that the distance really mattered, since most of them were illiterate.

When I thought about the women by name—red-haired, blue-eyed Maryam, gray-eyed Khadija with her long nose, and Nasreen with her Modigliani chin and jet-black hair—I felt reassured. I tried to imagine what they had been doing during my three years away from Iran. I had been writing up my notes on the Kurdish language, getting a degree, teaching, traveling. They had probably stayed in the village, with the exception of a few well-chaperoned excursions to the city at the discretion of the haji.

Perhaps I had to go away and come back to realize how these women never went anywhere, not during the three years I was away, not in any other years, except perhaps in times of war and migration, or, for unlucky girls, because of marriage to a Kurd from another country.

Through the winter when the snowdrifts and the oil stoves made life miserable, Maryam and Khadija and Nasreen had risen each day and done their work. Through the spring, they had walked through the flocks and touched the wobbly-legged lambs and kids. Every season of the year Nasreen and Khadija worked in the dark, smoke-filled kitchen at the back of the house. Now it was summer and harvest time, a season for picking apricots off the trees and cucumbers out of the garden. Soon it would be fall and the rain would come back. Through headaches and toothaches and menstrual pains and morning sickness, these women fed their household. Their stability reassured me in the midst of my gypsy search for personal fulfillment. They did not have to follow their own hearts; the road had been laid down for them centuries ago.

I decided I would stay with the women in the harem. I would wear their clothes. When I walked out on the plain or up into the mountains, I would be disguised as a Kurd. My light-brown hair and fair skin were hardly remarkable among Kurds. As far as I had plunged into a valley of paranoia and doubt I suddenly found myself soaring again into the fantasy and finery of being a Kurdish lady. One was no more real than the other, but maybe I would find the truth of how I felt somewhere in between.

At eleven at night my reflections ceased as the bus pulled up to our first rest stop and we stepped into a garishly lit room filled with tired travelers shoveling away at huge mounds of buttered rice. My stomach was so unsettled by the motion of the bus ride and my own emotions that I could only sit and pick sporadically at the plate of *chelow kebab* that Jared ordered. There was nothing wrong with *his* appetite.

Afterward we went back and stood outside our bus talking with some of the other passengers. One was an old woman who said she worked at the American Embassy in Tehran, but she could speak almost no English. Even her Persian was heavily accented by her native Azeri Turkish. The husband of the chador-draped woman sitting in the front seat suggested that Rezaiyeh was not a good place for us to be visiting.

"Foreigners should stay in Tehran," he advised. I knew he meant to be friendly, but I resented the implication. He told us that he had studied in Florida and hoped to go to California soon to continue his education. As we boarded the bus I wondered silently if his wife usually wore a chador or had donned it specifically for this trip to backward Rezaiyeh.

The bus rolled inexorably along the highway, its progress broken by hourly checks from the highway police. They looked at the speed graphed on the paper disc placed behind the speedometer to see that the driver had not exceeded the limit. The constant stops kept waking me, but I assumed that the number of buses falling over precipices had decreased since the highway patrol had cracked down.

After a while we began heading along the northeastern shore of the lozenge-shaped Lake Rezaiyeh, a huge dead salt sea that lies east of the Zagros range in northwest Iran. I opened my eyes in the pre-dawn light and stared across the salt flats to the blue, blue lake. A British adventurer in search of Kurds had called this lake gloomy, but ever since I had floated for hours on its surface, dipping cucumbers in the salt water and munching leisurely, Lake Rezaiyeh had become my favorite resort.

Gradually we began to see signs of human habitation-- a few villages that may one day become the real suburbs of Rezaiyeh. Coming toward the city itself, we saw more and more green. We passed the sugar-beet factory, then the turnoff to the airport, and finally we were at the circle with the statue of the shah's father, Reza.

As we rumbled down a wide street I felt the closeness of the mountains.

The *deevs* and *perries* of the night before had vanished and in the dawn we felt only mild, exhausted curiosity. Rezaiyeh was so *small*. This fact struck both of us like a revelation. When we had lived there, it had been our whole world, a world of greens and grays and browns next to the blue of the lake. One hour by plane from Tehran. A place not recommended for foreigners or educated urbane Iranians, for that matter, in spite of being the largest city in the province of West Azerbaijan.

Just when I thought that the rhythms of my body were forever linked to the vibration of the bus, the trip came to an end. One taxi driver had risen early enough to meet the bus, and he looked pleased, in his dour Turkish way, to have caught two foreigners. I was afraid we would find no one at home at Haji Ismail's house, and I waited in the car with the driver while Jared rang the bell. The house's tan brick facade with blue-painted iron bars on all the first-floor windows was unchanged. But behind the bars I saw broken glass and a thick covering of dust. For a minute I was afraid. Why had Haji Ismail left his house looking so forlorn?

The taxi driver agreed with surprising alacrity to drive us out through the mountains. Usually city cab drivers prefer to let the tank-like Russian Volgas handle the mountain driving but this driver was happy to take us in his Fiat.

By now the sun was up, but no one was on the street as we sped smoothly down the long boulevard, past the agricultural college where we had taught and out to the end of the asphalt in Band, where the houses are scattered against a mountain overlooking a lush green valley. Band is a village, but on the weekend it functioned as a resort for the vehicled class of Rezaiyeh.

The driver slowed down as his car bumped onto the graded gravel road. Now we were following the clear stream that flows from the mountains down onto the plain of Mergawar through the Band Pass and across another plain to the lake. The green of the mountains to our left and the fullness of the stream to our right surprised me. This was July, months past the rains. In July of the year we had lived in Kurdistan a drought had left the plain parched and brown.

The mountains rose straight ahead of us out of the wide circular plain. Below the patches of snow was the village, Dustan, set like an emerald on a larger tannish-green patch of drying vegetation. The high pyramids of straw piled along the the road entering the village told us that the harvest was already in progress.

Avoiding the creek that meanders through Dustan, the driver followed our directions to the one-story stone house of Maryam Khanim, Haji Ismail's second wife. No one seemed to be around. I felt odd, after having come so far, not to be greeted or even noticed. Yet the lack of notice only contributed to my growing feeling that I had never really been away. Nothing was strange—the town, the valley of Band, the river, the mountains—all were as we had left them, greener perhaps, but it could just as well be May now and the plain still soaked from melting snow. We might have simply fallen asleep in the tiny city nestled in the mountains. Perhaps we had just awoken and remembered we had an appointment to meet Haji Ismail in Dustan.

Before I went to Kurdistan for the first time, before I had even decided to go, I took half a dozen literary journeys there in the company of a group of mostly British adventurers. Decades earlier they had described their forays into "wildest Koordistan." Fear of bandits and the authors' physical discomforts figured prominently in these accounts. More interesting to me was the amazement of the Western men at the relative freedom of the Kurdish women. After the harems and black veils of Persian and Arab cities, they could not get over the sight of unveiled Kurdish women living and working alongside their men.

The books were often hard to follow, describing boring military campaigns or dwelling in detail on the geography of an area I couldn't picture. Still, I managed to learn a few things. The Kurds, like the Persians, were Zoroastrians before they were converted to Islam in the seventh century. Not surprisingly, considering the poor soil of the mountains, the Kurds have traditionally traveled from place to place, grazing their herds and flocks where they could find grass. The harsh winters in the mountains kept them in the mountain basins during the snow season and up on the peaks in summer when the plains became swelteringly hot.

I didn't read these accounts of Kurdish travels in the order they had been written, but rather when I could find them in the dusty corners of university libraries. Once I had read the whole collection I noticed a striking difference between the Kurdistan of the 1870's and the Kurdistan of the 1970's. The way of life was virtually unchanged; the clothing, the customs, were as they had been centuries before Westerners had described them. It was the geography itself that had altered. The greater Kurdistan of the nineteenth century had broken into pieces. Sections of families and tribes who found themselves on the wrong sides of the border were permanently separated.

Although parts of Kurdistan have been ruled at times by Kurdish chieftains and princes, Kurdistan has never really been united. The Kurds themselves trace their ancestry from the Medes, that early Iranian-based dynasty who conquered Nineveh in 612 B.C. and were themselves conquered by the Persians in 550 B.C. From about 600 B.C. onward, the area that is now Kurdistan was successively invaded by Seleucids, Parthians, Sassanians, Armenians, Romans, Byzantines, Arabs, Seljuks, Mongols, and Ottomans. When the colonial governments were weak or nonexistent, Kurds were quick to rule themselves. But, with the advent of modern armies and stable governments to direct them, Kurdish self-rule became less and less feasible.

By A.D. 1514 the partition of Kurdistan between the Persian and Ottoman (Turkish) empires was fixed. But the borders, high in the mountains of huge empires which owned no modern military equipment, were still not very significant in the daily lives of ordinary Kurds. Migrations took place according to the seasons and the availability of pasture rather than the dictates of central governments. The British adventurers of the nineteenth century were fortunate; even if they had to contend with bandits, they could still wander in Kurdistan without being bothered by border guards.

After World War I and the dissolution of these empires, the Kurds who had been Ottoman subjects were promised their own independent state by the Allies. As early as the late nineteenth century such forward-thinking Kurds as Sheikh Obeidullah had lobbied European governments for relief from Turkish and Arab pressure on Kurds to assimilate.

Following World War I, Kurds based their appeal for Kurdish statehood on Woodrow Wilson's Fourteen Points of January 1918. Wilson had proposed that the sizable ethnic minorities within the Turkish empire—the Kurds, Armenians, and Assyrians—be given the chance to set up their own states. The Treaty of Sèvres, signed in 1920 by the Allies with a puppet Turkish government, guaranteed that a Kurdish state would be set up within the year. Before it could even be implemented, it was rejected by the new Turkish nationalists led by Mustafa Kemal Ataturk. The new peace agreement, the Treaty of Lausanne, which was signed in 1923, made no mention of the Kurds.

Instead of getting their own nation, the Kurds found their cultural and political freedom more sharply curtailed than ever. The portion of Kurdish lands that fell to Turkey, the new republic headed by Ataturk, would never again be referred to as Kurdistan. The people would be called "Mountain Turks" and the language—now spoken by a quarter of the population of Turkey—would be outlawed.

In Iran I met scores of people and their descendants who had fled Ataturk's brutal suppression of Kurdish revolts in eastern Turkey. Kurds in the modern state of Iraq did not fare quite so badly. They had no control of the oil under their land—the British had helped to make sure that would stay in Arab hands—but at least they had their language and their native dress. In Iraq, Kurds form a larger percentage of the population than in any other country they inhabit. Because of this and the weakness of the successive Baghdad governments, they were able to mount a number of revolutions, which ended not in real defeat but in stalemates.

Iranian Kurds were not so lucky. They had one glorious year in which they set up a small Kurdish state south of Rezaiyeh in 1946 at the close of World War II. Then the Russian army which had been loosely occupying much of northwest Iran moved out, leaving the infant Kurdish state without protection. The Iranian army moved into Mahabad, headquarters of the new republic. The leaders were hanged and suspected sympathizers of those leaders were hounded for the next three decades. Without autonomous government, Kurds became just one of Iran's ethnic minorities.

In every modern state where Kurds now live, official sources, notoriously unreliable on population statistics in general, are especially shaky when it comes to Kurds. For years Iraq has been trying to "prove" that its major oil field in Kirkuk is not really located in a Kurdish population center, Turkey doesn't count its Kurds, since it doesn't admit to having any. Iran is loath to report accurately the strength of its restless minorities. Even if an attempt were made by one of these governments to obtain an accurate census in Kurdistan, Kurds would probably resist it as not being likely to benefit them. In no country except Iraq (and the USSR, where Kurds are a tiny minority) are the Kurds free to speak and write their own language.

It didn't take much reading for me to become intrigued. The Kurds were reputed to have the freest attitude toward women of any Muslim group in the area. I was in search of a language, and here was one that cried out for someone to study it. With a project like this I would not be confined to dull libraries and universities. I would have to go to the mountains and gain the confidence of those colorfully dressed women who wore no veils.

Tehran, our first stop, was not exactly what I had expected. There were mountains, but they were only vaguely visible under the heavy layer of smog that regularly permeates the atmosphere of that city. No one appeared to be dressed in Kurdish clothes and I heard no languages being spoken beyond Farsi and Azeri Turkish. In fact it was difficult to hear anything above the noise of the traffic. We wandered about for a few days, in a daze, trying to figure out if we were really in Iran, fabled Persia of Omar Khayyam and exotic fairy tales. We had flown over 6,000 miles east of New York, but somehow New York had gotten there ahead of us. It was a peculiar feeling.

Rezaiyeh was better. At least there were horse-drawn carts with bells, and mountains with no smog. There were also Kurds, visible on every street. Even in provincial Rezaiyeh, everyone wore Western clothes or some facsimile of them, except the Kurds. I wasn't so brash as to try to walk-up to these Kurds and speak to them in the stiff Kurdish I had learned at American universities, but I did expect that it would be only a matter of days or a week before I met some Kurds and began conversing with them regularly.

In my English classes at the local college I asked all of my students where they came from and what languages they knew. I thought I was being subtle, but it wasn't long before everyone knew that Ms. Kahn had the strange intention of studying Kurdish. A handful of Kurdish students came forward.

None were from the Rezaiyeh area and none spoke the dialect I was interested in. Furthermore, they didn't look like Kurds. They had grown up in cities rather than villages and dressed in suits—denim suits, if they could afford it. They wanted to get good grades in English, but they were intensely suspicious of my motives. I was just as glad I wasn't studying their dialect. In retrospect I realize that none of them would have agreed to spend time with me outside of class teaching a language that is discouraged by the Iranian government. As I later discovered, they were all sure I was an agent of the CIA.

I didn't start to feel desperate right away; there were too many other things to do. We found an apartment with the help of people at the college and hastily moved into five starkly bare rooms with a balcony and huge floor-to-ceiling windows, but no stove, refrigerator, heaters, shades or rugs.If you leaned against the walls, your clothes were covered with powdery white chalk. We spent all of our free time at the old bazaar and the shops downtown, faced with making large household purchases for the first time in our lives.

We saw many Kurds in the bazaar. At first I could not separate the locals from the refugees. A man sitting next to us on the plane from Tehran to Rezaiyeh had told us he administered the refugee camps that had been set up in the area to house and feed the thousands who had fled the bombing in Iraq.

This current revolution had begun the spring before our arrival in Iran, and the Iranian government was actively supporting the Kurds, giving them weapons and encouraging them to bring their families to safety in Iran. I was intensely curious about this war, especially when we discovered a number of American military experts who lived in Rezaiyeh and regularly traveled to the Iraqi border to give instructions on weapons use. They insisted they were instructing members of the Iranian army, and I did not press them. I was aware that I had no permission from the Iranian government to be investigating even the Kurdish language, much less a secret border war.

A large family of refugees lived directly behind our house. Like us they had recently arrived in Iran and were highly visible foreigners in the neighborhood. Their house appeared full of women and children. The balcony railing was draped with clothes in all colors of the rainbow—modern Western children's clothes alongside traditional Kurdish women's dresses of velvets and brocades. We would peer in fascination from our kitchen windows across the courtyard to their living room. Every now and then we caught them watching us back. One day, they hung curtains. In the street we continued to stare at one another, but neither side would speak first.

Everywhere we went in downtown Rezaiyeh, we saw Kurds. Men in fringed turbans were gathered in knots on street corners or sitting in the windows of tea houses. Women clustered together in the bazaar. Some wore black chadors around their finery, but unlike the Persian veils these tended to be sheer black lace which revealed the dresses underneath. Other women went unveiled, covered only by layered dresses, vests, and pantaloons made of velvets and satins dyed every color imaginable.

A courtyard populated with Kurds caught my attention. I passed it on my way to and from the college. A long gray-green Land Rover was usually parked outside the turquoise doors leading to the courtyard. I would stare at two rosy-cheeked young men polishing the car's surface or loading and unloading packages. They wore carefully pressed khaki *shalwar*, the wide-leg Kurdish trousers, gathered or ungathered at the ankle depending on tribal affiliation. The complete outfit includes a cummerbund at the waist and a turban. If the courtyard doors were ajar I sometimes caught a glimpse of a small man with a thin face dominated by a huge black fringed turban. Once I saw a short roly-poly woman wearing a bolero jacket of purple velvet. She was accompanied by a beautiful young girl with long black braids. I thought she looked like the heroine of a fairy tale.

While everyone else in town stared at me, the foreign unveiled woman, I stared at the Kurds. They appeared to be much more used to stares than I was, but not one of them spoke to me or answered my searching look. Over and over again the people I knew intimated that I should steer clear of these uncouth mountain people. It was beginning to seem that I would never meet any Kurds. I even had doubts that I had chosen the right language to study. Not only did all of the inhabitants of Rezaiyeh seem to speak Azeri Turkish—a branch of Turkic about as closely related to the Turkish spoken in Istanbul as Kurdish is to Persian—but their lips would curl in disdain whenever I mentioned Kurds.

Rezaiyeh, like all of the Iranian towns north and west of the Kurdish city of Mahabad along the shores of Lake Rezaiyeh, is run by Turks in the employ of the central government in Tehran. The highest officials are often from Persian-speaking parts of Iran, but the police station, the provincial governments, the schools, and the banks are all staffed by Turks. Before the rise of the Pahlavi dynasty, Rezaiyeh was called Urmia, a name so ancient that no one is really sure of its origin. But after the fall of Mohammed Reza Pahlavi, who had named the town "the place of Reza" for his much-hated father, Rezaiyeh was given back its old name.

For some people, like the Christian Assyrians who once dominated this part of West Azerbaijan, there never was any Rezaiyeh or Lake Rezaiyeh —only Urmia and Lake Urmia. These Assyrians trace their lineage from the remnants of the ancient Assyrian empire. Rezaiyeh's Assyrians as well as its Jews seem to have been living there from time immemorial. Both communities have been vastly reduced in the twentieth century—the Jews through successive migrations to Israel and the Assyrians through massacre.

In the late nineteenth century the Assyrians in Iran and just over the border in Iraq fatally attracted the help of European and American missionaries. In fact, the college where we taught had been built originally as a hospital by the Americans who came to help the poor Christians clinging to their ancient faith in the midst of the Muslim onslaught. Partially because this attention from Westerners roused the suspicion and envy of their Muslim neighbors, the Assyrians were subsequently massacred in large numbers by both Turks and Kurds in the early twentieth century.

The plain of Urmia then belonged solely to the Turks, despite Kurdish efforts to gain it. Even today Turks and Kurds continue to fight over Urmia. Tehran, which has no use for Turks except to use them against Kurds, intervenes when Kurds seem to be gaining the upper hand, as they did in 1946 and managed to do again following the fall of the shah in 1979.

During my stay in Rezaiyeh the real battles all seemed to be in the past. The Kurds we met boasted of having come into Rezaiyeh ten years before our arrival and "shot up the town" in retaliation for a Turkish raid on a Kurdish village. Even this sort of free-for-all had been stamped out by government authorities, at least temporarily. The Turkish city and its surrounding Kurdish villages were well infiltrated by secret police.

When we first came I didn't realize how many of the Kurds I saw were refugees or villagers simply passing through the city. I didn't yet know how my neighbors, the Turks, feared and despised these fiery mountain people whose villages surrounded their city. For many weeks I stared wistfully at the fairy-tale garb of the Kurds I saw on the streets, but for all I knew of them I might as well have been back in America perusing the pages of some obscure travel memoir.

CHAPTER 2

NEIGHBORLY EXPECTATIONS

The first time I saw Shehrzad, a buxom woman with huge, heavy-lidded eyes and black hair, she was standing in the doorway to her apartment vigorously motioning for us to come in, saying, "*Befermayeed, befermayeed,*" the all-purpose invitation that is the keystone of Iranian hospitality.

My inclination was to immediately walk into her apartment, but the Iranian who was with us politely declined her invitation. Instead of accepting his excuse, she became even more insistent, waving her hand toward the dark interior of her apartment and moving backward with a swish of her hips, indicating we were to follow. Again, the Iranian politely but firmly refused. Shehrzad nodded, and we walked out into the courtyard, where we looked up once more at the balcony of the second-floor apartment we were planning to rent.

"You are lucky," said the Iranian man, a teacher from the college. "Your neighbor is very friendly. The rental agent asked her if she would mind Americans living in the same house with her, and she told him she would welcome it. As you can see, she really wanted you to come in just now."

During our first days in our new apartment, Shehrzad smiled and repeated her invitation every time she saw us. As soon as I could, I accepted and found myself in a low, plastic-upholstered easy chair being served tea and sweets. The television set in front of me was turned on and I alternated between staring at the elaborately made-up face of an overweight female singer and trying to have a conversation with Shehrzad. Later, I met Shehrzad's husband, Houshang, a muscular medium-sized man who wore tight shirts and pants and spoke a little English. Over and over, they told me that we were always welcome in their house.

Our first weeks in Iran were hectic with all the difficulties of setting up a household in a foreign land, Shehrzad and Houshang were full of solicitude for the problems they imagined we were having. Houshang asked me how we found time to buy food and cook meals since we both worked full-time at the college and had no maid. I smiled noncommittally, thinking that it was true—we didn't have time. As if he had read my thoughts, Houshang immediately invited us to eat all of our meals with them. When he saw that the metal legs of our chairs were digging holes in the soft chalk floor of our enormous living room, Houshang offered to lend us two very large machine-made Persian carpets. Later, Houshang asked when we would be free to be his and Shehrzad's guests at the nightclub they frequented. Nightclub? I appreciated the offer of meals, although it was too generous to accept, and I gladly took the rugs, but this new offer made me slightly uncomfortable. I had not come to Rezaiyeh to visit nightclubs.

"Margaret doesn't like nightclubs very much," Jared volunteered awkwardly.

Houshang looked at me curiously. He had not expected to meet an American who did not go to nightclubs. "Well, perhaps she would like to go another time," he said graciously. "Please tell us whenever you are ready."

Gradually things settled down at the college, where our classes finally started two or three weeks behind schedule. Our house acquired a refrigerator, a stove, space heaters for the winter, and a few odd pieces of furniture which the college reluctantly loaned us after we petitioned the dean. Now that we didn't have to go shopping every day after work, I was forced to notice my growing loneliness.

It was not that people didn't act friendly. At the college everyone smiled and asked after our health continually. We always found people to sit with during lunch in the faculty dining room, but, in retrospect, this was probably because we didn't understand protocol and sat with whomever we pleased. In fact, every day, without knowing it, we committed enough social gaffes to set the teeth of all the Iranians around us on edge. Yet we went on, making more blunders.

No one told us we were demeaning ourselves by riding the city bus along with workers and students. No one suggested that we should not necessarily accept invitations the first time they were proffered. We spoke to the people around us with the easy familiarity that Americans take for granted, thinking that we were refined and sensitive compared to some of the other Americans we saw in town, particularly the United States Army weapons experts who sometimes came to lunch at the college as guests of an Iranian teacher named Mr. Khesheni. What we couldn't know was that Iranians lumped us all together—army, Peace Corps, researchers of Kurdish. But I only suspected the lack of friendliness on the part of people around us. I was never sure of it.

At first I spoke of my desire to meet Kurds only to people I thought were "westernized" enough to understand such a project. I knew this might be considered politically sensitive by the government, but it never occurred to me that it might be socially sensitive as well. When confronted with my bizarre interest and request, American- or German-educated faculty members only smiled politely and said they would do their best to introduce me to some—and here they paused—Kurds.

Our neighbors' courtyard

When Jared came home from the college in the afternoon, he took a nap, but I was always much too keyed up to sleep. I got into the habit of hanging around downstairs with our neighbors, the Jaffaris. Shehrzad was never without her welcoming smile, plate of sweets, and blaring television. She spoke of her plans to travel, to learn English, to do something besides care for her children. Although we were exactly the same age, she had married eight years before me and already had two children. Since she had a full-time maid, Nana, and a full-time mother, Maman, who lived with the family and spent most of her time taking care of the children, I could not see that her son and daughter weighed too heavily on Shehrzad.

Shehrzad's apartment was the structural duplicate of our own upstairs, but it gave no hint that it had once had an interior of bare soft chalk or bunches of wires protruding from ugly holes in the walls and ceilings. The Jaffaris' apartment was swathed in expensive fabrics. On the floor were carpets from Tabriz and Kashan. The windows were draped in velvet matching the requisite set of ornate velvet-upholstered chairs which were currently the fashion in modern Iran. No one sat on the floor anymore. The living room or guest parlor was partitioned off from a formal dining room by organdy curtains elaborately sashed and drawn back.

That dining room with its pale-blue Kashan was the scene of heavy gambling almost every weekend. Houshang, who was a government contractor, had more money than he knew what to do with. The cash was just piling up. A mere three years earlier the Jaffaris, although hardly poor, had not owned these rugs or custom-made easy chairs. Their old possessions, piled in the cellar of our house, were not nearly so luxurious. But now the Jaffaris were building a house, in another part of town, to go with their new wealth.

In the context of Rezaiyeh the Jaffaris were considered "fast." No one thought of them as good Muslims. They gambled, drank liquor, and danced. Shehrzad was supposed to be a loose woman according to various gossips around town. The strange thing was that if they had been in America they would have been ordinary, maybe even a little boring and prudish. Shehrzad for all of her gay abandon did not have much opportunity for affairs. It was inconceivable that she should spend time alone with any man not her husband or close relative. At sixteen she had had her first child, and her mother, who had grown increasingly pious with age, now lived with her. Shehrzad's mother insisted on wearing a chador and occasionally even draped Shehrzad's five-year-old daughter in a veil when she took her along to women's religious meetings.

The Jaffaris told us over and over how happy they were that we were their neighbors. They loved America. They expected to travel there. They wanted to practice English with us. They hoped we would show them the latest styles in clothes, in dancing, in living. I expected them to tell me about local customs, about traditions that had persisted over the centuries. This was the Iran I was interested in, not the Iran of imported cars and well-oiled rummy parties. But it was only very gradually that we became aware of how much at cross-purposes we were.

I hesitated to tell Shehrzad about my Kurdish project. As far as she knew I had come halfway around the world merely to teach English at an obscure little agricultural college. This seemed strange to her, and it was not long before she asked me why. Why would a foreigner, an American, choose to live in a place like Rezaiyeh? Shehrzad herself lived only for the weeks she could spend away from Rezaiyeh in Tehran. What could I be doing in a place so backward that it only had one real nightclub?

I took a deep breath and told her. "I came to study Kurdish. I want to write a book on Kurdish grammar."

It was as if she hadn't heard me. Shehrzad began talking about how much she wanted her son to go to a boarding school in England and learn to speak my language fluently.

"But what about your daughter?" I asked. "Don't you want to send her too?"

Shehrzad gave me a shocked look. First Kurdish and now this. Even modern-looking women like Shehrzad did not think of letting their daughters be independent. What would I suggest next? Rather than risk saying the wrong thing, I kept my mouth shut as she chattered on and on.

I continued to see Shehrzad. She seemed eager to spend time with me in spite of her busy social schedule. I knew that I was not getting any closer to the Kurds by lounging for hours in front of her large console television drinking tea and eating sweets. But at least I was improving my Persian, and, more important, I was avoiding being alone in a very strange land.

As I talked with Shehrzad the Kurds were always in the back of my mind. Perhaps she knew some Kurds and was not telling me. Maybe when we got to know each other better I would raise the subject again. In the meantime I tried to increase her confidence in me by saying nothing about politics, feminism, or Kurds.

It wasn't just Shehrzad. I had learned to be cautious about asking anyone to introduce me to Kurds. But more and more I was beginning to realize that I was not going to meet Kurds just by passing them on the street. At the college I kept questioning fellow teachers, administrators, and students. Several people mentioned that there was a biology instructor who was a Kurd from the Rezaiyeh area.

I went to his office and shook hands with a thin man wearing very tight pants and an equally tight shirt with a cravat at the neck. He could barely speak English. French had supplanted it during the five years he had studied in Paris. But he assured me that his native tongue was the dialect of Kurdish I was interested in.

After many polite phrases and eager invitations to come to his house, delivered in a mixture of broken English and French, he finally told me where he had been born. Not only was it outside the area I was interested in, but, after a half hour in his office, I was beginning to realize that his silk cravat, his brand-new Peugeot, and his oily manner bespoke a long estrangement from village life. When I stood abruptly to take my leave, he looked disappointed.

"But will you not come to my house?" he asked.

"Perhaps sometime," I said vaguely, rushing away from the close, perfumed atmosphere.

Every night in our apartment I would hear the sounds of Kurmanji, the Kurdish dialect I planned to study. I would sit next to our radio repeating the words I managed to recognize. Where were the voices coming from? The signal was so clear that I soon realized that Kurmanji must be broadcast right from Rezaiyeh, but the few people I asked didn't seem to know much about it. No, they never listened to Kurdish programs on the radio. But I kept on listening. If only the sound waves had been visible, I would have followed them to their source.

Although we couldn't seem to meet any Kurds, there were other people in town who wanted to get to know us. American army personnel and other expatriates were at the top of this list. But their pro-shah views and vehement dislike of Iranians made us cautious. Even if they had been the most charming, politically aware people in the world we did not want to spend our time with speakers of English, French, or German. If I couldn't speak Kurdish, then Persian was preferable. But, despite all the Persian speakers who said hello and asked our health every day, we didn't seem to have any real friends except the Jaffaris.

Everyone we had met except servants was Agha or Khanim—Mr. or Ms.—to us. Even people who were exactly our age and status gave us only their last names when we were introduced, so we were forced to address them formally. Only the Jaffaris downstairs had made it clear from the beginning that they wanted to be called by their first names without the titles. The Jaffaris were also the only ones outside of presumptuous storekeepers to use the familiar *to*, the Persian equivalent of the French *tu*, to us when we first met. They waited for us to reciprocate this sign of intimacy, but we couldn't—not because we didn't want to but because we had never learned the forms. Back at the university in the United States our Persian teacher had warned us that as foreigners we would probably never be privileged to address any Iranians in the familiar form. Even many Iranian children may not use *to* when speaking to their own parents. When we didn't return the Jaffaris' *to* they quickly switched to the more formal "you."

Reciprocity was a problem for us not only with language but with hospitality. The Jaffaris kept offering us food, but when we invited them to dinner they made it abundantly clear that they couldn't stomach what we cooked. Shehrzad simply pushed her food from one side of the plate to the other as she raved about how delicious it was.

After a while we fell into a pattern of accepting the Jaffaris' invitations without worrying how we were going to pay them back. Houshang's brother, a young electric-guitar player, took us on a car ride for our first view of the lake ten kilometers outside of town. Shehrzad and Houshang brought us along on one of their Friday outings to Band Village, where we sat in the car watching as they and their friends got in and out of each others' vehicles to talk. The weather was too chilly to stay outdoors for long.

During my daily visits to their apartment I held long conversations with Shehrzad's five-year-old daughter, who was just beginning to learn Persian from her parents. They wanted her to know something besides her native Turkish before she started school, which was officially conducted only in Persian. Jared and I often asked Houshang's and Shehrzad's advice on social customs in Iran, about whether we were making a mistake to accept an invitation too quickly or speak our minds too frankly or dress too conspicuously, but they always smiled and reassured us that we were doing everything perfectly. Despite their reassurance I felt more and more uneasy. If we were doing things so perfectly, why was everyone staring at us, on the kucheh, in the college, on the public bus, in such an unfriendly way?

The ideal occupation for an Iranian woman is to spend her time with female relatives or, if she is a bit less traditional, with female friends, whiling away the afternoon with talk and endless glasses of tea and sweet pastries. Naturally such a woman has a maid who is at home beating the dust out of the cushions or, in Shehrzad's case, using the imported vacuum cleaner on the expensive rugs. The grandmother looks after the children. Shehrzad's children referred to their grandmother as Maman, the French word adopted by upper- and middle-class Iranians for "mother." They called their real mother by her first name.

Shehrzad, when she was not at the boutique, the hairdresser, or the dressmaker, was with her friends or relatives. One day as I was passing by her door she invited me in. Looking around me I suddenly realized that my corduroy pants and plaid shirt were totally out of place. I was surrounded by women garbed in stylish calf-length skirts and boots or, in Shehrzad's case, a low-cut black evening dress.

When Shehrzad introduced me, they all stopped talking to each other long enough to give me saccharin-sweet smiles and Persian greetings. Then they went back to Turkish. I sat there trying to act like a part of this group, but instead feeling stupid and awkward.

Iranian women often made me feel this way: underdressed, overeducated, and generally out of it. What did it matter that many of them had not finished high school, that they had handed their children to the grandmothers so they could spend their time at afternoon tea parties, that none of them seemed to have the slightest idea about the politics or economy of their own country? They made me feel inferior. I was inferior. I couldn't even speak their language.

I stood up bewildered as they all trooped into Shehrzad's bedroom, where an unused imported exercise machine stood in one corner. Following them into the room I watched them step, one at a time, onto Shehrzad's scale. Groans of dismay. They were getting so fat that soon all those imported clothes they craved would look terrible on them. What could they do? The question was discussed in Turkish, so I couldn't follow it. They only remembered to speak to me again as they were leaving, when they switched to Persian once more to bid me effusive goodbyes.

The next day Shehrzad handed me a packet of capsules she had purchased at the local pharmacy, where everything from codeine to birth-control pills was sold over the counter. Shehrzad wanted to take these pills to keep from getting any fatter. Her doctor had recommended them, but she was still a little afraid. They were very strong and might give her side effects. Would I please read the accompanying literature, which was in English, and report back to her?

I looked over the literature and concluded, without knowing anything about pharmacology, that these pills were intended for people who had metabolic disorders that made them fat. As far as I could tell, Shehrzad's fat was not due to any metabolic disorder but merely to eating sweets and rice all day long without getting the slightest bit of exercise. But I decided that I should translate all of the English so that Shehrzad could read and decide for herself. A senior student at the college who was quite good in both English and biology agreed to provide a written translation, putting it all down in neat Arabic letters on a page in my notebook. Together we decided to advise Shehrzad not to take the pills.

"You must get exercise instead of taking the medicine," the student wrote at the bottom of the translation. Afterward this student, who was on her way to study in America, discussed with me the irony of Shehrzad's situation. In the old days fat was not considered unbeautiful on a woman. It signaled wealth, attesting to how much money her husband had. Now, the standard of beauty had shifted to a western look. In the space of a generation everything had changed—everything except the life-style that produces such fatness. Real out-of-doors exercise for women such as Shehrzad was unthinkable. She couldn't even get out of her car and walk since her clothing, class, and demeanor, not to mention her lack of chador, would have invited gross male harassment on the street.

When I returned home I rang Shehrzad's bell, ripped the page of translation out of my notebook, and handed it to her. She took it eagerly, but as soon as she started to read, she began to frown. When she came to the end she gave me a strange look and thanked me coldly. She never mentioned the matter of her weight to me again.

With Shehrzad and other Iranians like her, the patina of westernization was laid on so thickly that I usually could not see where it ended until it was too late. In the beginning I didn't believe that Shehrzad or another local somewhat older woman I know named Mrs. Jam could have prejudices that would prevent them from understanding or respecting me. Of course our lives were completely different, but I felt that was an accident.

Shehrzad and I were exactly the same age, but I considered it merely bad luck that she had never finished high school. It did not occur to me to condemn her, as Mrs. Jam did, for not getting her diploma by correspondence. Mrs. Jam, despite the burden of having infant sons and a husband to care for when she was only sixteen, had kept up with her studies and graduated. Not that it had made that much difference in her life as an upper-class married woman. She and Shehrzad pursued similar activities. The only difference was that Mrs. Jam was slightly more old-fashioned.

She, not her mother, raised her children, and she cooked for herself, letting her maids and handymen do the menial chores. It did not occur to me to suspect that both Shehrzad and Mrs. Jam saw themselves as better off than me.

They felt sorry for me having to go out without a car into a street full of men in order to earn my own living. I didn't wear fashionable clothes, and my house had hardly any furniture. In the beginning I never dreamed of how I was disappointing Shehrzad. When she had told the rental agent she was delighted that an American family was moving in, she had been under the illusion that we were real Americans—drinking, nightclubbing Americans who could afford seventy-five dollars to buy into one rummy game. We were hardly American at all by those standards. But Shehrzad might have been able to accept even that if it hadn't been for one extraordinary thing. All I seemed to care about were Kurds.

We were sitting around the television on the fake-leather French-style *mobles* when I decided to tell Shehrzad that I was having trouble finding Kurds. Since it was on my mind all the time now I could no longer avoid talking about it. Every new day that brought no Kurdish contacts made me wonder why I had come to Iran.

There was a silence, and then Shehrzad made a valiant effort to be friendly. "My husband knows some Kurds. He works in Mahabad."

I was astonished. Shehrzad had never mentioned that her husband worked in a Kurdish city. All I knew was that he was making enormous sums of money building things for the government. It had never occurred to me that he might be doing this in the real capital of Iranian Kurdistan. Mahabad is not an official capital, nor is it located in the province the Iranian government chooses to call Kordestan, but anyone who has read any Kurdish history knows that Mahabad is a center of Kurdish cultural and political activity not only in Iran but in greater Kurdistan as well.

For some reason I felt obliged to point out to Shehrzad that I wasn't really looking for Kurds from Mahabad because I wasn't studying their dialect, Sorani, but the Kurmanji dialect spoken around Rezaiyeh and to the north.

Shehrzad nodded uncertainly. What did she know or care about Kurdish dialects? She seemed glad that I didn't want to bother with Mahabad Kurds after all.

"Margaret, what do you think of my new dress?" she asked, holding a strapless lime-green chiffon gown up to her, waiting for me to admire it.

All I could think of was Mahabad. So what if I wasn't studying the dialect there? I was interested in more than dialects when it came to Kurds.

"But I *would* like to see it," I said.

"What? See what?" asked Shehrzad.

"Mahabad."

"Oh." Her face fell and then brightened. Well, why not? "Houshang goes there every day. We could all go. It would be fun." Shehrzad was obviously desperate.

When Houshang came home that evening it was arranged. In two days we would travel to Mahabad. I still did not know enough about relations between the Turks and the Kurds to realize that I would be visiting a Kurdish town in the company of the enemy. When Shehrzad had said that Houshang spoke some Kurdish, I believed her. When she said she would enjoy a trip to Mahabad, I think she almost fooled herself into believing it. Perhaps if I had called the town by its old pre-shah name of Sauj Bulaq she would have hesitated. Then she might have recalled the events of three decades ago, shortly before the time of her birth, events that had transformed both Mahabad and the rest of West Azerbaijan. Even to mention what had gone on during those long-ago days could be considered treasonous. Maybe Shehrzad had forgotten, or maybe she had never really been told. Even at the time of our stay in Iran the shah was still busily rewriting history through his propaganda machine to transform his non-role in the withdrawal of Russian troops from Azerbaijan into a spectacular triumph.

Sitting in Shehrzad's comfortable padded chairs, it was difficult to imagine the situation at the end of World War II, a war that Reza Shah had wanted to enter on the side of the Germans. In those days there were few automobiles in Azerbaijan. People traveled between the towns and villages in carts or on horseback. There was no electricity, no safe running water, no telephones. European furniture was far less popular, and no one had ever heard of an exercise machine. Few women walked on the streets. Almost none except Christians and Jews went unveiled.

Yet, despite the primitive conditions that prevailed then, the time of the Mahabad republic is remembered with joy not just by the inhabitants of Mahabad but by Kurds everywhere. To the Jaffaris, Mahabad was a lackluster little hole—dusty or muddy depending on the season. To them Mahabad was a city without a past. It was up to us to recognize the importance of a town that had once belonged solely to the Kurds

Our neighbors' kids

CHAPTER 3

MAHABAD VS. SAUJ BULAQ

The infant mortality rate is high all over Iran, Turkey, and Iraq, but in mountainous Kurdistan it is so high that a Kurd I met from Turkey had been named Mewan—"Guest." The local mullah who was always consulted in these matters suggested the name. Evidently God had been propitiated by this sign of humility, for the child eventually grew to manhood. But the Turkish government also had to be propitiated. In Kurdish, "guest" is *mewan*; in Turkish, *misafir*. From the time that this Kurd set foot in a Turkish schoolroom, he was Misafir. Only at home and around his hometown among Kurdish friends did he remain Mewan.

The Kurds of Turkey are used to such duality. The town where Mewan was born also had two different names—one imposed by Ankara and one that had been used as long as anyone could remember. In informal conversations out of government and secret police hearing, people always use the old name, even though it has been erased from the official map for years.

Just as Urmia in Iran was changed by the shah to Rezaiyeh, so was Sauj Bulaq converted to Mahabad, the difference being that "Mahabad" is a relatively innocuous word with Iranian origins while Rezaiyeh was named for Reza, the hated father of the last shah. But despite the innocuousness of "Mahabad," Sauj Bulaq has remained firmly Sauj Bulaq, a Turkic name meaning "cold water." Just the fact that the government imposed the new name on them was enough to make the Kurds reject it.

I was first corrected in my use of "Mahabad" by one of my Kurdish students who came from that town. This student, a tall, good-looking boy, was reputed to be descended from one of the leaders of the Kurdish Republic established in 1946. Like other Kurdish students in the college he was fascinated that I was studying his language. One day after class I spoke eagerly of wanting to visit Mahabad, a project that had been on my mind since I had arrived in Rezaiyeh. Mahabad, at the southern end of the lake, was only eighty kilometers away.

"Yes, it is a beautiful city," my Kurdish students chorused as they stood around my desk.

Now was the time, I thought, to ask if they knew a Kurd named Hassan whom I had met in the United States. His hometown was Mahabad.

But at the mention of his name I saw my students' faces harden.

"His brother was killed by SAVAK," one of them remarked.

"I thought he drowned on a camping trip in Minnesota," I said, feeling puzzled at this suggestion that the Iranian secret police had executed Hassan's brother. Maybe these students had never heard the actual details.

"Nobody who knows how to swim can drown," one student announced. "He was killed by SAVAK." The others nodded, staring at me suspiciously. Had I been sent by SAVAK to convince them otherwise?

And that was that, as far as my Kurdish students were concerned. Here in Iran where no newspaper carried reliable news they had inside information while I, after talking to Hassan in America, had only imagined that it had been a tragic accident. What was the truth? As long as it involved SAVAK, we would never know.

All dire events in Iran are surrounded by a thick fog. During our stay the Tehran airport terminal's roof collapsed under the weight of a winter snow, killing several dozen or several hundred passengers, depending on the source. For years and years students in Iran held commemorative strikes on the day they say that forty-four students at the University of Tabriz were massacred by the army. Yet eyewitnesses continue to allege that there were no deaths.

One hard fact did emerge from my conversation with my Mahabadi students: None of them was going to take the risk of showing me around the town. We made a few abortive attempts to take the bus there alone, but were soon defeated. The clerk at the desk in the dingy little bus station down by the Rezaiyeh bazaar refused to give us particulars. Evidently he had never seen two well-dressed foreigners who wanted to go to a place like Mahabad by bus. Everyone else in the waiting room was attired very shabbily, and they all stared at us as I scanned the walls in vain for some schedule or price list.

Now, a month after our arrival in Rezaiyeh, we had finally found a means of getting to Mahabad. The fact that we were going in the company of Turks—the Jaffaris—didn't bother me. I was overjoyed to be going at all.

In my mind I went over what I knew about the town. Friends who had served there in the Peace Corps eight years earlier had thoroughly described it to us. But things had obviously changed since then. Our friends had advised me to take only dresses to wear on the street in Rezaiyeh, but I soon noticed that pants suits had become de rigueur for the modern Iranian woman. They said we would not find clean water, a refrigerator, or a hot-water heater, all of which we immediately obtained.

Two corpses were propped up in the Mahabad bazaar on the day of our friends' arrival eight years earlier. These were the bodies of Kurds accused of challenging the authorities. At the time of my friends' stay the Kurds were still openly battling the government and the government was still making an example of them in the marketplace. By the time we arrived such methods were out of fashion. The hidden dungeons of SAVAK and the assiduous rural gendarmerie had the countryside pretty much under control.

If names in Kurdistan have a life of their own, then the innocent-sounding Chwar Chira, literally "Four Lamps," is a survivor of two executions. The leaders of the Kurdish Republic were hanged there, and later the Chwar Chira Circle, with its four streetlamps above a dusty intersection, was razed and the streets leading to it renamed. Because of Mahabad, Tehran will never trust the Kurds.

All Kurds are enemies, potential traitors and saboteurs, to the state that rules from Tehran. By seceding in 1946, the Persians reason, the Kurds have cut themselves off forever. To the shah and to Iranians of all political persuasions, Mahabad was an example of what Kurds were capable of, given the chance. Tabriz was likewise a symbol of Turkish nationalist dreams and their suppression.

Up until 1941, Reza Shah, the father of the last shah, had used harsh methods to bring the Kurds and other militant tribal groups under control. He had interned tribal leaders in Tehran, broken up their lands, and outlawed traditional dress. Then, in the midst of World War II, the British occupied southern Iran near the oil fields while Russian army troops moved into the northwest along the Turkish and Russian borders.

This was ostensibly to make sure that Reza Shah didn't enter the war on the side of the Germans, but, in fact, both countries had designs on Iran, particularly on its oil. Since the presence of Soviet troops effectively prevented the Persian army from enforcing order in Kurdistan, Mahabad (or Sauj Bulaq) grew steadily more autonomous. The Russians, who were more active among the Turks in the north, gave the Kurds a free rein.

In 1946, with Russian encouragement, two states broke off from the rest of Iran and declared their independence. The Azerbaijani Republic, the larger of the two, was based in Tabriz, 180 miles to the north of Rezaiyeh. It was run by Turks, who made their language, Azeri Turkish, the official language of the republic.

Until this time Azeri had been a nonstandard language, officially ignored by Tehran, discouraged for all public use. The Russians encouraged and aided the Azeri Turks in their declaration of cultural and political autonomy from Tehran. The new government of the Azerbaijani Republic was closely modeled on Soviet lines with an elaborate secret police organization.

Farther to the south, with much more tenuous support from the Russians, was the smaller Kurdish Republic. This was run by highly respected community leaders from Mahabad with representatives from the surrounding tribal areas. There was no secret police and relatively little Russian guidance. The army of the Kurdish Republic was initially made up of the followers of various local tribal leaders, but this was hardly adequate for repelling an organized invasion. Sooner or later the republic would have to defend itself. But when Mahabad got its first real general he was not welcomed with open arms.

At the time the Mahabad Republic was set up, a fierce middle-aged tribal leader named Mulla Mustafa Barzani was becoming established as the head of the Barzani tribe in northern Iraq. The Barzanis were famous warriors. Besides battling their traditional enemies such as the Zibari tribe they had more recently been fighting the British. In retaliation the Royal Air Force bombed Barzan province and other parts of Kurdistan.

The Mahabad Republic came at a time when Mulla Mustafa needed to get out of the mountains of Barzan, where he was slowly being drawn into a trap by the British in collusion with neighboring enemy tribes. In the 1940's the British were determined to enforce order in Iraqi Kurdistan by any means. They saw Barzani's tribal following as a direct threat to their plan to hand over the reins of power in Iraq to the Arabs, excluding both the Kurds and the Assyrians.

In contrast to Iraq, Iran was disarrayed and divided during World War II, presenting an ideal base for Kurds interested in governing themselves. Barzani decided to bring his men over the border, where he set up headquarters in Mahabad. At first Barzani got a guarded welcome.

Although in Iraq he had just escaped capture by the British, in Soviet-dominated Azerbaijan Barzani was suspected of being a British agent. Only later, when the Persian army moved close to Mahabad, were Barzani and his forces vindicated by their valorous performance.

Although the Kurdish state was hardly a democracy, it was a vast improvement over what had preceded it. The Persian police, secret police, and army were banished from the town. The Kurdish flag was raised, and the towns people literally danced in the streets. Newspapers, books, and schools in Kurdish soon appeared. Kurdish was used in the courts, which were administered by traditional Muslim judges. The president of the tiny republic, Qazi Mohammed, was himself such a judge.

Although the Kurds had enjoyed virtual self-government for several preceding years preceding, the actual republic lasted barely one year. During that time the Russians made promises about supporting both the Azerbaijani and the Kurdish republics. Western powers, on the other hand, did not want to see Soviet-backed republics in Iran. They agitated constantly for the removal of Russian forces.

At last the Soviets pulled out with little or no warning to the fledgling republics they had encouraged. The Azerbaijani Republic became a legend overnight—a reign of terror say some, a nationalist dream say others—and the Turks faced a coming decade of starvation. Weather and crop failure were partially to blame. But even at the time of our stay in Iran, nearly three decades later, people said that Tehran would never forgive Tabriz. What was once the largest city in Iran, capital of dynasties, was left to molder in its own dust, forgotten when plans for industry were drawn up, its population forced to emigrate to Tehran in search of work.

In Mahabad, at the other end of the lake, the Kurds were more sanguine about their fate. They assumed the Iranians would not take punitive action against them. They had not been so closely allied with the Russians, nor had they committed the excesses of the Turks to the north. Still, after several battles and some negotiations with the Iranian government, Barzani thought it wise to flee with his army.

He had been offered sanctuary in Iran but only if he and his men gave up all their weapons and settled in a place far from Mahabad. After he decided to leave, he and his men, traveling under great hardship along with their families, were hunted through the mountains all the way to the Russian border. Among the Iranian Kurds were some who had no love for the Barzanis. One tribe in particular, the Herkis, cooperated with the shah's army in harassing the Barzanis as they fled north.

Once again Kurdistan split along tribal lines, one group trying to benefit at another's expense. This seemed to be just what all governments wanted the Kurds to do. Thirty years later the last shah did not forget the Herkis. Herki villages boasted schools and clinics which had not been provided for other tribes.

Just before the Mahabad Republic fell and the Iranian army moved in, Barzani went to Qazi Mohammed, the president, to ask him if he too wanted to come to Russia. But Qazi, whether from naiveté or integrity, chose to stay behind in Mahabad. He felt he could not abandon the people who had gone in with him on this venture in defiance of the Iranian government. Perhaps he did not really believe that the government would be so foolish as to martyr him. Three weeks before the Barzanis left Iran, Qazi Mohammed and two of his relatives were hanged in the Chwar Chira Circle of Sauj Bulaq.

Even after reading the history of the Kurdish Republic, I still only dimly grasped its implications for relations between the Kurds and the Turks in present-day Iran. In 1946 two states had broken with Tehran and defied the central government to do anything about it. Both the Turks and the Kurds had received a great deal of encouragement from the Russians to cooperate with each other.

Yet, during the entire eleven-month existence of the Mahabad Republic, many of the Kurds north of Mahabad in the Rezaiyeh area had seen the Azerbaijani Turks and not the Tehrani Persians as the real enemy. The Azerbaijanis, for their part, had ignored the Kurds as much as possible. Since the cities west of the lake from Rezaiyeh up and around to Tabriz have Turkish majorities, the Azerbaijani Turks felt safe in excluding the sizable Kurdish populations in surrounding villages from representation or consideration. This pattern persisted up to the time of my stay in Iran. Kurds complain that teachers and students speak Turkish illegally in the public schools of Rezaiyeh, where Persian is supposed to be the official tongue. One way or another Kurds say they have been excluded by Turks as long as any of them can remember.

But it took time for me to appreciate the depth of ethnic prejudice in Rezaiyeh. My neighbors were all Turks, while my colleagues at work were mainly Persians. Just as I did not suspect how the Jaffaris felt about the

Kurds, neither did I have an inkling of how much the American- or European-educated professors at the college despised our neighbors. Our first journey to Mahabad, like many of our initial encounters in Iran, was a journey of two innocents.

We reached Mahabad via a highway still under construction. For miles we saw nothing but mud flats next to the lake and, at one point, an unexplained herd of camels—not an animal native to West Azerbaijan. As soon as we got out of the car on Mahabad's Pahlavi Street in the middle of the tiny downtown area it felt as if we had crossed a border.

The women on the street in Mahabad did not veil. They didn't need to —Mahabad had few Turks or Persians. The streets were full of Kurdish men dressed in bulky turbans and baggy pants pegged at the ankle. Kurds, I soon discovered, did not stare at me in the arrogant way of the Turks. Although Mahabad is more physically hemmed in by its mountains than Rezaiyeh—Rezaiyeh sits on a large plain while Mahabad is more properly a valley—Mahabad seemed lighter, sunnier. Perhaps it was the absence of the dark veils.

When we got out of the car I saw that Shehrzad did not appear to share my enthusiasm for this Kurdish city. She nervously wrapped her black crocheted shawl around her as she hurriedly guided us to a souvenir shop owned and managed by a Turk from Rezaiyeh. There, under her guidance, we spent the morning.

After we made some purchases I decided we should try to contact the family of Hassan, the Mahabadi I had met in America. As soon as I mentioned his name the atmosphere in the shop changed. The shopkeeper suggested that Hassan's brother might currently be in prison. But I refused to be put off.

Shehrzad reluctantly helped me make the telephone call to Hassan's family's house. By the time a fattish man looking nothing like Hassan showed up at the store their suspicion had infected me. I wondered if he was really Hassan's brother or a SAVAK agent. There was no way to know. Why had they speculated on his being in prison? Was he a criminal? I had not even been in Iran long enough to distinguish between the American and Iranian criteria for incarceration. Hassan's brother gave us his telephone number, written in crudely formed English numbers, and then he went away, much to Shehrzad's relief. He wanted us to call him to get together the next time we were in Mahabad, but we never returned.

The history of Hassan and his brothers is somewhat typical of what Mahabad residents have had to suffer over the years. In the 1950s, not long after the fall of the republic, still another brother, who was 13 years old at the time, had been rounded up with some other boys and detained in a small hut for a week. The police covered the floor with water a foot deep. He was accused of distributing seditious material and then released.

That brother, said Hassan, never recovered from the pneumonia he contracted during this torture. Only his lungs were damaged, but others were not so lucky. Those were the times when the most apolitical religious literature was considered seditious. Hassan himself and the brother who was killed on the camping trip had eventually managed to get away to the United States, ostensibly to be educated, but first they wanted to stay alive. Only after my return from Iran when I saw Hassan again did he make me understand why my Mahabadi students had just assumed that SAVAK had assassinated his brother in America. Deaths of people from Mahabad are often neither natural nor accidental.

As we walked with Shehrzad to the *mehmunserai*, the local government inn, we had a glimpse of the town. Dozens of men were hawking radios, cassette players, and other imported goodies along the main street. Mahabad was reputed to be a Mecca for smuggled Western goods, since Kurds on both sides of the border cooperate easily with one another to avoid customs. The smuggling chain has no doubt been broken now that the Iraqi government has used fire and defoliating agents to put a twenty-five-kilometer-wide stretch of scorched earth between its Kurdish villages and those of its neighbors, Iran and Turkey.

After lunching in a private room at the *mehmunserai* (no women were eating in the public dining room), Jared and I wandered by ourselves through the tiny mud kuchehs off the main street. The winding alleys and the mud construction of the houses reinforced our feeling that we were really in another country. Our own house was made of concrete with bits of colored glass and broken mirrors stuck into the facade.

Later, when we drove to Houshang's construction site, we saw that Mahabad would soon boast houses like ours. Houshang's houses were being built in long, dreary, straight rows. Pipes rolled around in the dust of the unfinished street, and the area had a depressingly bare aspect quite unlike the traditional maze of kuchehs with their low walls and small gardens. I felt that I would have gladly given up our hot-water heater and refrigerator to live in old Mahabad.

Our day in Mahabad was soon over. Houshang was finished with his work, and Shehrzad was freed from the burden of having to show us around. We were following the course of the river out of town when, without warning, Houshang turned off the main road onto a beautifully straight graded gravel street.

After a few kilometers we pulled up to a circle, exactly like the circle that signaled the beginning of Mahabad except that this one had no statue of the shah or his father and no grass in the middle. Inside this circle stood a collection of men, some old, some very young, all dressed in various soiled and torn articles of Western-style clothing. I did not see a single pair of wide Kurdish trousers or a turban. Shehrzad was fuming in the front seat as Houshang alighted and began talking to a small knot of men. Jared and I decided to get out too and take a look around.

As soon as we exposed ourselves outside the car, the remainder of the crowd drifted in our direction to have a good stare. The sun, which was rapidly sinking, threw long shadows over the whole scene, making the sunburned faces of the men even darker. As they stared at us, I sensed an overwhelming hostility directed toward our clean, untorn clothing, our pale, protected faces, our undisguised curiosity.

Suddenly Jared said to me, "Don't you see what's strange about this place?"

I was jarred by the note of discovery in his voice and frowned. Obviously the whole place was very strange. We were surrounded by a group of very poor, hostile Turkish men who were standing in the road eyeing a couple of strangers. Across from this dirt circle with surrounding gravel roadbed was a tiny collection of shack-like stores selling fruit and vegetables and some dusty dry goods.

"There are no cars," exclaimed Jared. "They're building this beautiful boulevard and this ridiculous circle in the middle of nowhere. None of *these* people can afford a car. The government is building a road which is not going to be of any use to them."

Before Jared could elaborate any more, we saw Houshang getting back inside the car. Hurriedly we got in too, and Shehrzad chided me. She said that the men here were not used to seeing women. Houshang, as if to smooth things over, suggested that we take a side trip to another valley to see some interesting archaeological ruins. But Shehrzad reminded him that the sun was setting. The two of them argued for several minutes, and then Houshang admitted that it would not be safe to drive around the mountains after dark. It seemed that Iraqi planes often flew overhead, bombing Kurdish villages on the Iranian as well as the Iraqi side of the border. Houshang laughed as if this were a great joke. I felt a chill.

The day after our trip to Mahabad the feast signaling the end of Ramazan, the month-long Muslim fasting period, was celebrated. I heard the sound of holiday guests as I was passing the Jaffaris' half-open door. Shehrzad, seeing me go by, came over and invited me in. I was introduced to a cousin who worked in Mahabad as a tobacco inspector.

"Mahabad is an awful place," he said in response to the news that I had just been there. The rest of the Turks in the room nodded.

"But Margaret likes Mahabad, don't you, Margaret?" prodded Shehrzad.

"Yes," I said as everyone stared at me.

"Margaret *likes* Kurds, you know," Shehrzad gushed. "She wants to learn Kurdish." The cousin's eyes almost popped out, and no one else said anything.

Shehrzad smiled. "Foreigners are interested in these things," she explained, and someone changed the topic of conversation.

After our trip to Mahabad I looked at the crumpled piece of paper with the phone number of the man in Mahabad who had said he was Hassan's brother. He had been insistent that we should call him as soon as possible. But how? I hesitated to ask Shehrzad to let me use her phone. Then someone told me that the phones in Mahabad were not yet linked up to those in other provincial cities. I didn't know what to believe.

I was beginning to get the message that in Iran when someone refused to give you information about how to get from Point A to Point B, as in the bus station when we first tried to get to Mahabad, or when he said maybe you couldn't call one town from another, he was trying to say something else.

When Shehrzad had said in Mahabad that she didn't know any other place to take us except the Turk's souvenir shop, she was telling us that we shouldn't be anywhere else. She and Houshang had carefully tried to restrict our visit there to the inside of their car, the government-run *mehmunserai*, and a shop owned by a Turk. When we broke out of the boundaries they set, rudely insisting on seeing Hassan, going for walks, and getting out of the car at the circle, they had naturally been upset. They knew better than we did where our place was.

Everyone in Iran had a place. Servants and workers had theirs on the city buses, which cost three cents to ride. Clerks and other white-collar workers had theirs on the college-owned "staff" bus or the buses provided by government offices. Those were free. Professionals like ourselves are required to be in cars, which, at the time of our stay, cost $4,500 and up. This sense of place is so strong that a colleague of ours, when he was forced by pressing finances to sell his car, walked several miles instead of taking the staff bus.

In Rezaiyeh, Kurds have their place—outside of town. That was part of what was so annoying about the refugees. They insisted on being visibly Kurdish in a Turkish city. Mahabad was just the opposite. There the Turks did not belong. Perhaps that was why the government was building an artificial town on Mahabad's outskirts—to bring in Turks and Persians and make the area a little less solidly Kurdish. The more mixed Kurdistan became the harder it would be for its inhabitants to break off from the central government again. The Iraqi government has been using this method for years to "thin out" its part of Kurdistan.

Unbeknown to the shah's government, time was running out. It had carefully made sure that no army recruits from Kurdistan or indeed from any of the strongly ethnic areas would be posted among their own people. It had sent governors and mayors appointed in Tehran who would be sure to have no language and no sympathies in common with the people they administered. It had lured tribal chiefs into its pay. But the dream of the republic and the names Sauj Bulaq and Chwar Chira persisted among Kurds despite SAVAK's best efforts to eradicate them.

CHAPTER 4

RADIO REZAIYEH

I was sitting on a long couch facing some half-open venetian blinds, trying to look at the large, friendly face of Mr. Goherkhaneh rather than at the distracting lines of light behind him. But the rest of the room was getting blurry, whether from my astigmatism or from nervousness, I couldn't tell. Thirty people were watching me conduct my thrice-weekly Kurdish lesson, As a field linguist I was used to taking responsibility for organizing and directing any language instruction I might need, but at the radio station I often felt as if I were pulling Kurdish out of my teacher's mouth rather as one might pull teeth.

These excruciating lessons were held in the office of the manager of Radio Rezaiyeh, which, in addition to its main programming in Persian, broadcast shows in Azeri Turkish, Kurmanji Kurdish, and Assyrian. Although these programs were supposed to attest to Tehran's tolerance toward its ethnic minorities, some people alleged that the nonstandard languages were deliberately "Persianized" in the broadcasts. Even people who were not concerned with linguistic issues recognized that aside from the music, the Kurdish programs were basically a vehicle for the shah's propaganda.

At the bottom of the radio station's hierarchy was the tea man, standing at attention at the farthest end of the room from Mr. Goherkhaneh, waiting for a chance to approach the desk with half a dozen large porcelain cups rattling on his tray. Mr. Goherkhaneh usually directed that I be served first, with the other notables in the room receiving their tea in order of importance. Most had to go without, but they were not disappointed, since they had come for the entertainment, not the tea. I was the foreign woman who had walked into the station last week with a letter of introduction from an Iranian teacher at the college. Mr. Goherkhaneh had electrified the staff by announcing that I was to be taught Kurdish. So, at specified times on Saturday, Tuesday, and Thursday, other diversions ceased and everyone went to the office of the station manager to watch, listen, and make whispered remarks.

Once again I was among Turks, pursuing the study of Kurdish. This time, though, there *were* a few Kurds. The head of the Kurdish broadcasting staff, Mr. Asyabee, was half Kurdish, half Turkish. He was a stout, self-important man with an early Elvis hairdo and a preference for bulky knit turtleneck sweaters. It was clear that he relished the role of teacher in front of such a large audience. His answers to all of my awkward requests for verb forms and translations of vocabulary items were loud and deliberate. He was so pompous and concentrated so obviously on performing rather than imparting any information that I soon began to distrust the Kurdish he gave me.

The station manager, Mr. Goherkhaneh, if he hadn't been a Turk, would have been a far better instructor than Mr. Asyabee. Whereas Asyabee affected boredom and sophistication, Mr. Goherkhaneh was straightforward and enthusiastic, so enthusiastic in fact that he even encouraged my aspirations to learn Kurdish. As king of the station he presided over my lessons and made comments to the effect that I was very clever, which he pronounced "cleever." He was sure that I would be able to learn everything there was to know about Kurmanji, the northern dialect of Kurdish, in less than two months, at which time, the implication was, I could go on to something more complex and useful. I, on the other hand, doubted that I would ever learn the language, working in such a circus.

One day Mr. Asyabee had some other business and Mr. Goherkhaneh assigned me to study with Mr. Asyabee's sister, the next person in the hierarchy of Kurmanji broadcasting. She was a hugely pregnant, sloe-eyed woman whose ability to speak Kurdish seemed to have atrophied from extreme boredom. Like Mr. Asyabee, she was half Kurdish, and since she was married to a Persian, she didn't have much use for Kurdish. The next time I came to the station I was moved down to Mr. Gahi, a better-looking, more debonair version of Mr. Asyabee. Mr. Gahi was a great flirt with a good sense of humor. Teaching Kurdish was not high on his list of priorities, but since Mr. Goherkhaneh had ordered him, he made an effort to answer my questions.

Mr. Gahi was a poorer, older version of the French-educated "Kurdish" man I had met at the college. Without the advantages of a French education or a Peugeot, Mr. Gahi was trying to put his past village life behind him.

He managed to fool me with his stories of drinking and carousing around town like a single man, but he probably didn't fool anyone else. He sat at his desk all day on the telephone, shouting "*Qurbanet*" into the receiver. Literally this means "I will die for you," but Mr. Gahi used it loosely to show his callers what an elegantly magnanimous man he was.

At last my patience paid off, and I encountered the only person at the station who cared about Kurdish. When Mr. Gahi found other activities to occupy his time, I was passed to Mr. Khalili, who had always wanted to be my teacher. He immediately suggested that we leave the station manager's office and work alone in the next room.

Mr. Khalili proved to be a spectacular teacher in comparison to his predecessors. It was not just that he cared whether I learned something that was correct, but that he loved his language. He had collected all sorts of underground literature that had been printed in Kurdish. Later I learned that he wrote poetry in Kurdish. Although Kurdish has never been an officially recognized language in Iran or Turkey, the list of works clandestinely published there is impressive. Kurdish books legally printed in Iraq were also smuggled across the border and guarded jealously in Iranian villages.

Mr. Khalili managed to obtain a copy of *Mam o Zeen* for me by telling a villager that he had lost his own copy. Radio Rezaiyeh regularly broadcast lyric verses from this great Kurdish epic with musical accompaniment, but, as Mr. Khalili pointed out, it was unthinkable to put the explicitly nationalist portions on the air. *Mam o Zeen*, the story of two tragically separated lovers, *à la* Romeo and Juliet, is really an allegory for the tragic fate of Kurds, separated and denied unity by the Turks, Persians, and Arabs as well as their own intertribal warfare.

Ahmedi Kani wrote *Mam o Zeen* in the seventeenth century, and it has been reprinted many times in Turkish, Iraqi, and Sviet Kurdistan. Kurdish writers who came after Khani have dealt with topics ranging from love to the beauty of the Kurdish mountains. But none has failed to mention the nationalist aspirations of the Kurds. Writing in Kurdish is in itself an act of defiance. Musa Anter's Kurdish-Turkish dictionary is as unacceptable to the Ankara government as his *Birina Resh*, "The Black Wound," a play about the disease and death of many Kurdish villagers from chemically treated grain handed out by the government.

Mr. Khalili tried to teach me elementary Kurdish. At first I was excited, but gradually I became frustrated. I felt that I could not make enough progress to suit him. He wanted me to be able to read poetry and understand abstruse metaphors while I was still working hard on conjugating verbs. I had studied some Kurdish in the United States, but Kurdistan, since it has no single, standard language, is split by numerous dialect differences. Whatever I knew from before had to be repurposed into the local pronunciation, and there were still many, many words that I did not know.

I was sometimes afraid that the forms Mr. Khalili gave me were too literary, too erudite for a language like Kurdish. Kurdish is primarily an oral, not a written, language, spoken by villagers who use it to conduct the business of life. It is also employed creatively to tell jokes, sing songs, and narrate long stories. The Arabic, Turkish, and Persian loanwords in Kurdish are an integral part of the language the way Latin and French words are in English. But Mr. Khalili, a Kurdish patriot, was always trying to purge his language for me. He would substitute authentic Kurdish roots that no one else knew for the Persian or Arabic words that everyone used. I was beginning to realize that if I wanted real, down-to-earth Kurdish, I would have to go to a village and talk with the people there. I suggested this to Mr. Khalili, but he put me off, saying I wasn't ready.

Not long after, Mr. Khalili abruptly decided to take me to a village. Everyone else on the programming staff sat around in Rezaiyeh, making recordings, drinking tea, and going home in the afternoon for noonday meals followed by protracted naps. Mr. Khalili, on the other hand, as the lowest man on the staff, was required to spend the entire day in a village, recruiting farmers for the agricultural question-and-answer sessions that were aired weekly.

After he asked me to come along, he asked pointedly whether my husband would be coming as well. His tone made me uncomfortable, and I wondered what he thought I should do. Mr. Khalili and I were already getting strange looks at the station because my lessons were now held in private. I was sure, as I got to know him better, that he never spent time alone with any women, except his wives.

Since there were no classes at the college on the day scheduled for this expedition, Jared was free and so I brought him along. Mr. Khalili, dressed as usual in a black suit, white shirt, and black tie, was waiting for us along with Mr. Gahi's brother, the official driver. Noting the driver's flirtatious manner, I was glad I was not alone.

We took a western route out of the city, a road we had never traveled on further than Band Village. Mahabad, to the south, is reached via a tree-lined boulevard that turned into a two-lane road meandering through village after village. The road to the west was quite different. Once we had passed through the lush valley of Band, the landscape here was barren and desertlike, especially now in October, the tail end of the dry season.

Looking out at the circular plateau ringed by mountains I felt as if we were traveling across the face of the moon, so different and alien did this landscape appear to me. We passed Kurdish shepherds standing by the side of the road, staring alternately at our jeep and their flocks of sheep. We passed families huddled together waiting for the rural bus. Mostly we passed nothing but rocks, leaving a huge cloud of dust behind us as I looked back, wondering how we could find our way back across the arid, boulder-strewn plain.

As we emerged from the next pass through the mountains that separate the first circular plain of Mergawar from the next circular plain of Tergawar, I noticed a slight increase in the amount of vegetation. Tergawar's stone villages were once inhabited by Christian tribes who, for a time, had shared the mountains and plains with the Kurds. These were the Assyrians. They, along with the Armenians, had embraced Christianity long before most of the rest of the Christian world.

Assyrians had lived in uneasy peace with the Kurds for many years, but world events—attentions from Russian troops who occupied Azerbaijan around the time of World War I, and the Western missionaries—brought the wrath of their Muslim neighbors down on their heads. Some villages east and south of Rezaiyeh are still inhabited predominantly by Assyrians, but in Tergawar the Assyrians are gone—driven out, or murdered. The Kurds took possession of their trees and churches.

The Herki, one of the largest tribes of today's Kurdistan, with an estimated 30,000 members in Iran and Iraq, dominate Tergawar. Part of the tribe lives here in the old Christian villages, while part remains in Iraq near the town of Erbil, or Hewler, as the Kurds call it. But despite their geographical separation, the two groups have remained very much united. All the years that the Iranian and Iraqi armies confronted each other along their mutual border, the Herki were somehow allowed to pass in order to graze their flocks in the mountains of Iran each summer.

While other tribes were forced to choose one country or to be forever split, the Herki were allowed to live as their ancestors had, camping in settled villages in the winter and in tents on mountaintops in the summer, without worrying about national borders. But the year that I came to Kurdistan marked the end of this way of life, even for this privileged tribe. Watchers along the border were destined to wait in vain this coming spring for the first sign of the tribe and their flocks making the long trek from Iraq.

Although a century earlier nearly all Kurds were pastoral nomads, by the time I got to Kurdistan few tribes could live like the Herkis. Most were confined to villages, with a few lucky ones permanently settled in cities, enabled by dint of education or imagination to give their children a better future than village life could offer. These Kurds and their descendants often stop thinking of themselves as having any tribal affiliation. But in Iranian villages, tribes were still all-powerful, commanding far more allegiance than the Iranian government.

In Iran alone there were estimated to be sixty tribes with 500 to 3,000 plus families apiece. Some of the larger tribes were subdivided into *tayfa* or clans. The minimal social unit in Kurdistan is the extended family rather than the individual. Quite a few villagers were considered tribeless. They were called Kurmanj or more pejoratively *doodi boodi*, somewhat equivalent to our *hoi polloi*. These Kurmanj were attached to villages and landlords as peasants or serfs. Although they might fight for a particular tribe they did not wear the particular dress that distinguishes one tribe from another—for example, the red and white turbans of the Barzanis or the green sashes of the Sayids.

"Sheikh" in Kurdistan was the title reserved for the head of the village, clan, or tribe, although it can also be used in its more usual Islamic sense of religious leader. Other titles used by Kurdish notables included "Beg," and "Agha," both originally Turkish, as well as the Mongolian-derived "Khan."

Outside of Kurdistan, "Agha" and "Beg" have lost some of their cachet, since "Agha" in Iran and "Bey" in Turkey are the usual titles for men—like our "Mr." Reza Shah, the last shah's father, outlawed the title "Khan" because he wanted to be the only *Khan* in the country. Kurds seem to have ignored that edict, among many others. They not only call some of their leaders Khan, but, unlike any other Muslim people, attach it to the names of distinguished women as well as men.

Completely ignorant of both the past and future of Tergawar, and still knowing little about the hierarchy of Kurdish villages and tribes, I saw only the rocky landscape softened by a tiny stream here or a village and a patch of trees there. I didn't even appreciate the preeminence of the village where we were heading. Mawana was the headquarters of the great Rashid Beg, one of the leaders of the Herki at the time that the tribe had played such a strangely ambivalent role in the formation and dissolution of the Mahabad Republic.

Mr. Khalili, of course, had mentioned none of this to me. He had said only that we were traveling to a typical Kurdish village where, for the first time, I would see how village people— real Kurds—lived. I could talk to the women and understand something of their lives. I was so wrapped up in worrying about how these long-imagined Kurdish women would react to me and in wondering how they would even understand me, in my curious broken Kurdish, that it didn't occur to me to speculate on what Mr. Gahi's brother and Mr. Khalili were going to do in their dark suits and black ties in a "typical" dusty village.

Even the shining metal roofs of the clinic and high school just outside Mawana did not tell me how unusually blessed this village was. As far as I knew, all villages had such amenities. I was becoming more and more apprehensive about the crowd of raggedy children who had gathered to stare when we got out of the car. They looked so poor and strange. I did not know that even the children of the wealthiest tribal leaders wander around in ragged, cast-off adult clothing, their little sunburned faces gray with grime. Ironically, it was the poverty and dirt of Mawana, one of the richest villages in northern Kurdistan, that struck me first.

Mr. Khalili spoke to me kindly but firmly.

"You must go with the women," he said.

I looked around and wondered where that was when I saw two older girls dressed in neat Kurdish costumes approaching from the entrance of one of the two-story buildings in front of me. Mr. Khalili and Mr. Gahi quickly led Jared off in another direction. I was left alone, my heart pounding.

"*Te kheyr hati*," they said many times over so that I would know I was welcome at their house. Then they motioned for me to follow them inside, up some rough stone stairs to the second floor, where one of them took out a huge skeleton key and unlocked a crudely made wooden door.

In contrast to the bare, dirty hall, the room inside was alight with color. The pillows and wall hangings and coverlets reminded me of the handicrafts I had seen at the shop in Mahabad. Not a single surface was left bare. The hand-cranked sewing machine and the radio cassette player which were perched on shelves cut into the wall both had elaborately quilted covers. At one side of the room was a high double bed with a pile of handmade coverlets, and on another side was a low dressing table covered with ornate perfume bottles. Two older women with jet-black hair and blue dresses with black vests sat on the rug next to the table. They rose when I entered with the two girls. Behind us trailed some of the children from the courtyard.

"*Te kheyr hati*," they all said and quickly presented me with a plate of small, wormy-looking apples. Feeling obliged to take one immediately, I carefully peeled off the skin and ate it while they watched.

As soon as I had finished, without warning, they gathered around me as one woman brought over a pile of clothing. Somehow, without the medium of language, I grasped the idea that they wanted to dress me up like a Kurd. For a moment I wondered uncomfortably whether I would have to take off the corduroy slacks and sweater I had worn to the village. As if to answer my question, one of the women threw the first dress of white-and-gold tulle over my head; the rest of the outfit quickly followed.

In a couple of minutes I was completely swathed in Kurdish garb. The woman then lifted a collar of gold chains and charms from around the neck of one of the girls who had greeted me and put it around my neck. I looked down at the gold, wondering if it could possibly be real—there was so much of it. Next, a heavy black turban, edged in pompoms, was wound around my head, with bits of my own hair woven in.

Finally, they attempted to remove my glasses and paint my eyes with kohl, the black substance traditionally used all over the Middle East as an eyeliner. At this I balked, refusing to be made up. I put my glasses back on, and they sighed when I told them that I never wore makeup and never went without my glasses. Then they pointed me toward the dressing-table mirror, watching eagerly to see my reaction.

I stared at my reflection, feeling as if I were in a dream. A minute before, I had been standing in the dusty courtyard being scrutinized by a crowd of children, Now I looked as if I had joined a medieval pageant, with the long, pointed sleeve endings wrapped around my wrists and a weighty headdress perched on my head. But before I could muse about my appearance any more, my hostesses were taking me somewhere else. I clutched my skirts to avoid tripping as we descended the stone stairs. Outside, in the bright sun, the two girls backed off, holding their headscarves over their mouths while I began walking toward my husband, who was seated at a card table with the men under the trees in the courtyard.

The men nodded to me when I came over, but did not stand up. In villages men do not stand for women unless they are very important women and the men are very unimportant men. Mr. Khalili looked at me approvingly. Later Jared told me that the men had been hinting to him, before I came out, that he was in for a surprise.

This was our initiation into one of the standard entertainments that Kurds have to offer foreign women who visit. Even Persian women from Tehran vacationing in Rezaiyeh were waylaid by my Kurdish friends in the bazaar and taken home to be dressed and photographed. I could never figure out who was supposed to be more amused by this—the dressers or the dressee. Since photographs were an essential part of this ritual, I handed Jared my camera and he took a few pictures of me, but when he came closer to the house where the girls were standing, they instinctively turned away from the camera, their scarves over their mouths.

I went back to the men, and Mr. Khalili asked, "Are you having a good time?"

I looked at him and then at Jared and then at the other men. Was I having a good time? It was simply impossible to evaluate what sort of time I was having. All I could do was wonder what they were going to do to me next. But, of course, I told Mr. Khalili I was having a wonderful time. He beamed. Jared looked at me strangely, and I wondered what kind of time he was having. Later I discovered that the men had been trying to persuade him to take another wife. The offer was sparked by his telling them that he very much wanted me to learn Kurdish.

They replied, with some logic, "If you want a wife who speaks Kurdish, why not get one who really knows the language? You could take one of our girls as a second wife."

Jared then explained that it was also important that his wife know English. The men assured him with some dishonesty that they could find a village girl who knew some English. Finally Jared said that he would have to be friends with his wife before he could marry her. That stumped them. Kurdish husbands and wives are not friends, especially not before they are married.

Meanwhile, my two hostesses decided to take me on a walking tour of the village. I grasped my camera in one hand and my long skirts in the other, though they continually advised me to drop the hems and let the edges of the dresses drag in the dust. I ignored what I thought was their polite offer and kept holding the white-and-gold tulle out of the dust, for it was inconceivable to me to let such finery be covered by the dirt.

I had yet to fully appreciate the fact that these women wore such clothes every day and that they did not have time to worry about a little dirt. No wonder. The whole village seemed to be covered with dirt. Again, the strangeness and the poverty struck me as we walked behind the large brick edifices where my hostesses lived. Here, on the winding mud pathways, I saw conical mud huts and deep mud courtyards and what seemed to be dozens of eyes staring at me out of sunburned faces.

The cone-shaped huts with the straw roofs floated by in a blur as I lifted my skirts higher to cross a little stream in our path. My two escorts, who were better dressed than any of the audience, led me over to a toothless woman weaving on a crude loom in the yard in front of her hut. 1 stopped and examined the coarse black wool fabric, asking what it would be.

The answer: a chador. Startled, I looked around. Was I so disoriented that I had failed to notice villagers wearing veils? All of the women standing along the path had their heads covered only by scarves. Not one wore a full-length veil.

"Chador?" I repeated questioningly. The woman gave me a look, no doubt wondering if I understood her language, and added, "For the mountains." Then I understood. A chador in the old meaning of "tent," not in the city meaning of veil. In Kurdistan, the only things that are black, besides the vests of some of the women, are the tents that bloom on the mountaintops when the weather gets warm enough in spring to take the animals up to graze.

On our way back to my hostesses' house, we saw a pregnant woman spinning yarn on a drop spindle. She did not want to have her picture taken, but my hostesses prevailed upon her. I profited by knowing so little Kurdish and being so ignorant of village custom that I did not feel guilty about accepting her reluctant agreement. Later on, I would not be able to photograph strange women in villages so easily.

Closer to the house, we passed a bald man chopping wood with an ax. He was happy to have his picture taken. As I passed and photographed these exotic characters—the toothless weaver, the pregnant spinner, the bald woodsman—I could not help feeling that I was in a fairy tale. Pretty pictures, vignettes of an alien life, flashed by me but how could I know anything about the way these people lived? I was in the company of the two princesses of the village. Their house was strange to me too, but at least it held familiar things like beds and sewing machines and windows set at right angles. What lay beyond the mud doorstep of the weaver?

After our tour past the mud hovels of the village, I looked at the house where my hostesses lived with new eyes. The yellow, manufactured bricks, the metal window frames, the second story had all seemed quite ordinary when I first saw them. There are thousands of such buildings in Rezaiyeh, many in better condition. But in Mawana, there are only two, and every brick, every piece of iron, had been transported through the mountain passes on a dirt road. Rashid Beg had built these houses and populated them with the progeny of his wives and his son Amir Khan's wives.

We went back inside, past the animals housed on the bottom floor. It was so dark, after the bright sunlight, that I could hardly make anything out until we reached the stairway, which had a window at the top. Inside the room where we had been before I quickly took off my borrowed finery, relieved that I no longer had to worry about getting it dirty. Then we settled down on the rug and faced one another.

I had finally gotten their names straight. Shireen, or "Sweet," was the dark, heavy-set one, while Parweneh, "Butterfly," was just like her name, ethereal and blond. Shireen, the younger of the two, began the questioning.

"Do you have any children?" she asked.

"No."

"Why not?"

"Uh, I haven't been married for very long."

"Then you will have one in a little while?" she asked, looking at my stomach.

"No, I don't think so."

"How do you know?"

I sat wondering how the conversation had gone so far so fast. How old were these two girls, anyway? How detailed did they expect me to get about the form of birth control I used? I pictured my diaphragm, a device not known in Iranian Kurdistan, and I tried to summon the words to describe it.

Finally Parweneh prompted, "You take pills?"

"*Taqriban*," I replied in Persian. *Taqriban*, literally "approximately," is an Arabic word useful for giving vague answers all over the Middle East.

Now it was my turn to ask questions. Being too reticent to ask anything intimate, I limited myself to Kurdish names for objects in the room. We played this game for a short while with varying success. I understood so little Kurdish—although they politely assured me that I spoke their language fluently—that they kept switching into Persian. Since they had attended school through the fifth grade they knew quite a bit of the standard language and assumed that I, as an educated stranger, would of course know Persian far better than their own unwritten tongue. I couldn't seem to make them understand that it was nonstandard, no-prestige Kurdish that I had studied in the United States, not Persian.

Without explanation my hostesses went to confer with the maid in the corridor. The maid then came into the room, carrying a metal basin and a plastic pitcher with a narrow spout. One of my hostesses retrieved a bar of soap and a towel from the cupboard and handed them to me. Awkwardly, I held my hands out while the maid poured. Then I lathered my hands with the soap, rinsed them in more poured water, and dried them with the towel.

As the two girls washed their hands, Parweneh explained to me, "My father has many of these."

I stared at her. Many of what? Basins and pitchers? Bars of soap? When she pointed to the girl pouring the water, I understood. Her father owned many maidservants.

Parweneh's father's maid was the first of many I was to meet in Kurdish households. Right from the beginning I was uncertain how to act with servants. It made me nervous to have someone performing the function of a water pipe and faucet in front of me. Maidservants also spent hours washing clothes by hand, cleaning foodstuffs, baking bread, and doing other time-consuming chores. But it was not only the hardness of their lives or the menialness of their chores that made me uneasy; my inability to recognize servants was also a problem. Service in a partially feudal, not very monetary economy is a fluid thing. Although Parweneh said her father "owned" servants, in other villages I saw that anyone could be called into service at any time, depending on the situation and the status of the people involved.

Peasants often waited on landlords and their families as a matter of course, without any regular wage. Villagers who came into the city temporarily on errands and stayed at the sheikh's house routinely served the regular inhabitants. Kurds who were full-time servants often seemed to be like members of the family. They lived in the houses of their employers and their clothing was often indistinguishable from that of their betters. Conversely, real members of the family sometimes seemed like servants.

New brides waited on mothers-in-law, sisters on brothers, and younger sisters on older sisters. Even the sheikh, the highest man in the village, might wait on someone if it was appropriate. Aristocratic Kurdish men, pampered from childhood by the women and servants around them, turn into the most deferential hosts if there is no one else around to serve the guest. But service in Kurdistan is primarily "in the family," for when I tried to find a Kurdish woman rather than a Turk to work in my house I was told that Kurds did not work for strangers.

When dinner was served, not having been to a village before, I could not appreciate what an elegant and munificent repast it was. It did not even occur to me to wonder how often my hostesses ate meat, involving as it did the labor of the shepherds to graze the sheep, the slaughtering, and the problem of storage in a place with no refrigerators, not to mention cutting and cleaning. Our mutton stew contained not only meat, but home-grown vegetables as well. Then there were potatoes fried to crispness over a non-adjustable, non-gas flame. Finally there was the bread, painstakingly baked every morning, made from the flour ground by the mill I heard humming when I walked outside the village. Of course not many villages had their own power mills.

After the meal, Shireen and Parweneh suggested that I must be tired and ought to lie down and take a nap. But I felt wide awake. Besides, I did not know how to gracefully stretch out my legs in front of them, having read in a book that it is the height of rudeness in the Middle East to point your soles at someone. As we all sat cross-legged on the floor facing one another I could see them wondering how they were going to amuse me. The language barrier, hour after hour, was becoming tedious.

Finally they hit on the idea of teaching me how to dance. Parweneh jumped up and took down the cassette player from the shelf, removed its cover, and put on a cassette. As a scratchy recording began to play, the two girls clasped hands and slowly began to circle the room in a stately rendition of a traditional Middle Eastern line dance. They pointed first one foot and then the other and shuffled sideways. At their urging, I stood up and attempted to follow them. Then, after an awkward few minutes, we all sat down again. I wondered if that was all there was to Kurdish dancing. Casting about for something else, they pulled down the family picture album and I looked at picture after picture of stiff, non-smiling Kurds. I tuned the pages politely, trying and failing to make some sense of all these strangers.

Then Shireen asked, "Are you coming to Parweneh's wedding?"

I looked at her quizzically, trying not to get my hopes up. I had heard about the fabulous extravagance of Kurdish weddings and I was dying to be invited to one. But then I saw that Parweneh was blushing and frowning.

"I'm not getting married," the blond girl said, looking angrily at her sibling.

"Yes, she is," Shireen assured me.

I looked from one to the other, still hoping that somehow this was a real invitation to a real Kurdish wedding, but, at the same time, I felt that there probably was not going to be a wedding if the bride-to-be denied it. Perhaps this was another ritual, like dressing me up. Foreign guests were jokingly invited to weddings that were not scheduled to take place.

"How old are you?" I asked the girls, thinking that might provide me with a clue as to whether Parweneh was really getting married or not.

"Fourteen," answered Shireen.

"Fifteen," said Parweneh, the supposed bride.

"Will you come, then?" Shireen prodded me as Parweneh made faces.

"I don't know," I said doubtfully.

At that moment the maid appeared in the doorway, and everyone stood up in relief at the news that Mr. Khalili had summoned me. They would be able to get in their after-lunch naps after all. After I thanked them and shook their hands, I hurriedly wrote down my address in Rezaiyeh and urged them to visit me when they came to town. They had told me, in the course of our conversations, that they often came to Rezaiyeh, and I imagined that they were free simply to leave wherever it was they stayed and walk or take a taxi over to my house.

The maid led me down the stone stairs and then motioned for me to go over to the men. Once more I was boldly examined by a number of male eyes. I sensed hostility and contempt in their gaze, although I did not know then that they had been offering Jared another wife. Mr. Khalili again asked if I was having a good time. I stood, waiting expectantly for everyone to stand up so that we could leave, but no one moved.

"Aren't we leaving?" I asked Jared, in English.

"No, I think Mr. Khalili just wanted to see how you were doing."

I stared back at the entrance to the harem, bare of children or adults in the hot autumn sun. Now I would have to go back, for I could not continue to stand and be stared at by these men. Slowly I walked away, getting all of the way up the stairs alone until Shireen opened the door in surprise, looking at me in consternation. Guests are never supposed to be left alone in a village.

Shireen and Parweneh gallantly roused themselves to be my hostesses for yet another hour. We drank glass after glass of tea and tried to keep a conversation going, but everyone was relieved when a little boy came and told us it was time for me to go. Again we said goodbye, but this time the two girls accompanied me all the way down the stairs and outside to make sure I was actually leaving.

Back in the jeep, swirling through the clouds of dust in the mid-afternoon sun, I learned that Mr. Khalili's fancy Swiss-made tape recorder had not been working well enough to record anything. For him, the day had been a waste. Then why had we stayed so long? I wondered to Jared. For your sake, he answered.

"Now you know something about village life," said Mr. Khalili, smiling.

I nodded politely. The scenes of the day had frozen in my mind like unconnected frames in a foreign movie. Dust, glittering dresses, drop spindles, mud huts, sunburned faces, strong-tasting yogurt, and dust, dust, and more dust. I had sat until my buttocks were sore, trying to converse with two girls.

What did they do when I was not there? I had no idea. It did not occur to me to wonder why I had been entertained by a fourteen- and a fifteen-year-old. I just assumed that their mothers were off doing something more useful than entertaining foreign guests. But, where were they? My notions of what people and especially women did with their time were still hopelessly tied to the United States and a milieu that bore no relation to this village.

"Is Parweneh really getting married?" I asked Mr. Khalili the next time I saw him for a lesson. He glanced at Mr. Gahi, who was, for once, not on the telephone.

"She already got married, last Thursday."

At the surprised look on my face Mr. Gahi laughed loudly. "Parweneh threw herself into the fire," was what he said.

I imagined the Indian custom of burning a wife on her husband's funeral pyre, and it turned out I was not so far from the truth.

"We say she threw herself into the fire because she married an old man," explained Mr. Khalili.

"A deaf old man with two other wives," added Mr. Gahi, chuckling.

I continued to stand there, conscious of the fact that I was looking very sour and that the two men perceived me as a typical Outraged Western Woman. Now I knew why Parweneh's face was so red.

"Shireen told me that Parweneh was getting married, but Parweneh said it wasn't true," I said.

"Yes, that is the custom," said Mr. Khalili. "Our brides should be shy. Her father was the one who arranged the wedding. That's why there was no one in the village the day you were there. All of the women came into Rezaiyeh to prepare for the party."

I stared at them, wondering how I had missed so much. Why had Mr. Khalili chosen to go to Mawana? Who was Shireen and Parweneh's father, and why had he chosen to marry his daughter off to a deaf old man with two other wives?

It was too alien, too stark. Even in Mahabad, I had not pictured Kurdistan like this. I thought the Kurds were different. Their women didn't wear veils and worked alongside their men. Where were the democratic ideals of the Mahabad Republic?

I returned to the radio-station routine, coming to study with Mr. Khalili according to the schedule we had agreed on. Sometimes he would be gone for the day, visiting another village on a reportage trip, and I would wonder why he hadn't told me or, more worrisome, why he hadn't invited me to come too. He made vague promises, but never again would he take me to sit with the women. Had I embarrassed him or annoyed my hostesses in

Mawana? I mulled the events of that day over and over in my mind, wondering what Shireen and Parweneh had thought of me.

Stacks of letters arrived at the radio station every week. I saw them piled up on Mr. Asyabee's desk and asked what they were. Questions and comments from listeners in the village. The better my Kurdish became, the more closely I was able to follow the radio broadcasts. I realized that an important part of the programming was translating the official news from Persian into Kurdish. This "news" was pared down to its essentials for the Kurds. "The shah is a great and glorious ruler." "The Iranian army can vanquish all foes." "Oil will enrich the poorest villager in Kurdistan." "Stay tuned and listen to Kurdish music."

Many villagers did stay tuned, huddled around the battery-powered radios that were their only contact with the outside world. I wondered how much of the news they believed. I wondered what Mr. Asyabee did with those letters and why Mr. Khalili went out and did "reportage" in the villages.

The more time I spent with Mr. Khalili, the more I was aware that there was some mystery surrounding him. He was a strikingly uncomfortable man who looked progressively more unhappy and unhealthy over the year I spent in Iran. Once he told Jared that he never slept at night and that he had lost a lot of weight because he couldn't eat. His clothes hung from his body, and some days his skin looked ashen. I sometimes had him read poetry and tell stories into my tape recorder, and once, in order to get him to speak informally, I asked him to recount the story of a time he came close to death. At this request, he turned paler than usual and said that if he complied, he would be forced to relive an experience so horrible it would keep him from sleep for weeks.

Mr. Khalili was far too serious for the job he had been hired to do. If only he could have been satisfied with reprocessing government propaganda into Kurdish. If only he could have regarded his treks into the countryside as outings on which to lord his importance over the villagers and get favors from them.

From listening to the nightly broadcasts I finally learned that Mr. Khalili was supposed to be disseminating agricultural information via the home-grown question-and-answer sessions he tape-recorded in village mosques or schools; but these expeditions were like throwing seeds on the dry, infertile, rocky soil of the mountains. No one in the government had given any serious thought or money to the question of how to motivate these villagers to change their farming methods in order to produce more. Mr. Khalili was simply the last link in a chain that went nowhere—a fall guy for the misconceived agricultural policies of the shah. He told me that when he had first taken this job he had had high hopes of doing something for his countrymen. Just thinking about his earlier ideals made him laugh bitterly.

I was flattered by how much Mr. Khalili chose to reveal about his feelings at a time when a person with such feelings stood in great danger. But perhaps Mr. Khalili had already faced that danger. Perhaps he had already been imprisoned and tortured. Such an experience could have explained his terrible anxiety. But I never asked. For the most part, our talk was limited to what might have been and, in the still optimistic days of the Kurdish War of 1974, what might yet be.

The more I talked with people at the college, the more I realized that everyone in Iran was afraid. Hardly anyone was willing to discuss politics. From the time I had first contemplated going to the radio station and announcing my intention of studying Kurdish I realized that I would be blatantly exposing myself to the secret police. A policeman always guarded the door of the station, and it was obvious, from listening to the nightly news, that there was no separation between press and government. I took the risk of being asked what permission I had to be studying this semi-outlawed language, or worse, of being considered a spy or an agent come to stir up nationalist feeling among the Kurds in Iran. As a woman who taught English at the college, I seemed innocuous enough, but there was no telling for sure. Suppose I made an enemy. Suppose Mr. Goherkhaneh, a Turk, got seriously annoyed that a foreigner wanted to learn Kurdish instead of Turkish. Suppose. There was nothing concrete to worry about yet, but there soon would be.

CHAPTER 5

A LESSON IN TA'AROF

It took me a long time to appreciate just how visible I was as a foreigner in Rezaiyeh. I was used to living invisibly in big cities like New York, but even my sojourns in small American towns had not prepared me for the scrutiny I would undergo as a foreigner in Iran. Rezaiyeh has a population of about 150,000, swollen during the time of my stay by the flood of Kurdish refugees from Iraq. Amid this large native population were a handful of foreigners— perhaps fifty Germans, Americans, French, and Poles, as well as some less noticeably foreign Turks and Egyptians. A number of the foreigners were wives of Iranians who had studied in Europe or America, and I soon noticed that almost all of them kept a low profile, staying at home as much as they could, depending on servants or husbands to do their shopping.

The possibility of staying at home did not occur to me, at least not during my first few months in Rezaiyeh. We had no car, so every day I was out on the street alone, hailing orange taxis, going to the produce market, the bazaar, the radio station, the college. As soon as I walked from the relatively deserted kucheh where our house was to the main street, the calling would begin.

"Hello, meesus. How are yoooooooo," would echo down the street after me. At first I looked at the people, mostly men and boys, who were yelling at me. My ears were alert to possible greetings from real friends, and the crudest, least English-sounding ogler could get my attention. Slowly, I learned to walk stiffly and never smile, never acknowledge that I heard anything. I managed to wrap myself in a psychological veil so thick that if a friend greeted me on the street, chances were good I would ignore that too, only realizing too late that it had been someone I knew. A Polish engineer who worked at one of the government offices in town decided that I was a very unfriendly person because he had greeted me on the street three times and I had ignored him on all three occasions.

Unpleasant junctures in more personal encounters with Iranians were not as easily ignored as street harassment. We had never before had the experience of being asked pointblank by virtual strangers, "How much money do you make?" "Why don't you have children?" Many of the Iranians we were introduced to asked us these questions in our first conversation with them. The questions were put so directly that we didn't know how to let people know that it was none of their business without seeming incredibly rude.

With no information to guide us, we assumed that Iranians must ask each other these very same questions and, presumably, give some answers. Persian is a language that is well developed to handle the nuances of every social interaction. Unfortunately, since we didn't know it well enough to use it to our advantage, we were always left tongue-tied, either giving out more information than we felt comfortable about or ineptly insulting our listeners with our feeble efforts to deflect their queries.

One day I mentioned this problem to the wife of the teacher who had helped us find our apartment. She immediately grasped what I was talking about.

"Yes, the people here are very *fuzool*," she said. "It's awful the way Turks gossip about everything. They have no manners at all, the way they will ask you about anything."

She came from Meshed, a city far away in northeastern Iran, and, like all of the people I talked with who were not native to Rezaiyeh but were forced to live there, she hated the place.

"You call the people *fuzool* when they ask such questions?" I asked, trying to learn the new word.

"Yes."

"Is that a polite word, I mean, can you actually call people that without having them get angry?" I was beginning to be aware of the power of epithets in Iran; the response can be overwhelming to an American who is used to giving and receiving casual insults. In Iran, there is no such thing as a casual insult.

"If people are *fuzool*, then you may certainly call them *fuzool*," she said. I filed the word away for future use and that night repeated the whole conversation to Jared.

"*Fuzool*," Jared repeated to himself, learning the word that described some of our least favorite behavior.

Sometimes we found ourselves in the company of Iranians who wanted information from us and who knew how to get it in more subtle ways. We were not attuned to the social niceties necessary for surviving in a police state. Even the normal conversational game of one-upmanship played daily between Iranian acquaintances was far beyond us. Many Iranians were very aware of how naive and uninformed foreigners—especially Americans—are in their complex society, and some were able to use this knowledge to their own advantage.

One day we were sitting at a table in a local confectionary when a Kurd joined us, saying he was a friend of Hassan, our friend from Mahabad. Somehow, this stranger told us this in such a way that it did not immediately occur to us to wonder how he knew that we knew Hassan. Our new tablemate then led us through a conversation for about twenty minutes which culminated in an invitation to accompany him to his house. In those days when we received so few invitations and knew so little about Iranian etiquette, our first and overwhelming impulse was to accept.

We found ourselves standing in the man's tiny kitchen, where his wife was making tea, and he was suddenly asking us all sorts of questions about Hassan. It was as if he had drugged us up until this point—lulled us into unsuspecting compliance by his gracious invitation and adroit verbal manipulation. Wide awake now, we managed to extricate ourselves after drinking the required glass of tea.

Later we wondered why it had taken so long for us to realize that this man was no doubt an agent of the secret police. Maybe it was because he was Kurdish and we hadn't expected to find Kurds in SAVAK. We didn't know that the Rezaiyeh branch of the secret police was headed by a Kurd from Kermanshah. He was reputed to be on very good terms with the aristocracy of Mawana, the village we had just visited.

Only our neighbors, the Jaffaris, didn't make us uncomfortable with their questions. They were curious about how much money we made, but they were obviously making so much more that it was not an awkward issue. Anyway, if they asked us questions, we usually felt relaxed enough to ask them questions back. The relationship seemed to be on an equal footing. It was a while before I noticed that they paid too much attention to everything we did. They noted and criticized our comings and goings, the people who came to visit us, even the accent I was acquiring in Persian. One day, Shehrzad burst into laughter when I pronounced a common Persian word to her.

"You sound like a Kurd," she said accusingly.

It was true. Kurdish and Persian are so close together that it was sometimes hard for me to keep them apart, especially as I was trying to learn both at the same time. I explained this to Shehrzad, but she was not impressed. The implication was that an American accent was preferable to a Kurdish accent when speaking Persian. That made me feel more self-conscious about speaking to her, but, still, I did not question the goodwill the Jaffaris seemed to have for us. I did not really appreciate how closely they were monitoring my activities, because I could not imagine that they cared that much. It was my own delusion that I was going around Rezaiyeh, a private person on private business, unnoticed and uncommented upon by the locals.

I was becoming such an unremarkable sight at the radio station that the policeman at the door now rarely even raised his head when I entered. Since I was no longer under intense scrutiny, I was able to pay more attention to other visitors. Not only did letters arrive at the station from Kurdish villages, but people, mostly men, came as well. They would hang around the room where the Kurmanji staff sat at their metal desks. Depending on their importance, which was usually obvious from their dress, these visitors would either be assiduously ignored or deferentially served tea.

Some old men in ragged clothes would sit patiently in front of Mr. Asyabee, waiting for him to look up from his microphone or papers in order to hear some special plea. Others, well-dressed middle-aged tribal leaders, would monopolize the staff conversation for several hours at a time. My Kurdish was not yet good enough to follow word for word what these colloquies were about. I imagined, from a village point of view, that Mr. Asyabee and even Mr. Gahi and Mr. Khalili must have seemed like important men, capable of granting all sorts of unimaginable favors.

One day I saw a man in a shiny gray suit with a black turban and many gold crowns on his teeth sitting at the station. We were briefly introduced, and then he went back to his tête-à-tête with Mr. Asyabee. Later I ran into him again when Mr. Gahi gave me a ride out to the college in his car. Both men seemed vastly amused to be alone in a car with a foreign woman. I heard the man in the gray suit asking Gahi all sorts of questions about me. When I interrupted and answered him in Kurdish, he was astonished.

"So she speaks Kurdish," he told Gahi, as if I could only speak, but not hear. "Where did she learn?"

"A Kurd from Turkey taught her in America," Gahi answered.

The stranger's mind worked fast. "Was it a boy or girl?"

Gahi paused and looked at me. Since Kurdish has no gender, "he" and "she" being rendered by one sexless pronoun, Gahi had no way of knowing. I had never mentioned the name of my teacher.

Anxious to take an active part in the conversation, I quickly informed them, without thinking, "A boy."

"Aha." They nodded at each other significantly.

I didn't realize it at the time, but my reputation was now fixed in Mr. Sheikhzadeh's mind. For that was the name of this peremptory stranger—Sheikhzadeh, "the progeny of the sheikh"—and it soon became apparent that he had come to the radio station this day to invite the Kurmanji staff to a feast in his village.

Now he graciously included me in the invitation. Before I could answer, Gahi smoothly interjected that I was married, and Sheikhzadeh included Jared, although, as I later learned, he did not believe I was really married. In spite of the leers, I accepted. After Mr. Khalili's incomprehensible silence, at this point I would have accepted an invitation to visit a Kurdish village from almost anyone.

The day of the feast dawned sunny and dry, like almost all of the days since we had come to Rezaiyeh that autumn. As Jared and I walked toward the radio station we saw many people promenading along the street. Although it was officially a day of mourning, a *vafat*, for some martyred saint of Shi'e Islam, everyone seemed to be having a good time.

At the station I noticed Mr. Asyabee looking over my dress critically and muttering to Gahi, "Look, she's wearing a dress to a village while she wears pants in the city."

After my experience in Mawana I had tried to copy Kurdish clothes as best I could with my comparatively skimpy wardrobe. My pseudo-Kurdish outfit was put together with a long heavy skirt with embroidery at the hem, a blouse, and a crocheted vest.

Two cars were going from the station to Sheikhzadeh's village, because, in addition to the regular staff of three men, there was a relative of Asyabee's and Mr. Gahi's brother. As foreign guests, we were immediately invited to ride in style in Asyabee's foreign-made sedan while everyone else had to take the bumps in the jeep. We drove down one of the main streets in town until the road seemed to disappear into an uncultivated park or pasture where sheep were grazing. Without stopping at this seemingly impassable detour, Mr. Asyabee merely pulled to the right and began traveling along a dirt path next to some trees. If we hadn't actually been driving on it, I would never have known this for a road.

On the edges of the city were orchards where leaves were falling, and gardens lay fallow inside the confines of low stone walls on either side of our route. After awhile whole villages appeared, mud houses surrounded by mud walls.

Mr. Sheikhzadeh's village came less than six kilometers from the city via a remarkably straight graded gravel road that promised something more than the small dried-mud village at the end. Mr. Asyabee pulled his car into the rutted mud street that ran between the walls surrounding the houses.

A huge sheepdog came out to bark at us, and then we saw Mr. Sheikhzadeh himself in the doorway, beaming his big gold-toothed grin. He was dressed as formally as he had been the day I saw him in the city, with the shiny gray suit and the black turban. The jeep full of the other guests soon pulled up behind Asyabee's sedan. When everyone had disembarked we began the ordeal of going through the doorway in the appropriate order.

As the only woman present, I was ushered through first. Jared, as a foreign guest, was invited to go next, but he refused, stalling the entire procedure. Soon after our arrival in Rezaiyeh, Jared had become aware of the Iranian system of etiquette known as *ta'arof*. He found it extremely amusing the way his students would never precede him through a doorway, and he delighted in pushing them through first, much to their embarrassment.

Jared had easily grasped one of the first principles of *ta'arof*: No matter how important you were and how obvious it was to everyone that you should therefore go first, you must always defer to those around you. Unfortunately, Jared had not grasped the second principle of *ta'arof*: Everyone *must* ultimately go in the appropriate order. He had also failed to appreciate the underlying seriousness of this peculiarly Persian ritual. To Jared it was all a game, but to Iranians, *ta'arof* was a way of life.

This time, unlike with his students, Jared was a rank amateur among older, more experienced Iranians. He was made to conform and, after a short, good-humored struggle, he came through the doorway after me, followed by Asyabee, and then Gahi, with the rest coming in a fixed order known only to themselves. Mr. Sheikhzadeh, as host, walked through last.

Still in the same order, we filed through the garden, up the concrete stairs, and into a brick house. Inside the central hallway, one by one, we removed our shoes and then passed through still another doorway, which led to the room on the right of the hallway. There we all sat down on a flowered Persian rug with a red background. I was surprised to see a television and asked if the village had electricity. Since it was only six kilometers from Rezaiyeh, it was not inconceivable that it would, but I had heard that the policy of the government was to withhold electricity from all villages.

Sheikhzadeh's village proved to be no exception, since his television turned out to run on a car battery, His house was heated in winter by an oil-burning stove with a pipe that ran up to the uncovered rafters of the house. On the wall he had hung an outdated picture of the shah and his first wife, the sister of King Farouk of Egypt. But there was also a much more recent photograph of the shah presenting some sort of award to our host. What had he done to deserve that? I wondered.

Jared and I sat on one side of the room while Mr. Sheikhzadeh and the staff sat on the other, facing us. No women or family members appeared except a buxom, rosy-cheeked girl who I later learned was Mr. Sheikhzadeh's daughter. She bustled in and out serving tea with downcast eyes, not saying a word in the presence of all these men.

At first Sheikhzadeh devoted his attention to me. A shaft of sunlight illuminated the spot where I was sitting, and I squinted as he quizzed me about one Kurdish vocabulary item after another. I soon found out that he worked as village schoolmaster, an unusual occupation for any rural Kurd. Most of the schools in villages were run by army recruits, the so-called literacy corps, which was made up of young draftees.

A college education, sometimes even a high school education, was sufficient to qualify them to teach village children to read and write. Perhaps the idea was not flawed in principle, but I never heard these schools praised by any Kurd who cared about education. Since army recruits were deliberately sent to parts of Iran away from where they had been raised, none of the teachers assigned to Kurdistan spoke Kurdish, and, of course, they were not trained teachers. They seemed to be tolerated rather than welcomed, and in some parts of Iran they had even been murdered. I imagined the students in Mr. Sheikhzadeh's village felt themselves lucky to have someone of experience with such an obvious flair for pedagogy, but I wondered if he used Kurdish in his classroom.

Suddenly, in the midst of our question-and-answer session, Mr. Asyabee broke in impatiently and said something in Turkish. From then on, the entire conversation was in Turkish. Asyabee, Sheikhzadeh, Gahi, Gahi's brother, and Asyabee's relative were all conversing animatedly in a language neither Jared nor I could understand. No one seemed to notice except Mr. Khalili, who was not saying anything either. He looked as uncomfortable as I felt. What were we doing in a Kurdish village with a bunch of Kurds speaking Turkish to each other?

After a few minutes of being ignored, I suddenly realized that we were being included again. This time Asyabee had switched into Persian to address Jared peremptorily.

"A month, how much you give?" was what he said.

Jared and I were momentarily confused. In the case of salaries, the verbs in Persian are reversed from what you would expect from their English translations. To "give" means to "get" and vice versa. As soon as I grasped what it was he wanted to know, I was stunned, Why was Asyabee asking us to name our salaries in front of the entire radio staff in a village where we were strangers? Quickly, I explained the question to Jared. The room was silent as everyone stared at us, waiting for a reply. Jared and I looked at each other. What were we supposed to say?

Jared rose to the challenge, putting a blunt thought as obliquely as his rudimentary Persian would allow.

"*Fuzool*, what does it mean?" he asked.

I looked at Asyabee and recognized the reaction I had seen on the face of a hotel clerk who was blatantly trying to cheat us on our first day in Rezaiyeh. Jared had replied to the clerk's lies with a mild Persian obscenity he had learned from some Iranian students in the United States. Like the clerk's, Asyabee's expression went totally blank.

I caught Jared's eye and frowned. Why had I taught him the word *fuzool*? Jared looked back at me, puzzled by the expression on my face. He could read my anger, but he noticed no change in Asyabee. Why was I making faces? For a few minutes there was an awkward silence. Asyabee, with the eyes of his social inferiors upon him, felt obliged to brazen it out.

"I'm sure I make a lot more money than you do," he said to Jared.

"I'm sure you do," Jared agreed.

After that Asyabee shifted his sitting position so that he was no longer facing us. The conversation seemed to go back to normal. I no longer knew whether it was in Turkish or Kurdish or Persian. My ears rang. If Jared had picked up the game of *ta'arof* faster than I had, I had become aware of the power of insult much sooner. Somehow I had sensed, from the moment we had entered Iran, that people seemed to be waiting to take offense.

If you failed to say hello to the grocer when you entered the store, you risked not being waited on. If you didn't ask someone's health, people might think you were snubbing them. Many other subtleties were lost on me. But one thing I had been sure of since the moment I saw that hotel clerk's face: An insult was not to be laughed off in this country.

To me, the reaction in the room had been unmistakable. It was as if everyone present had sucked in their breath. Where did these Americans come from that they thought they could speak so plainly to a man as important as Asyabee? He had preceded everyone except the foreign guests through the doorway. And now these guests that he had honored had insulted him. We did not yet know the etymology of the word *fuzool*. But that was a mere detail. Later, Jared would discover that to tell your maid that she was speaking nonsense, in the mildest possible terms, was to give her reason to walk out of your house immediately and never return.

Somehow, the party continued. Lunch began to be served, with the daughter laying first one and then another fragrant dish out on the plastic cloth she had spread in the middle of the floor. I kept running over in my mind Mr. Asyabee's reaction to Jared's words. Perhaps it had been my own oversensitive imagination. Perhaps his annoyance had passed. His face registered nothing when I looked at him.

Someone (the daughter? the wife? other unseen females?) had obviously spent a great deal of time preparing a varied repast. I almost forgot about the unpleasantness as I stared at the chicken, the vegetables stuffed with herbed rice, the homemade pickles, the pilaf, and the yogurt. Conversation stopped as everyone began reaching to fill their plates.

As I picked through the meat on my chicken I found that I had the wishbone. Suddenly it occurred to me to try to lighten the mood by asking about a Kurdish game I had read about. Did people really play it, or was it a figment of some British adventurer's imagination? I would soon find out.

Mr. Asyabee's eyes gleamed when I held the bone aloft.

"*Jinakh!*" several people in the room named the game immediately.

"I'll play," said Mr. Asyabee. "What shall we promise each other?"

I didn't understand that he was trying to set stakes, but in the confusion of being told the rules by everyone present, Mr. Asyabee's demand passed unnoticed. We began to play without knowing what the winner would gain. The object of the game, which is merely triggered by the breaking of the wishbone by both players, is for one person to hand the other person something and have it accepted. Asyabee immediately picked up the ballpoint pen I was using to record Kurdish words and tried to hand it to me. I would have accepted and thus lost the game, but Mr. Khalili reminded me. After a few more attempts on Mr. Asyabee's part, the game went into remission. The daughter came and led me first to the outhouse and then back inside to the room on the other side of the house. In the meantime, Asyabee began playing a new and far more sinister game with Jared. This was not a Kurdish game, but rather an old, old game that has been played in Iran for centuries. No doubt playing it with an uninitiated foreigner like Jared gave it a new twist for Asyabee.

While my host's daughter began laying out a set of her clothes for me to dress up in, all of the men, except Mr. Khalili, remained sitting in the other room. Later, we wondered whether the conversation would have been the same if Mr. Khalili had not decided to go for a walk when Mr. Asyabee began to speak.

"Do you want to come to my house and smoke some *teriyak*?" Mr. Asyabee asked Jared apropos of nothing as soon as Mr. Khalili had gone.

Jared stared at him. First he had asked about our salaries and now he was offering opium. Mr. Asyabee's notions about Americans seemed as stereotyped as those of the rudest villager. Jared shook his head. No, thank you, he did not care to smoke opium.

"Why not?" persisted Asyabee.

Jared shifted uncomfortably. The other men were watching closely.

"Because the police might come," he answered simply.

"The police never come to my house," Asyabee said meaningfully.

Jared watched uneasily as Asyabee withdrew a card from his pocket and held it out for the American to see. It was some sort of ID.

"I am an officer in SAVAK," announced Asyabee.

No one said anything as it finally dawned on Jared that something was seriously amiss. Mr. Asyabee was letting him know in the most blatant way possible that he was a member of Iran's dreaded secret police. What would happen next? Jared looked at the faces of all the men. They were noncommittal. What was he supposed to say? The subject seemed to be dropped as fast as it had been raised, but with our knowledge of Turkish, they might have spent the rest of the afternoon commenting on what fools we were.

The men came out of the room en masse and were joined by Mr. Khalili. Jared quickly informed me in English of what had happened while I was duly presented in my borrowed finery, which was not nearly so fine as the outfit I had been given to wear in Mawana. There was no bib of gold and a machine-made sweater instead of a black wool vest. Although Mr. Sheikhzadeh was more educated and more prosperous than anyone else I ever saw in his village, he was not on the same level as Rashid Beg.

We strolled along the crumbling mud wall that surrounded Mr. Sheikhzadeh's property, a bare, dry piece of land this time of year. In the distance Rezaiyeh looked like a sprawling oasis, the green of its irrigated trees and gardens fading into the blue of the lake behind. Walking across Sheikhzadeh's field, we passed women washing clothes by hand in a stream. The wind snapped at my skirts as Jared took photographs of everyone present.

Mr. Asyabee wanted to be in all of them. Mr. Sheikhzadeh rushed along attentively at the side of the head of Kurmanji broadcasting. Asyabee was behaving in a rather patronizing fashion toward our host, but then I had never seen Asyabee when he was not patronizing the people around him. But he had not succeeded in making Jared toe the line. Asyabee had tried to humble the foreigner by demanding to know his salary in front of a group of strangers and had ended up being embarrassed himself. To a man such as Asyabee this was intolerable. I wondered how far he might go to even up the score.

Soon the men were too cold in their thin Western-style suits to stay outside in the wind. We went inside, where Mr. Asyabee grabbed a cup of tea off the tray and tried to hand it to me. I refused. Perhaps if I won the game of *jinakh*, I would also win the day from Mr. Asyabee. Then, the conversation took another Asyabee-directed turn. This time he had decided to discuss *ta'arof*.

Ta'arof, the system which had guided everyone on the order in which they ought to go through the doorway, is a Persian word derived from the

Arabic verb "to know." In Arabic, the form *ta'arof* means something like "knowledge" or "realization," while in Persian it has come to have somewhat different connotations, although, in a sense, it was still a matter of knowing.

In Iranian culture, *ta'arof* codified all social interaction except between very intimate friends and family. And even in these latter relationships it was always possible to distance yourself by reverting to *ta'arof*. *Ta'arof* is a way of managing people and situations with maximum grace and minimum vulnerability. At times it resembles a dance, an ice-cold minuet where partners never touch, but everyone comes off looking beautiful, at least from a distance. Under the rules of *ta'arof*, you must offer up everything, even your own life. Thus, *qurbanet*, Mr. Gahi's constant refrain into the telephone at his office, is a byword in *ta'arof*. So is *befermayeed*, the phrase Shehrzad used whenever she invited me into her apartment. In the best sense, *ta'arof* can be overwhelming hospitality, endless offers of tea and sweets and tables groaning under an elaborate display of tantalizing dishes. Of hospitality far into the night, as long as the guests choose to stay. No host ever yawns. The refreshments never run out even if servants and family members have to sneak out the back of the house in silent search of food and drink to replenish what has been consumed.

But there is another side to *ta'arof*: the burden implied by receiving. Everyone wants to offer and no one wants to accept. If someone says "*qurbanet*" to you, you may nod politely and offer to die for him instead while neither of you has the slightest affection or regard for the other. In the ultimate exaggeration of the concept of *ta'arof*, neither the offer nor the refusal has any meaning whatsoever, except as the most abstract politeness. Someone might offer you a magnificent feast and have nothing but stale bread in the house. You would of course reply that you have already eaten even if you are going hungry for lack of money to buy food.

Young Iranians had claimed to us in America that *ta'arof* is outdated hypocrisy, an obstacle to friendship. Kurds told us that there was no tradition of *ta'arof* among Kurds. But we had to find out for ourselves to what extent and in what ways and situations people actually used *ta'arof* in Iran. Sometimes the very people who most denounce the system were the most dependent on it.

At the mention of *ta'arof*, Jared immediately commented, "There is no *ta'arof* in America." By this he meant that it is not important who precedes you through the door, that people usually accept the first time you invite them because, in general, Americans mean the invitations they proffer. Later, in a more honest appraisal of our own culture, we had to admit that there is certainly *ta'arof* in America. The next time we heard Americans say, "We simply must have you to dinner," when we knew they had no intention of ever inviting us, we realized that Americans too are capable of *ta'arof*.

Jared's comment that there was no *ta'arof* in America was just what Mr. Asyabee wanted to hear.

Thereafter Asyabee began ostentatiously preceding Jared through doorways, taking his tea before Jared, and, in general, comporting himself exceptionally for an Iranian. Each time he broke one of the rules, he would excuse himself by saying, "There is no *ta'arof* in America."

Finally, and mercifully, the day's outing seemed to be at an end. Mr. Sheikhzadeh stood at the doorway, wishing us all goodbye while the native speakers showered thanks on him for his hospitality. Asyabee allowed me to go through the door first, but carefully made sure to precede Jared. Once again, we were in Asyabee's car, and, this time, since he had his mind on the driving, I managed to hand him a lighted cigarette. He accepted and I won the game of *jinakh*.

"What shall I get her?" he asked his cousin, who was sitting in the front with him. "Maybe a dress or something." Hearing this, I thought perhaps the hostilities had ended.

We invited everyone to come to our house for tea when we returned to the city, and Mr. Asyabee accepted immediately, confident that "there is no *ta'arof* among Americans." But, in a more Iranian vein, he first drove to a pastry shop in order to present us with the gift that is obligatory the first time you are a guest in someone's house.

Mr. Asyabee was civil, even friendly, at our house, but he also seemed more cocky and acerbic than usual. He kept repeating, "There is no *ta'arof* in America," and then he would disregard the rules of *ta'arof*. By American standards he was not being impolite, but by Iranian ones, he was extremely rude. As far as I could tell, Mr. Asyabee was much more Iranian than he was American. Still, the day seemed to be ending on a better note than I had expected.

Mr. Asyabee had accepted our hospitality. He had even brought us a box of cookies. I couldn't see that I was still reading behavior according to my own culture. The cookies were a mere gesture, *ta'arof*. Mr. Asyabee may have had his own reasons for coming to our house which had nothing to do with friendliness. In Iran, form, like the chadors I saw at the Tehran airport, lies on the surface. What lies beneath is not easy for any foreigner to see.

The next time I presented myself at the radio station, the policeman nodded to me as usual and I walked into the room where all the Kurmanji broadcasters sat. The first thing I noticed was how busy everyone seemed to be for a change. Mr. Asyabee and Mr. Khalili were buried in their papers, while Mr. Gahi was on the telephone. No one even seemed to notice that I was standing there. Finally Mr. Gahi got off the phone.

"I'm sorry, Margaret Khanim, but Mr. Khalili is too busy to work with you today," he said.

At that moment my thin, nervous-looking Kurdish teacher got up and rushed out of the room, barely glancing at me as he passed. My heart froze. I tried to catch Mr. Asyabee's eye, but he was busier than all of them translating the day's non-news which had been prepared by propaganda experts in Tehran and sent to Rezaiyeh. This was clearly the most important job of the Kurmanji staff. Mr. Asyabee would sit at his desk, translating orally into the microphone of a large reel-to-reel tape recorder and then copying his translation to be sent back to Tehran and checked by the authorities.

I continued to stand in the office, uncertain what to do next. It was a new experience to be there and not be noticed. Before, there had always been a waiting line of people who wanted to catch my attention, wanted to ask some question about English or about the United States, wanted to show me that they existed. Now, I was the one who did not exist. There was no joking, no flirting, no helloes. Red with embarrassment, I felt tears stinging my eyelids. I started to walk to the door.

Mr. Khalili, who had returned from his urgent mission of a few moments ago, said to me, "Sit down, Margaret Khanim." Then the tea man served me tea and some unimportant person came by and greeted me. When I finished the tea, I got up and left. No one even looked up.

Because I always doubted my perception of things in Iran, I decided that I should make another trip to the station. I waited a few days to gather my courage and then returned. Perhaps they really had been busy the day I was there. Perhaps some directive had been issued from Tehran which was actually forcing them to adopt a more intensive work pace. Perhaps I was too sensitive. Maybe everyone had just gotten used to me and I was no longer the focus of attention. I couldn't be the center of a three-ring circus forever.

The second time I could not mistake what was happening. No less important a personage than Mr. Goherkhaneh told me that Mr. Asyabee said the Kurmanji staff was too busy to help me with my work on Kurdish. Mr. Goherkhaneh himself was friendly, but busy. He seemed to have no personal grudge against me, but his attitude was that if Mr. Asyabee didn't think I was worth anyone's time anymore, then he was probably right. In any case, whatever Goherkhaneh's feelings about Asyabee were, it was not worth his while to get into a confrontation with him over a foreign woman wanting to learn Kurdish. Once again, it seemed that I was destined never to learn this language I had come five thousand miles to study.

Depression and paranoia set in immediately. I vented my anger on Jared, whom I accused of being unforgivably self-indulgent in his reaction to Asyabee's question. Since it was fruitless to blame Mr. Asyabee for creating the whole situation, I blamed my husband and wondered if he would ever learn to conform to Iranian social rules. What I didn't know was that the two other Kurmanji radio staffers in the room blamed only Asyabee, and were, in their own ways, biding their time for an opportune moment, when Asyabee wasn't around, to tell us how they really felt.

Our first encounter was with Gahi, who was parking his car on the street near our house one Friday when he happened to notice me. He called out a greeting and I waved and continued walking on my way back from the corner grocery. But Gahi called out again.

"Why don't you come to lunch with me?"

"No, thank you," I called back, sure this was mere *ta'arof*, not a real invitation.

"Have you eaten?" he asked.

I came closer to answer him. "No."

"Then why not come?" he asked, sounding as if he seriously meant his invitation.

"What about Jared?"

"Let's go and get him," replied Gahi, holding the door open on the passenger side of his car. We drove around the block to pick up Jared, and

I was almost sure that he really meant this invitation.

Mr. Gahi took us to the Iran Kuloob, where, amid the Friday-afternoon family crowd eating kebab and rice with raw eggs, he was at his most charming. At the end, he insisted on paying the bill, a preordained matter in Iran, since he had done the inviting. Several times during the meal and again as he drove us back to our apartment he made a point of saying how much he liked Jared. The message was subtle, as messages in Persian tend to be. Without ever mentioning Asyabee or referring to the incident in Mr. Sheikhzadeh's village, we now knew that Mr. Gahi sided with us.

Mr. Khalili, true to his nature, was less subtle. I ran into him one day while walking down the *kucheh* where the station was located. He called to me to wait and then, when he had caught up with me, said bluntly, after we had exchanged the required greetings, "Mr. Jared speaks the truth."

I looked at him and he looked at me. Even Mr. Khalili had his limits. He was not going to come out and tell me straight out that Asyabee was *fuzool*. I took the opportunity with Mr. Khalili to try to clarify what had happened.

"Mr. Asyabee got really angry at Jared when we were in Mr. Sheikhzadeh's village," I said. "In fact, he is still really angry at us."

Mr. Khalili looked at me uncomfortably, "No, he's not angry at you," he said slowly.

"Of course he is. Jared called him *fuzool*." We had later discovered that the word *fuzool*, which means "nosy" in Persian, was derived from an Arabic word for "shit."

But Mr. Khalili ignored the impropriety of using *fuzool* and focused on something else.

"He couldn't be angry. He came to your house and drank tea with you."

Mr. Khalili was referring to a Kurdish rule of hospitality: A guest in your house cannot be your enemy. Although Mr. Khalili had spent many years in the city, his mind was still in the village, with the traditional Kurdish code. Mr. Asyabee, on the other hand, had been born and raised in the city. He was more Turkish than Kurdish.

Despite the reassurance from Gahi and Khalili, I could not stop thinking about Mr. Asyabee. Why had he made such a point of claiming to be a member of SAVAK? Suppose he should file a report saying I was a spy, entering Iran and residing in Rezaiyeh under false pretexts? My Iranian government contract with the college specified that I could be fired immediately for regularly engaging in any professional activity other than teaching English. There would be no legal redress and no explanations.

Gradually we began to solicit other people's opinions.

"Is it polite to ask someone how much money he makes?" we queried colleagues.

"No," was the almost universal answer.

"Then why do so many people ask?"

"Because they don't know better. They are uneducated," came the slightly embarrassed answer. Obviously that wasn't the real reason, because some of these very same, very well-educated people had asked us about our salaries. However, most of the people we questioned did agree on one point. "One should never use the word *fuzool* to a member of SAVAK." The obvious corollary, which no one bothered to spell out, was: Don't use the word *fuzool* to anyone, because anyone could be in SAVAK.

Soon after *l'affaire* Asyabee, Jared went downstairs and had a long conversation with Houshang Jaffari. The two of them laboriously worked out a formal apology to Mr. Asyabee, which went something like this: "I humbly ask your forgiveness. You know I don't know Persian very well, and sometimes I don't know what words mean. I confused the word I used with another word I meant to use, but, if I have given offense, please forgive me."

Jared insisted to Houshang that he had known the word he meant to use, but Houshang told him firmly that any other apology was unthinkable. Of course Asyabee knew very well that it had not been a mistake, but that was not the point. It was the form, the *ta'arof*, which was important.

Fortunately, for our very culture-bound self-respect, no opportunity presented itself at which Jared could easily offer this apology. I never went to the radio station anymore and we never ran into Mr. Asyabee on the street. I began to realize that an apology would not even gain me anything. Before the incident, my Kurdish lessons, even with Mr. Khalili at the helm, had been becoming more erratic and less satisfactory. Mr. Khalili was often not there when he said he would be, and he was plainly tired of my relatively slow rate of progress. And more and more, I wanted to talk to some Kurdish women, women whose Kurdish was not changed by false notions of correctness.

I had come to Kurdistan thinking that as the first female researcher of the Kurdish language, I would also be the first to talk with women. For all anyone knew, Kurdish women might speak a completely different language from the men. In an American Indian tribe men and women use different grammatical forms. I had specifically stated, in my dissertation proposal, that I was going to compare men's and women's speech. But I never talked with any women, except Miss Asyabee, who, like her brother, I no longer viewed as a real Kurd.

I had begun, even before our trip to the village feast, to ask Mr. Khalili to help me find a woman speaker to converse with. But his response was less than promising.

"I don't know any Kurdish women," he said. Perhaps it was the demure thing to say in such a sex-segregated society, but we both knew it was ridiculous. The man had two wives and plenty of female relatives. I wondered where he kept them all stashed.

Kurdish women did appear on the street, and because they were Kurds, they were by far the most visible women there partly because many went unveiled and even under chadors you could see the glitter and swish of their fabulous attire.

I watched them more wistfully than ever. I would never be comfortable sitting in a roomful of men, but in the reception room of one of these women I imagined myself sitting easily, notebook in hand, learning many things, and not just about the language. I looked again hopefully toward the refugee family that had moved into our neighborhood, but they had secretive, unapproachable expressions on their faces as they hurried in and out of the *kucheh* via their beat-up Land Rover.

Once again, I was thrown back on the hospitality of our neighbors, the Jaffaris. There were other Americans in town, but they had long since decided we were pariahs because we did not spend our nights at the U.S. Army headquarters, drinking and watching American movies.

Often we sat home alone at night, bored with each other and our failures, but too proud to go and show the other Americans that we were not succeeding. They all told us they had long ago given up trying to be friends with any Iranians. When the Kurmanji ninety-minute program was not on the radio, I tried to tune in the BBC. All the paperback novels I had brought with me were soon read.

What we needed were friends, but we kept coming up against *ta'arof* and worse. We wanted to discuss our impressions and feelings about Iran. We desperately needed feedback about what we were doing. From the Jaffaris we got invitations and smiles. From the Iranians at the college we got smiles. It was getting harder and harder for us to remember that once, back in September and the beginning of October, in the first month of our stay in Rezaiyeh, there had been someone we could talk to, someone we trusted, someone who listened with more than a smile.

He was someone we knew apart from the Jaffaris, apart from the teachers at the college. The time we spent with him was time away from Iran, in a third world. For, with Ameer, we had not been bored, and we had

Visit to village with Mr. Khalili (center) and Mr. Asyabee (far right)

not been held at a distance as with most Iranians we knew. Rather, we had been mesmerized by a boy who had woven a magic Kurdish spell around us.

CHAPTER 6

AMEER

More than the Jaffaris, more than Mr. Khalili, more than any other person we had met since we came to Iran, Ameer, a tall, skinny boy from Bukan, was our hope for finding Kurdistan. Ameer had been standing around with the other students when they talked of how SAVAK had killed my Mahabadi friend's brother in America. Ameer too had been sure that he was executed, but Ameer had not drawn away from me like the others. Instead, when all the students had gone away talking in hushed tones to each other about their suspicions, Ameer had followed me to my office and offered to teach me Kurdish—his native Sorani dialect, southern Kurdish, but still Kurdish.

Ameer told me he knew a lot of Kurmanji, northern Kurdish, and would be able to teach me the difference between the two. He immediately suggested that I should travel to his home town south of Mahabad and meet his family, Ameer could not stop talking about what we would do together, how he would teach me Kurdish and take me to places in Kurdistan. I stared at him in wonder. How had this first-year student from a small Kurdish town learned to speak English so fluently? And why did he seek me out when the other students backed away?

The first time Ameer came to our house was on Friday, our day off. He offered to accompany us to Mahabad, but I was sick with bronchitis.

"I know Mahabad almost as I know Bukan," he told us.

I coughed happily, thinking that we would go as soon as I got well. But Ameer never offered again, and we went with the Jaffaris.

Ameer fell into the habit of coming to my office, a dark room with a rubber-topped metal desk and a sooty oil-burning heater in the corner. None of the other students ever knocked on my door, except when grades were being given out. They ignored my repeated announcements of office hours. But, from the beginning, Ameer was not like the other students. They were distant, sometimes hostile, while he was friendly and enthusiastic. Their English was useless for real conversation, while Ameer chattered away in English that was not colloquial exactly, but slipped easily from his tongue. And Ameer was Kurdish. Above all, he was Kurdish. He had appointed himself my pied piper of Kurdistan, and day by day he led me along, dancing on a path he strewed with imaginary flowers, telling me of the beauty of Bukan, the friendliness of his family, and, most fascinating, the political thoughts and aspirations of the Kurds.

Ameer became an integral part of our lives without us even realizing it was happening. Besides offering to teach me Kurdish, he made himself available to help us deal with the complexities of getting settled in Iran. If we needed to find something in the bazaar, he said he was ready to go with us. He could translate, he could guide us, but most of all he could just spend time with us—time that alternately went too fast and too slowly.

During the week when we taught, shopping for food and household items ate up all of our spare time. In one tiny store after another we would stutter out the items we sought. Sometimes the storekeeper couldn't understand us; sometimes we couldn't understand him. For all the time we spent looking, the number of purchases we made was small.

We made lists and lists of cleaning utensils, spices, soap—things we regarded as essentials—but we couldn't find half of them. On Fridays when the bazaar and most stores were closed, we would find ourselves suddenly with nothing to do, no one to visit, no one to talk to, Ameer made Fridays bearable, even fun. Once or twice we walked around downtown with him, but usually he simply sat in our house for hours, facing us intently across our metal table, nervously chewing sunflower and melon seeds and pistachio nuts, talking, talking, talking. And we talked too.

He wanted to know everything about America; we wanted to know everything about Kurdistan. What did his father do? What was his town like? How many brothers and sisters did he have? Was there a high school in his town? What did the people do in winter? What did the people of his town think of the Kurdish War in Iraq?

He made us feel that we could ask him anything, and the distinction between his answers—some straightforward, some evasive—was blurred by our fascination with anything he chose to tell us. He delighted in saying extravagant things. He described his town in spring, with the flowers on the mountains. He told us that he had seen Israeli tanks and soldiers going over the border to Iraq and he assured us that the Kurdish War there was not at all the way we had thought it was.

"Kurds are not fighting Arabs," he said. "Kurds are fighting Kurds."

He called Barzani, the aging tribal military leader who had once defended Mahabad, an imperialist and a fascist, who had sold his people out to the American government, offering the Americans oil in return for support of the Kurdish cause.

"Real Kurds fight on the other side," he declared.

Ameer listened to all the radio stations that broadcast in Kurdish— from Iran, Iraq, and the Soviet Union. He was fascinated by the Soviet Union.

I said that as soon as my books came in the trunk we had sent by air freight from Boston I would show him what had been printed about the Kurds and Kurdish in my country. There didn't seem to be enough hours in the day to talk to Ameer. While everyone else we met was reticent about politics or the Kurds, silent in response to the feelings we expressed about being foreigners, Ameer was a fountain of information, of reaction, of feeling. He stayed for meals at our house when, after the visit of the Jaffaris, I despaired that we would ever have Iranian guests. He criticized our food openly, humorously. I was not offended. How could I be? Ameer's way of putting things was so charming.

"Like chewing gum, isn't it?" he remarked while laboriously grinding away on a piece of stew meat that I had cooked for only three hours instead of the required seven. I laughed. He told us that his mother's cooking was famous. We would be able to taste it ourselves, soon enough.

Except for Houshang and Shehrzad, we called every Iranian that we had met by a title plus their last name; even our students were Mr. This and Miss That. When we spoke Persian we always used the polite form of "you," like the French *vous*. Since Ameer was our student, by Iranian etiquette it was unthinkable that he should be on a first-name basis with us. But when we first met we didn't know this and he chose to ignore it. He immediately began calling me "Dada Margaret," using the southern Kurdish title for "sister." Jared he addressed as "Kak" or "Elder Brother" Jared. We always called him by his first name.

Our relationship with Ameer began in a cocoon. We spent time with him alone, away from other Iranians. No one else, except perhaps the Jaffaris, could compare to Ameer in warmth. Electricity bounced off this boy with the oversize head and the huge brown eyes framed with long, thick eyelashes.

"Your eyelashes are beautiful," I actually told him one day.

"Oh, yes. In my town, I am famous for my eyes," he replied seriously, taking off his glasses so I could see them better. His mother was famous for her cooking; he was famous for his eyes. From Ameer's point of view, everything and everyone in his family, his town, was famous. Kurdistan was a magical place. He didn't have to convince me. Hadn't I come 5,000 miles because I believed the same thing?

In retrospect, it is a little hard to understand why and how we fell so completely under Ameer's spell. In many ways, he was an ordinary, unlovely adolescent, full of egotism and crazy ideas. We knew he exaggerated, and we began to realize that he was evading many of our questions.

What did his father do? He would never really answer. How had Ameer learned English so well? It seemed unlikely that he had picked it up from occasional American tourists passing through Bukan, as he claimed. Where did Ameer live while he was attending college? These things never became clear. But there were no awkward gaps in our conversation.

The difference between the Jaffaris and Ameer was linguistic as well as emotional. While we struggled along in stilted Persian with our neighbors, Ameer was able to pour out his heart to us in English. And we poured out ours. We told him about everything—our lives in America, our hopes and disappointments in Iran, our feelings of utter estrangement and alienation from the Iranian social scene.

The times we walked on the street together I complained of how the men would stare at me with an unpleasantly hostile, bold look in their eyes. I felt as if they would rape and kill me, given the chance. Ameer said he understood. He spoke of the decline in morals among the student population, the way girls would telephone the boys in the dormitories at night, begging them to come out with them.

"Disgusting!"exclaimed Ameer. "These girls have no brothers to protect them, to tell them what is right."

Jared and I were amused. There was no doubt that Ameer was sexist, but there was something so innocent about him and so fierce. He even professed to be disgusted by Googoosh, the most popular singer in Iran, who had entranced everyone else.

"She is a bad girl, the way she acts," was his judgment.

Jared and I wondered. Were all Kurdish boys this prim? Amid the lasciviousness that lies just beneath the surface of all encounters between men and women in Iran, Ameer was an oddity. He refused to stay for a minute in our house alone with me. If Jared was going out, then Ameer would leave also. But, later, when I knew more, his calling me by my first name began to seem like a sign of intimacy that would be criticized at the college.

Eventually, critical eyes did come to rest on our relationship with Ameer. The first belonged to the teacher from the college who lived across the kucheh from us.

"You are friends with this boy?" he asked, after seeing Ameer come out of our house with us.

"Yes," said Jared. "We like him very much."

The teacher studied Jared's face for a minute. "Such boys are dangerous."

"Why?" asked Jared.

"Because they want too much love. I know this student. He wants everyone to love him. Such boys are dangerous for women." The teacher glanced at me obliquely.

Jared and I laughed off the sense of uneasiness that momentarily assailed us. By now we knew that none of the other teachers would dream of having any of their students to their houses. The social barrier between students and teachers in Iranian colleges was complete.

Five weeks after our arrival in Rezaiyeh, when my trunk had finally arrived from America and was ready to be picked up at customs, I naturally turned to Ameer. We made plans to leave the college immediately to go and pick it up. Before we left, I told Ameer that all of my books about Kurdish and Kurdistan were inside the trunk. He looked at me, a veiled fear in his eyes.

"But SAVAK will take the books away from you."

"Why? I am an American. Besides, they won't know what the books are. They are in English." Ameer was doubtful, but he came with me as promised.

Outside, while we were waiting for a taxi, one of the drivers swung his orange car around in the middle of the road in front of the college and came full speed directly at me. I leaped back out of the way, my legs moving awkwardly in fear. Ameer stood his ground, and the taxi squealed to a halt a couple of inches from where I had been.

"What's the matter, Dada Margaret? Were you afraid of just a taxi?" he said, laughing at me. "You must not be afraid of death. *I* am not afraid."

At the customs office, Ameer waited with me as the officials pried open the lid of the trunk, their faces falling at the sight of eight pairs of Jared's socks squashed on top. Underneath, they quickly spied the books and began talking to each other excitedly. Ameer intervened, and they soon quieted down. I was handed a piece of paper to sign and the trunk was once again mine.

"What happened?" I asked Ameer.

"They wanted to send the books to the SAVAK office to be examined, but I told them they are for your work at the university. Then they lost interest."

Ameer negotiated for a taxi to convey the heavy trunk to our house, and, with the driver, helped to carry it up the stairs when we arrived. He had insisted on paying all the fares down and back from customs. When the taxi driver left I chased Ameer back down our stairs, trying to put the sum of money I owed him in his hand. At last I succeeded in jamming it into his shirt pocket. I stared at him, wondering how he could afford to be so generous. Ameer had said he wanted to borrow some of my books, but when I offered them, he put me off, saying he was afraid to be seen with them.

One day, shortly after we picked up the trunk together, I heard Ameer in the office of the head of the English department explaining that he would not be in class for a month or two. What was this? I listened, but I could not find out what the reason was. Later I confronted him. How could he leave after barely six weeks of classes, in his first year of college? He looked at me mysteriously, his huge eyes made huger by seriousness.

"I cannot to tell you, Dada Margaret.

"Why not?"

"I don't want you to worry."

Jared and I discussed it for several days. I imagined that Ameer was going to join those fighting in Iraq. Hadn't he spoken many times of how that was where he wanted to be?

"Are you going to Iraq, Ameer?" I asked him.

Ameer looked at the floor sadly. "I cannot tell you," he said. "You must not know."

For several days, whenever I saw him, I would ask him why he was leaving. He would always laugh ruefully and refuse to talk about it. The head of the English department, a self-important American who had warned me several times that Ameer was "too friendly," also refused to tell me, saying Ameer had given him the reason in confidence. I was hurt at Ameer's lack of trust, but I was also terribly curious and worried. I thought Ameer was romantic and headstrong enough to do something really dangerous. In fact, I almost convinced myself that he was indeed going to fight with the "leftist Kurds" against Barzani in Iraq.

At last I had it out with him in my office. He was going to Tehran for an operation in a hospital. He had kidney stones. This time, I allowed myself a little doubt, a little skepticism. Why had he made such a big deal about it and acted so mysterious? Ameer was capable of making even kidney stones seem like a dark tragedy.

"I do not know what will happen to me, what will be the result of this operation," he confessed to us the last time he visited our house before he left.

"It will be all right," we assured him glibly.

He looked hurt by our lighthearted reaction. "You do not know Iranian hospitals. You do not know Iranian doctors. This is not America."

By the time he left that evening, he had managed to scare us too. We wondered if we would ever see him again.

Many, many things happened to us in Ameer's absence, but none of them seemed quite real, because he was not there for us to discuss them with. As they say in Persian, the salt had gone out of our life, out of our conversation, out of our thoughts. He was not there when we returned from Mawana or when I was ostracized by the radio staff. Finally, when there were no Kurds at all who would talk to me, Ameer was doubly not there.

By the time Ameer left we had acquired beds, a table, chairs, a refrigerator, a stove, and the rugs Houshang had loaned us. But we were still looking for things in the stores. Shopping was an ongoing challenge that I looked forward to only when I was in my most relaxed, Persian-speaking mood. Even then, it was not much fun to be alone in the crowd.

Male passersby constantly stared at me, touching if they got the chance. I almost never left a store without feeling I had been cheated by the merchant because I was a foreigner. When it came to large purchases, I always tried to find someone local to accompany me.

One day I asked the wife of the neighbor who had helped us find our apartment if she would go to the bazaar with me. I needed her help to buy a small rug for Jared's birthday. She agreed. The day of the planned shopping trip, I went happily to her house, looking forward to touring the bazaar in the company of someone who would know what was going on. I was in such a good mood that I hardly noticed that Nazi wasn't even dressed when I arrived. I played with her baby and admired her own beautiful rugs as I waited for her to get ready.

At last she had on her street dress and a sweater. She handed the baby to the maid and we went out the door. As we were walking down the street, I told her how much Jared wanted one of these rugs and what a surprise it would be when he saw it. I was allowing almost a month before his birthday to be sure of having enough time to find the right one, but I hoped, with Nazi's help, I would find one this very day.

Suddenly, without saying anything, she hailed a taxi as we were halfway down the block. It stopped; she got in and explained through the window that she didn't have time to help me after all. Then the taxi drove off in the direction of the bazaar, leaving me dumbstruck next to the open gutter.

I could not figure out what happened except that before she left there had been the usual heckling from all the males hanging out on the street. Nazi's dyed red hair and natural green eyes coupled with her short dress and provocatively low-cut bodice were calculated to look fashionably Western. Probably the men took her to be a foreigner as well.

"Do they always do this to you?" she had asked me accusingly just before she fled.

I got the distinct impression that she thought it was my fault, that I had actively done something to provoke the harassment that she had been forced to share.

I was still brooding about Nazi Khanim's incredible rudeness when the Jaffaris started talking to us about a wedding that might be celebrated in their family. Houshang's brother, a middle-aged engineer, had picked out a local eighteen-year-old to be his bride before he went on a business trip to Japan. While he was away Shehrzad speculated that Mahmoud, the brother, would break off the engagement on his return, realizing that he could do better than this uninteresting hometown girl who, Shehrzad implied, was mainly distinguished by having blond hair. Later on she relayed that Mahmoud had decided to go through with the ceremony, because he said he was tired of being single in Rezaiyeh. As soon as the date was set, the Jaffaris assured us that it would be very interesting for us to see an Iranian wedding, and we, in turn, expressed our delight at being invited. Privately I hoped the groom's attitude would not ruin the festivities.

However, the whole thing turned out to be very festive and surprisingly European, from the bathroom of the bride's father's house, which boasted a European toilet and tub, to the quantities of prohibitively expensive Johnnie Walker Red whiskey. This was liberally poured into the highball glasses of most of the males and some of the females present. The bride, who was quite stunning in a European wedding gown with a long train, seemed to be really enjoying her wedding and did a modified belly dance in front of the assembled guests.

Later in the evening, a man who was drunk cornered Jared, angrily demanding to know, "How much does the Iranian government pay you to teach here? You are a rich American. We don't need you." The man kept his grasp on Jared's elbow until Houshang came over and made him apologize.

"He didn't know what he was saying," explained Houshang. We nodded. outwardly polite, inwardly skeptical. This was a case of *masti rasti*, the Persian equivalent of *in vino veritas*, if we had ever seen one.

Up until that moment we had felt extremely welcome at the wedding. Everyone had been very solicitous, offering us food and drink, coming over to talk with us, smiling at us constantly. The drunk man's outburst did not ruin our evening, but it made us wonder what was really on the minds of all those smilers. The more we lived in Iran, the more we learned to look beneath the smiles.

There had been no Ameer around to discuss these depressing incidents with. There was no Ameer to weigh the possibility that Mr. Asyabee would report me to SAVAK. There was no touchstone, no sounding board, no way to get our worries and our gripes and our misunderstandings off our chests. Jared and I were locked in a psychological cell with each other, and our relationship was not thriving in our isolation.

At the end of a month, Ameer sent us a warm letter from a relative's house in Tehran, I replied immediately, telling him how much we had missed him, how much had been happening to us, how much we needed to talk to him. A few weeks later, before the advent of winter and the rains, he was standing in the sunshine at the entrance to our courtyard.

"Ameer," I cried out and hugged him, knowing but not caring that men and women never hug each other in public in Iran and never hug each other anywhere if they are not closely related by blood or marriage. Jared came downstairs and hugged him too.

Our reunion took place over lunch, but there was no time to begin to utter everything that was on our minds. We had to return to the college in the afternoon, so we waited impatiently until the next time we would see him. Now that Ameer was back, I felt that Kurdistan, with all its romance and possibility, might open up for me.

Two nights later, he came to dinner at our house. This time, the meat was cooked perfectly. Everything was just to an Iranian's taste, because, in Ameer's absence, we had hired an elegant Turkish man to cook for us three nights a week. This way, we reasoned, we could have Iranian guests without the disappointment of watching the food go untouched.

As Azeez and I began putting the plates on the table, Ameer came over and asked, "Is Azeez going to eat with us?"

I looked at Ameer uncertainly, guilt striking my liberal heart. "No, he never does."

"Then I will ask him. Is it all right with you?" said my student, going into the kitchen after Azeez without waiting for my answer.

"Of course," I replied faintly.

An uncomfortable, blushing Azeez was made to sit at the table and pretend to eat steak and salad with us. He knew Ameer from the college, where Azeez worked days in the student cafeteria. By the rules of Iranian *ta'arof* it was bad enough that a student and his teachers should sit down as equals, but it was utterly unthinkable that an Iranian university student, his teachers, and a servant should be eating together at the same table. Even as a foreigner, I sensed this. Yet Ameer, as always, had been able to bend us to his will with the merest suggestion.

He had announced that a new social order was about to be born in Iran and, confident of his influence over us, he had decided to inaugurate it in our house. Jared and I felt strange. Azeez rushed away from the table and Ameer's attempts to converse with him before tea was served. I don't know whether Ameer even noticed how uncomfortable Azeez was.

Once more we fell into a pattern with Ameer. He would drop by our house on evenings and weekends. Again, the three of us sat for hours, talking. But things had changed somehow—not with Ameer, but with us. After close to three months in Iran, we were less naive and far more suspicious. We were not as sanguine about our prospects for making new friends, and we were beginning to pay more attention to the nuances of what we said to other people and what they said to us. Still, this was Ameer, one of our first and only friends. His English had gotten a little rusty in Tehran, but it came back in the rush of conversation.

He never taught me Kurdish, although that had been the original reason for us to meet. Occasionally, the three of us spoke a little Persian, but we could see that Ameer was impatient with our efforts. Once Jared accused him of not wanting to teach me Kurdish, and Ameer assumed his characteristic hurt expression, lower lip stuck out, as he brooded over this insult. Of course he planned to teach me Kurdish, but it was very important for him to learn English. Everything would come in time. Stung by the reproach in his eyes, we backed down.

There was also the question of visiting Ameer's town, Bukan. When would he take us? For a long time, we simply waited for him to suggest a date. Then, after his return from Tehran, we brought it up ourselves. But Ameer always put us off. Now was not a good time. There would be snow in the mountains. But Ameer took the bus there himself once or twice, and we knew other students from Bukan who occasionally went home. Why couldn't we go too? And why had Ameer lost all interest in going with us to Mahabad? We told him what had happened with the Jaffaris and how we wanted to go again in the company of a Kurd, but Ameer made it plain by his evasiveness that he would never take us.

Several weeks later, Ameer remarked that his father was coming to Rezaiyeh to visit. When he saw the look of interest on my face, he immediately added, "And I want him to meet you. I have told him all about my English teachers, Kak Jared and Dada Margaret."

It was then arranged that Ameer would fix an Iranian stew at his house and we would come and eat with his father. On the day that Ameer had invited us, he arrived at our door three hours early.

"What have you done with your father?" I asked him, peering down the stairs to see if anyone was standing there.

"Oh, he went home already," said Ameer.

"But what about the dinner you were going to make?"

"Oh, that. Was it important to you? I will make it here in your house."

I looked at Ameer coolly. What was he up to? Surely he realized that it was meeting his father, not eating the stew, that I cared about.

"What's the matter?" asked Jared. "Don't you want us to come to your apartment?"

"Well, it's not very nice there, not very nice for my English teachers."

Ameer didn't stay very long that day, sensing, no doubt, the questions we had. Suddenly the evasions about teaching me Kurdish and visiting his town, all the unanswered questions about his father—who he was and what he did—even the way Ameer constantly sidestepped telling us where he lived, began to surface and gather force in our minds. He was still making no moves to teach me Kurdish. Now he had offered to introduce us to his father and then, without explanation, had withdrawn the invitation.

"Why do you think he didn't want us to meet his father?" I asked Jared.

"I don't think his father ever came to Rezaiyeh," he answered.

"Then why did he tell us he was coming and why did he make such a point of inviting us?"

"We've been invited places before that people have no intention of actually taking us to," Jared pointed out.

It was true. *Ta'arof* reared its hypocritical head every time we gave or received an invitation. We had gotten to the point where we wouldn't let ourselves get excited over any invitation, no matter how tempting. And we could never be sure if the people we invited would really come or not. Wait and see was always our attitude as the appointed hour approached. Ameer at least had almost always come to our house when he had said he would, which was a far better record than other people we knew, including the Jaffaris. The Jaffaris obviously preferred to be on the giving rather than the receiving end of hospitality with us. Ameer seemed to be the opposite.

Ameer's mysterious behavior wrung a confession out of Jared. He told me that he had recently gotten very depressed because one of his favorite students at the college, a classmate of Ameer's, had told Jared he would teach him cuneiform script and then, after one fascinating lesson, had refused to meet with him again. The reason: He would lose all his friends if he was seen hanging around with an American teacher. Jared had decided that Ameer probably felt the same way. Thinking back, we remembered that despite all his offers, Ameer had walked on the street with us only a few times in the beginning of our relationship. Since that time he had reneged on or evaded all invitations and offers to see us anywhere except inside our house, usually at night.

Ameer didn't come for a week, and then he showed up suddenly one evening at nine o'clock.

"Where have you been?" Jared asked sourly.

"I have been very occupied looking for a new apartment. A better place where it is more suitable to invite you to come to dinner."

"Hah," said Jared.

Ameer looked hurt.

"You don't want us to come to your house for dinner," said Jared. "In fact, why do you hang around with us at all? Are you in SAVAK?"

Ameer turned pale. No one said anything for a minute. I felt an overpowering urge to change the subject. How had we come to this degree of distrust? Why were we questioning this boy as if he were a criminal? What had happened to all the warmth, all the love? I stared at Ameer, who was saying nothing to defend himself, nothing to reassure us, and I let Jared go on.

"Why did you invite us to meet your father when he wasn't here?"

"I am very sorry about that. He had to return to our home suddenly. To be truthful, my father and I don't get along very well. We were fighting and he decided to leave."

"I don't believe you," said Jared.

Ameer looked down. Said flatly, "I don't believe you" is a strong statement anywhere. In Iran, where lying routinely greases the wheels of social interaction, openly questioning someone's words is unthinkable.

I had a flash of insight into what Ameer was thinking.

"I don't think Ameer believes what we say either," I said.

"Is that right?" asked Jared.

"You don't believe that I have really come to Iran in order to write my doctoral thesis on Kurdish, do you, Ameer?"

Ameer looked at us, almost hopefully. "Well, you are very young to be getting a doctorate."

"I told you I am twenty-five years old."

"You are not twenty-five," said Ameer confidently. "None of the students believe that you are twenty-five. You look much younger than that."

"Why would I lie? Why would I pretend to be older than I am?" I demanded.

Ameer refused to answer my questions or even to look at me.

"You don't believe that I am working on Kurdish either, do you?"

"No, Well, maybe you are working on Kurdish. You say you are interested in Kurdish. But how can you be doing research when you are not at your university? People do research in a university. You are in Iran now, so you cannot be doing research."

I had guessed that maybe Ameer had accepted our stories tentatively. I had expected to find doubt, but instead I found total disbelief, denial of everything I had said I was, everything I had told him I cared about. I had talked incessantly of my academic work, my plans for research, my reasons for wanting to come to Iran in the first place. All of that talk, every word, had been judged by this small-town boy and apparently had been debated by his classmates. Every word had been weighed and rejected. I resisted an impulse to touch my face to reassure myself I was real. I looked at Ameer and couldn't believe I had ever liked him. At this moment he looked ugly, even horrible. How could I go on talking to him?

"Do you think we are in the CIA?" Jared asked calmly.

"No, I think you are not like that," said Ameer.

"Then what *are* we like? What *do* you believe?"

Ameer looked at us pleadingly. "I have not known you very long. I don't know who you are. It takes a long time to know someone, to trust them."

"But how can you get to know us if you don't believe anything we say?"

Ameer did not answer.

Ameer did not leave right away, although Jared and I both felt, without saying anything, that we could hardly stand to sit and look at the huge hurt eyes and the stuck-out lower lip a minute longer. It was as if we had gorged ourselves on pistachios until the very sight of them made us ill. It was not Ameer we saw in front of us, but our monumental naiveté, gullibility, vulnerability, and betrayal. And it wasn't only Ameer's distrust, but Nazi's ditching, the drunk man's insults, Mr. Asyabee's anger, and Mr. Khalili's reticence. Kurds and Turks alike had met us, judged us, and overwhelmingly rejected us. Now I was looking at another broken thread, my last thread on the spool that was going to lead me to Kurdistan.

Ameer continued to sit at our table, staring at first one of us and then the other. He really could not believe that we had turned against him so completely. He had kept his doubts to himself, sitting silently all those hours, all those weeks, that we had spilled out our hearts to him. Why had we forced him to say what was on his mind? It had all been so pleasant. He had been learning a lot of English. Why were Americans so blunt, so insensitive, so final? We stared at him stonily and at last he got up to leave, tears glittering behind his glasses.

On and off, Jared and I debated the possibility that Ameer was a SAVAK agent assigned to find out what we were doing in Iran. As a last defense against our anger he had suggested that his trust had been destroyed against his will, that he had had terrible experiences growing up in Bukan that we, as Americans, could not imagine. What? What? I pressed him this time and he could not be vague. He said that he had been brought before the secret police for putting out a student newspaper in high school. His father had been called from home to stand with him and be interrogated.

Were you tortured? I asked unsympathetically. Imprisoned? No, none of those things, he admitted. Just scared to death. But Ameer's confession came too late and at the end of too many other revelations. I didn't know what to believe. He *was* a Kurd. That much I knew, because he hung around with the other Kurdish students and spoke Kurdish, But beyond that I couldn't tell.

Who had won over his wavering loyalty? Was he moved by money, by fear, by Kurdish nationalism? If he hadn't trusted us, why had he been so willing to discuss politics? That was a bad sign in Iran, where only SAVAK agents were reputed to talk about such things.

Now we were truly alone, cut off. This was not like the incident with Mr. Asyabee. We could not admit to other people what kind of relationship we had had with this boy. Such a confession would only do more damage. We could not discuss it with Ameer, our former confidant. I ticked off the people I had asked about introductions to the Kurds, I thought of the Jaffaris, the radio staff, the teachers at the college. They had all been eliminated.

In America it had been easy to contact Kurds, the few that were living there before I left. I simply called them up and introduced myself. But in Iran, where telephones were not common, it would not do to walk up to people's doors and say I was studying Kurdish. Without the appropriate contacts, without relying on years of built-up trust, face-to-face communication was meaningless. It was like trying to cash a check at a big-city American bank without any ID. People would just assume that you were up to no good.

The break in trust between us and Ameer was like a break in reality. From now on, every word, every action, took on a double, hidden meaning. I was now more alert than I had ever been to people's remarks. When someone drove us home from the college and said at the end of the ride, "When are you going to buy a car?" I realized that every faculty member owned an automobile except us—that other faculty members resented having to give us rides and, at the same time, felt we were traitors to our class because we rode the city bus along with the workers and students.

I was no longer eager to accept any invitations, because I could not distinguish between those that were real and those that were gestures. In fact, I began to have the sensation when someone offered us something of being picked on, singled out. It felt like teasing, these invitations and smiles and hellos that meant nothing.

Invisible barriers appeared on all sides. I began to lose all the perspective and confidence I once had living in a society where I knew how to act and how to find information when I wanted it.

The fall-winter rains were beginning, and the sky and the mountains appeared closer, making me feel hemmed in. Where was Kurdistan? I looked toward the mountains, where the first snow had turned the peaks into cones of white. Were the Kurds only on the other side of those mountains, in Iraq or Turkey? No. They were right here, under the same sky, looking at the same mountains. I kept looking for the right person who would introduce me to the right people—for the magic words to say that would make the jinn appear.

PART TWO

ON THE EDGE OF KURDISTAN

CHAPTER 7

A CONFUSION OF WOMEN

To be alone in Iran was to be cursed. At first people pitied us, but if they thought we were deliberately avoiding other people, they would soon become suspicious. The unspoken rule seemed to be that women, in particular, should never be left alone. Whenever Jared went to the neighbors' to practice speaking Persian and I didn't come, they would urge him to go back to our house and get me. After I made it clear that I worked in the evenings, going over my data, they would peer out of their windows in amazement, watching the crazy, solitary American woman at her typewriter.

As outsiders, we soon learned that we could not expect to spend time with people as individuals. Almost every occasion that we invited someone to go somewhere with us, at least one extra person would show up. This was one reason going to see the Kurdish women—when I finally met them —made me nervous. They were always in a group, while I was always alone. It was unthinkable for any of them to venture out of the house alone. We could make no dates to meet in a teahouse or a restaurant; women were never seen in teahouses or restaurants except in the company of their husbands or fathers.

I had two choices open to me: Either I could go to the house of these women and deal with them *en masse*, or I could not see them at all.

Besides not having my mother or any other relatives to form a protective social buffer, there was the astonishing fact that Jared and I had not been related before we were married The Kurds always asked about this, wondering how we could have met. At least we must have been related by marriage so some kindly in-law might have mentioned me to Jared's mother; then we could have met with decorum, backed by our respective family groups. Instead we saw each other alone, far from our families and in an impersonal university where no one could know what our behavior had been before we were married.

At long last Mr. Khalili had decided to introduce me to a Kurdish woman. He telephoned my office at the college to tell me the news and make an appointment for us to go to her house together. I could hardly wait. As I taught my classes, ran errands at the bazaar, and went to sleep that night I kept thinking about this Kurdish woman.

When I appeared in the doorway of the Kurmanji staff room the next day Mr. Khalili picked up the phone, dialed a number, and told a person on the other end that we were on our way. Mr. Khalili said nothing about the house where we were going. All I knew was the name of the woman he had talked with on the phone—Maryam, or more politely, Maryam Khanim, Lady Maryam.

We emerged into a street I recognized, Pahlavi, one of the main thoroughfares in town. Just past the shop of a greengrocer I often patronized, Mr. Khalili led me up to a pale-blue metal door where he rang the bell. A woman with a pink face and wisps of blond hair escaping from under her bright-orange kerchief answered. After Mr. Khalili had told the pink-faced woman who I was, he said goodbye to me and left. I stared in dismay at the black-suited figure walking away down the street. Who would introduce me to Maryam Khanim? I sensed that the woman at the door was not my hostess, but who was she?

Before I had time to panic, the smiling pink-faced woman reached out for my hand and led me inside. The metal door shut with a thud, and, in the dim light, I made out a bare, dingy hall with a couple of tame gray doves running around and cooing on the tile floor. Deftly, the woman reached out and lifted my purse and my heavy reel-to-reel tape recorder off my shoulder. I hadn't taped anything since I came to Iran; in fact I had made a rule to myself that I would not even try to tape anyone until they knew and trusted me. Yet, I carried the machine around like a talisman. I was beginning to be afraid that no one would ever get to know me or trust me. Maybe I would just have to start taping wherever I could.

The pink-faced woman with her glittering Kurdish clothes now motioned for me to precede her up the stairs. These were bare, grimy tile like the floor of the hallway. The windows facing the street along the stairwell had streaks of dirt over the frosted glass. At the top of the stairs we reached another hallway with a large refrigerator.

All at once, I was standing in the doorway of a room where a collection of shoes and plastic slippers lay on a mat. I heard the swish of skirts, the murmur of voices, and, without warning, I was face-to-face with a roomful of Kurdish women.

They were all standing up, waiting for me to enter. Awkwardly I bent to unlace my knee-high boots; several people cried out for me to leave them on, but I could see that no one else had worn shoes into the room. As I entered in my stockinged feet, I saw the room was as padded and decorated as a jewel box. Someone ran to a corner to fetch a folding chair, but I refused this as well—no one else had a chair.

I was standing in the center of a circle of ladies—real ladies with long flowing dresses, layers of gowns and pantaloons and hand-knitted socks—in a boudoir filled with color, every surface decorated by crocheted doilies and machine-made tapestries. Mirrors and elaborate perfume bottles filled with liquids of all colors stood on a dressing table in the corner. I was dazzled.

Someone was pushing me to a seat under the window. Someone else was rushing over to a pile of suitcases and extracting a satin-covered pillow which she was thrusting behind my back as I attempted to sit down. Fully conscious of all the attention directed at me, I desperately wanted to lower myself to floor level. At last I was arranged to their satisfaction. I kept trying to cover my bare knees with my skimpy brown shirtwaist. Now I would have to open my mouth and speak. The room fell silent in anticipation.

The woman next to me, in a pale-aqua overdress with layers of other shades of blue peeping out from underneath, introduced herself in a low, hoarse voice as Maryam. Slowly, so slowly I felt they would soon lose patience, I answered their questions about who I was and what I was doing in Iran, how I liked it here, whether Iran was better or America was better.

I could not take my eyes off Maryam. She had several gold teeth in the front of her mouth. Her hair was red, perhaps from henna, but it suited her pale complexion perfectly. Her eyes were a clearer, truer blue than any of the blues in her clothing, and her chin jutted out, giving her face a masculine look that went with her assertive manner and low voice. Since she was my hostess, I assumed she was also the owner of the house.

Tea was being served. The pink-faced woman was coming through the doorway with a tray of small glasses filled with strong-looking reddish-brown tea. Another woman wearing a red tulle dress embroidered with sequined butterflies had gone to the wooden wardrobe that stood in the corner and extracted four china boxes. These she placed around the room on the rug. The boxes held lumps of sugar, *qand*, for placing between your teeth while you sipped the tea.

I stared at the lumps, trying to pick the right size. In too much of a hurry, I chose a huge one and then awkwardly tried to bite it in two. The women kept watching, and, in a few seconds, one of them was crying out for the servant to get me a spoon.

"No, no," I protested, vehemently enough that the spoon was not brought.

My teeth became gritty with sugar as I drank one glass of tea after another. Every time I finished a glass, the servant or the woman in the red dress would come over and refill it.

"This is my bride," Maryam told me, putting her arm around the woman in red who had just served me tea. I stared at her, wondering what that meant. I knew that the word *buk* meant bride, but how was she *Maryam's* bride? I did not yet know that brides in Kurdistan are not, strictly speaking, the property of their husbands, but of their husband's family, and, most particularly, of their husband's mothers.

I had read that the most common type of marriage in Kurdistan is between the children of two brothers, the so-called FaBroDa alliance. This custom is convenient from two points of view: It keeps the land in the family and it tends to lower the bride price, which can be quite exorbitant. Looking at Maryam and Khadija, I wondered whether they had been related before Khadija's marriage to Maryam's son. Physically, they looked completely different, and it was impossible for me to judge, in this highly formal situation, what their feelings were toward one another. But already I had sensed Khadija's youthful exuberance in contrast to Maryam's controlled strictness.

Now Maryam was making a point of telling me that Khadija, her bride, would also help me learn Kurdish, for Maryam seemed to be quite impressed with my intention to learn her language. While the other women had eagerly questioned me about my personal life—are you married, where is your husband, do you have children, why not?—Maryam had immediately set herself the task of making sure I knew the Kurdish names for all the objects in the room.

The awkwardness of my Kurdish echoed in my ears. Maryam was being very polite, waiting patiently for me to stumble out my answers, repeating things if I looked confused. But it took me an extra second or two to process even the simplest sentence, and it is a rare speaker of any language who can put up with this for long. I myself had told my students at the college that I would not slow my speech for them because that wouldn't be "real" English. But these Kurdish women, none of whom had been to a day of formal schooling in their lives, were patient enough to speak "careful Kurdish" for me.

With my tape recorder lying idle, I had been using phonetic notation to copy all of the words Maryam told me. Now, one of the women present wanted to know if I could really reproduce those Kurdish words the way they were supposed to sound. One by one I read over the words I had transcribed. The women murmured among themselves. They could see that I was not using the Persian alphabet. How were the sounds coming out so accurately in a strange Western alphabet? Tape recorders they had seen before; it was writing, as a record of sound, that amazed them. As far as they knew, their language couldn't be written. It wasn't used in schools; there were no standard dictionaries for spelling.

Gradually the women talked to me less and to each other more. Not only was there the language barrier to contend with, but the cultural one as well. I was too unsure of what was appropriate to ask about anything except their language. But, despite the silence between us—silence that I would come to accept as normal after I knew them better—communication continued. Each person took time to look at me closely and smile. Khadija, Maryam's bride, was grinning at me almost constantly. I saw amused warmth in those gray eyes ringed with black kohl.

Khadija was not as forbidding as Maryam; her chin didn't jut out, nor was she as striking with her pockmarked skin and hooked nose. But, to me, Khadija looked like the friendliest, most approachable person in the room. Somehow, without knowing it, I had sensed our common bond. In this room, Khadija, the new bride, was still an outsider, like me.

Time passed and tea kept being served. I had no idea how to stop the flow that poured into my glass, I saw the rays of sunlight slanting more and more sharply into the room, turning the confetti of color darker and richer as I began to watch the large battery-operated clock ticking on the wall.

Only two hours had passed since my arrival, but I was exhausted and buzzing from the caffeine in the tea. How could I take my leave? I began to worry about the words I would need to extricate myself politely from this room as it got darker and warmer and closer. Awkwardly, I began to scramble to my feet.

"What are you doing, Margaret Khanim?" asked Maryam, stopping in the midst of another conversation she was having.

"I have to go home now," I said clumsily, realizing belatedly that there was going to be no graceful exit for me. I simply did not know how to manage one.

"Stay, stay," cried some of the other women.

"Yes, you must stay," echoed Maryam.

"But I have to go home and prepare dinner," I said.

"Eat dinner with us," responded Maryam.

"My husband is waiting for me."

"Go and get your husband and bring him for dinner."

Were they serious about inviting a man in? Where would this escalation of invitations end? The invitations did not feel like *ta'arof*, but what did I know? As always, I was tempted to accept. But I had finally learned. Never again would I take another invitation at face value.

"Thank you very much," I said, feeling the smile glued onto my face. "But I must go."

I knew that my refusal had been accepted, because now all the women stood up, in a great swishing and bustling. I looked frantically around the room, wanting to grab my tape recorder and leave quickly so that everyone would not have to continue to stand. Khadija retrieved my equipment before I could reach it and then followed me out of the room. Before we could go back down the steps together to the front door, I had to stoop once more and re-lace the boots I had left on the mat. Everyone in the room continued to stand, calling out many goodbyes before I straightened up. At the door downstairs, Khadija handed me my purse and recorder and wished me goodbye.

I walked out into the gray dusk of early evening. Men in dark, shabby suits were hurrying home from work, while women shrouded in black chadors were shuffling from one little food shop to another, tucking their baskets under their veils. The vivid colors of the afternoon were gone, but when I turned and looked back, there was Khadija in her red tulle dress and her orange scarf leaning out from the doorway of the house like a genie halfway out of the lamp spout.

Maryam had assured me, in response to my awkward questions, that she was happy to help me with Kurdish. I knew I should go back to her house soon and take her up on her offer, but I hesitated. Here was my first real group of Kurdish women contacts, who lived half a dozen blocks from my house, who had been as friendly and welcoming to me as any group of people I had ever met. And yet I was afraid of them. Perhaps they were only being polite. They certainly had better things to do than sit around all afternoon drinking tea and speaking Kurdish to a foreigner.

With some prompting from Jared, I managed to take myself to the house on Pahlavi Street several days later, where I found Maryam sitting with two older women from Mahabad. The room was not as crowded as it had been on my first day. Counting Khadija, there were only four besides myself. The Mahabadi women's clothes were different from my hostesses'. They were wearing short jackets and wide cummerbunds wrapped several times around their waists, making them look more rotund than they already were.

The north-south division of Kurdish customs and language cuts across Iraq and Iran with the Sorani dialect spoken in the south and the Kurmanji or Bahdinani dialects to the north. All Turkey's, Syria's, and the USSR's Kurds are Kurmanji-speaking. Although Kurdish nationalists like to say these differences are trivial, several northern Kurds pointedly remarked to me that northern women's clothing was more attractive. Because Kurmanji women wear no bulky cummerbunds at the waist, their costume gives them a more desirable hourglass figure. But even if the northern Kurds came out ahead stylistically, linguistically, at least in Iraq, they are disadvantaged. The children of Iraqi Kurdistan must all learn to read in Sorani despite the fact that for some it is very different from the northern Kurdish spoken at home. I had a hard time understanding the accents of these Mahabadi women.

This time Khadija, sitting next to me, did more than smile silently. She picked up strands of my hair and admired them. Then she looked into my face and announced loudly, "Isn't Margaret beautiful?"

I was speechless. But Khadija didn't seem to mind my embarrassment at all and continued absentmindedly touching my hair and looking at me as if I were a child.

After Khadija's effusiveness, Maryam and the Mahabadi women didn't seem very warm. But neither were they unfriendly. The Mahabadis, like all of Maryam's previous guests, wanted to know the essential details: what I was doing there, how I liked Iran, whether I was married, whether I had children, and why not. This time, once the conversation shifted away from me and I had drunk three or four glasses of tea, I decided to leave. Maryam urged me to stay, but not as insistently as the first time. I went away wondering how she really felt about my dropping in.

I let a week or more pass before I went to Maryam's house for the third time. The afternoon I finally returned to the house on Pahlavi Street, Khadija, Maryam's bride, welcomed me. Seeing her alone like that made me imagine that maybe we could spend the afternoon in a tête-à-tête. Then we arrived in the doorway of the women's sitting room. It was crowded with guests. I hesitated, but Khadija was behind me, gently shoving me into the room. As I leaned over awkwardly to unlace my boots, everyone rose except one woman with a wooden cane placed by her side.

"*Te kheyr hati,*" they all welcomed me in unison. I hurried to sit in the place they indicated. My neighbor was the woman with the cane. She and I were the only ones provided with blankets and pillows. Everyone else sat on the bare rug.

Maryam introduced each woman by name. I tried to remember them by their clothes and features; but it was difficult to focus on anything, as I felt their stares and heard their whispering. Tea was served, and after I was asked the usual questions about whether or not I liked Iran and whether or not I had a husband and children, the conversation reverted to normal. There were so many women present that they could not sit silently while one of them interrogated me.

As I was drinking my tea and trying to pick up a word here and there, a slender woman with a very pale complexion and dark hair came into the room. Maryam put her arm around the woman's shoulder and spoke to me.

"Margaret, this is Zeinab. She has just returned from Tehran, where she got her teeth fixed."

The woman smiled at me, and I saw the glint of gold in her mouth. As soon as Maryam started talking to someone else, I turned to my neighbor.

"Who is Zeinab?" I asked. "Is she Maryam's sister?"

The woman with the cane looked at me uncomprehendingly. Then she began to laugh, "She is the wife of the haji," she said.

"The haji?" I repeated blankly. "Haji" is the title given to men who have made the haj, the pilgrimage to Mecca.

"Haji Ismail, of course," a woman at the end of the room called out.

The women were all watching me now. They had known a stranger was in their midst, but they had not realized how ignorant I was.

"Don't you know who Zeinab and Maryam and Susin are?" someone asked me.

I shook my head.

"They are *hevi*," said another. I noticed that the three women named were silent, letting the others explain. I wrote the word *hevi* in my notebook and raised my head.

"They are all married to the haji," someone said. The women laughed a little uneasily this time, as if it were not quite right to be talking about the haji.

"Don't men in America have more than one wife?" asked Zeinab.

"There is a law that forbids them to," I said.

Everyone started talking at once. "I told you America is a good place," I heard my neighbor with the cane say to the woman on the other side of her.

I was still mulling over what they had told me. Who was Haji Ismail? Today I had caught a glimpse of a group of men passing by the doorway, but they had seemed to be in transit, as if they didn't live here.

I thought I could go back to being invisible, but another woman started talking to me.

"Margaret," she said. "Is it true you want to learn our language?"

"Yes," I replied.

"Aisha has been to England," someone commented..

"Do you know English?" I asked her eagerly.

"Not really," she answered. "But I want to learn and I will teach you Kurdish. Come to my house any day."

"Thank you," I answered, wondering if she meant it. She had not given me her address. I looked at Aisha more closely as she began to speak to someone else. Her dress of pale-green gauzy material embroidered with silver thread and her emerald ring and huge dangling gold earrings were elegant. Gaudy colors and colored glass set into real gold did not seem to be her style.

"Are you going to Aisha's house?" the woman with the cane asked me. I did not realize that this was Aisha's mother.

"I don't know," I said awkwardly.

"Please come. I am not very busy," Aisha assured me. "Like you, I have no children."

"Can I teach you English?" I asked, obsessed with the idea that I could not simply ask her to speak Kurdish with me and give nothing in return.

"All right," said Aisha. The women around her giggled.

"*I* could never learn English," said one woman in a sarcastic voice. "But of course Aisha's husband is very learned. He is a doctor."

"What languages do you speak?" I asked the woman.

"Kurdish, of course, and Turkish and Persian," she replied.

"You speak three languages!" I said, admiringly. "You could certainly learn English."

"No, no," she protested. "I don't write."

This gathering seemed unusually large, and Maryam looked strange with an old fur jacket thrown over her Kurdish clothes. When it occurred to me to ask what the occasion was, I discovered that Maryam was leaving the city to spend the winter in her village. Disappointment washed over me. Just as I was getting to know her, Maryam was going off to some village where I would never be able to see her. The woman who gave me this news watched my reaction intently.

"You don't think Maryam should go to the village, do you?" she asked.

I looked at her, startled. How had she guessed what I was thinking?

The woman then suggested, "If Maryam goes to the village, her husband will start looking around for another wife."

At this, most of the people in the room dissolved in laughter. I felt confused. What was the joke? Who was Maryam's husband, and would she really risk losing him by going to the village? Where did *he* live?

Toward the end of the afternoon Maryam said to me, "I want you to teach my son English this winter."

I nodded enthusiastically. Now I would have a good excuse to return. Maryam's son went to high school and would be spending the winter in the city.] preferred the idea of trading English for Kurdish with him and with Aisha to the vagueness of dropping over for tea. When I learned that the son, Raheem, would be home in an hour, I waited, drinking three glasses of tea. After the third I set my glass on its side as I had seen other women do. But when Zeinab came over to refill my glass she laughed and drew the attention of the entire company to my overturned glass and then, to my chagrin, she set it upright and poured me some more tea. This time I simply left it, and afterward, in the company of Kurds, my overturned glass was always treated the same as anyone else's.

When the rest of the guests left, Maryam led me into the bedroom where we had sat during my previous visits to her house. Two handsome boys with blue eyes and chins like their mother's stood when I entered.

Taha, the elder son, shook my hand and looked me straight in the eyes when we were introduced. But Raheem stared at the floor, refusing to acknowledge my presence.

Since Raheem would not speak to me there was no way even to make an appointment to have a lesson. I then turned to Taha, asking if *he* wouldn't like to trade Kurdish for English lessons, but he laughed as if I were making a joke. Maryam then spoke rapidly to Raheem, who continued to avoid my gaze. In the midst of our mutual awkwardness, I heard a commotion outside the room. The doorbell had rung downstairs, and a minute later I saw Jared walking into the room. All the women who had remained standing about suddenly rushed off into another room, giggling and holding their headscarves over their mouths. But Maryam stood her ground. I introduced Jared, and then it was time to go. I wished Maryam a good winter, and she responded by inviting me to visit her in the village, but I had no idea where that was and there was no time to ask.

With Maryam's departure I was less sure of my welcome. I debated endlessly with myself and Jared about the advisability of returning on this or that day. I usually managed to find something else to do. At last, having run out of excuses, I found myself facing the blue metal door.

Not only was Maryam gone this time, but Khadija had also disappeared. Maryam's co-wife, and Nadia, Maryam's other bride—were snickering as they told me that Khadija had been dragged off to the village by Maryam "to do some work," as they put it. I could not rid myself of the impression that they were laughing at me as well as at Khadija.

As I sat with them, Zeinab worked the wheel of her hand-operated sewing machine while Nadia nursed her son, a strikingly ugly one-year-old with a large shaved head. They were talking to each other so quickly I could barely catch anything they were saying. Both of the women hardly glanced at me. Every once in a while I made an effort to join their conversation. They looked at me as if they were trying hard not to laugh. My confused doubts grew and grew until finally I could stand it no longer. I walked home slowly, pausing to look in the windows of the shops without really seeing any of the merchandise, trying to make sense of this last, puzzling encounter.

Long before I knew about the divisions and loyalties of Maryam's family, I sensed them. Both of Maryam's daughters-in-law were outsiders. Not only were they not from the same family as Maryam and her husband, they were not even from the same tribe. Khadija was an approved choice. An earlier alliance between her uncle and Maryam's stepdaughter had paved the way for marriage negotiations between hers and Taha's families. Nadia's marriage was another story altogether.

Although eloping is an accepted method of marrying in Kurdistan, it did not make Maryam happy when Nadia ran away with her next eldest son, Massoud. There had been no negotiations, no festivities, and no prior parental approval. The bride and groom had made their own choice, but it was Nadia more than Massoud who had to live with that choice. I once heard Maryam comment disgustedly that Massoud had never finished high school because of this early marriage—he had been only sixteen.

Once he was out of school he was forced to live permanently in the village with his new wife. This meant that Nadia, unlike Khadija at the time I met her, was basically Maryam's servant. She cooked all meals, squatting for hours over huge metal caldrons set on a hot fire. She stacked grape leaves between layers of salt in large crocks and pickled an assortment of vegetables for winter. Besides all of her chores for her mother-in-law she bore four sons in quick succession. Nadia was famous for her sharp tongue and salty wit in addition to her beauty. When I didn't speak Kurdish well, she made me nervous with her quick repartee and mocking laughter. But later on I wished I could know her better.

Although I still felt friendless, I had already been claimed by part of Maryam's family. Khadija was the selected daughter-in-law, wife of the eldest son; Nadia was the runaway. Maryam was the second wife of the haji; Zeinab was the third. These women spent days, weeks, even months together in the same house in the city.

In the village, as I was to learn, they were one another's main company. Yet, they were always competing, always trying to get a bigger share for themselves and their children. They held on tight to their possessions, their friends, even peculiar American acquaintances. So with Maryam and Khadija gone I had no friends.

As at the radio station, there was also the problem of the ever-present group. No one seemed to do anything alone. But how could anyone but a small child learn to speak in a circus? I became convinced that I needed to find one person, one teacher, to sit down with every day and laboriously go over Kurdish words and grammar.

I had to recognize the part my own culture played in this decision. I needed structure. I needed to know what structure others were operating under. I simply could not understand what Kurdish women did with their lives, what hours they were free and what hours they were working, when they were happy to receive guests and when they wanted to be alone.

As long as I felt I was somehow interrupting them and intruding into their lives I could never be comfortable. If only I had had a Kurdish fairy godmother to come and tell me that most of the world does not live on a fixed schedule. But even in the Kurdish equivalent of "Cinderella" there is no fairy godmother, just a Red Cow. I had no Red Cow, just my own preconceptions. So I kept on with my search and, in the end, I managed to find one Kurd who did operate on a schedule, someone who was as much at home in the right-angled universe as I was.

Maryam's Two "Brides" – Nadia and Khadija

CHAPTER 8

A SELF-POSSESSED 15 YEAR OLD

I rushed to the gate at the front of the college grounds. This was the second time I had arrived too late. Dara Ahmedi, my prospective tutor of Kurdish, had already been escorted away. This time to see the dean in person.

"That boy said he came to teach you Kurdish," commented the guard, looking at me incredulously.

A little while later Dara reappeared at the gate and the guard reluctantly let him onto the college grounds, "just this once." The dean had made it clear enough that he didn't want Dara here, and no one, no matter how important, was allowed past the police at the gate without the dean's permission.

Had it been necessary for Dara to tell the guard that he had come to teach me Kurdish? In America I wouldn't have thought twice about such an announcement, but in America they didn't have armed police to ward off spies and potential revolutionaries at the gate of every college and university.

My tutor didn't seem to be showing any ill effects of his trip to the dean. He walked with a firm jauntiness that looked all the more crisp because of his carefully pressed plaid pants and his neat blue cotton blazer over a yellow jersey turtleneck. I had not expected him to have such pink cheeks or such cool brown eyes. He didn't look at all like his nephew, a certain Mr. Haqzadeh who had an extremely toothy grin and a pair of narrow eyes that shifted frequently from side to side.

Dara's own eyes were set wide apart, and his expression was open and calm. Of course, I reasoned to myself, his looks might be as deceptive as his nephew's; Mr. Haqzadeh was not shifty in the least. Dara's nephew was five years older than his uncle and was one of our few students who were actually interested in learning English. Mr. Haqzadeh had voluntarily involved himself in my search for a speaker of northern Kurdish. Out of all the people I had questioned, he alone had proved successful in finding me someone. This was all the more surprising since Mr. Haqzadeh himself was a Turk, not a Kurd.

In the privacy of my office I introduced myself by writing my name on the blackboard. Dara in turn introduced himself as Mr. Ahmedi, writing only his last name on the board alongside my full name. In Iran, people never introduce themselves by titles. It is up to the other person to add the title to the last name. I had already called my tutor Dara and referred to myself as Margaret, but I was not going to be accused of condescension toward Kurdish boys. The tone of our lessons was set—Mr. Ahmedi it was.

When I raised the question of money, there was only the faintest hint of embarrassment, nothing like the dramatic scene we had gone through in arranging the salary of Azeez, our cook. Then we had talked back and forth —Azeez blushingly insisting he could not discuss the issue with us, Jared giving him money and Azeez then attempting to return it to us in an earnest persistence that only hinted at the grand *ta'arof* manner.

With Dara the money question was simple. He did not argue with my figure, a dollar fifty per hour, which was about half what a bricklayer in Rezaiyeh made in a ten-hour day. He simply nodded and smiled, faintly. Much, much later he told me how important the money had been to him and his widowed mother, who lived in an inaccessible village, far from any opportunity to earn a cash income.

My first hour with Mr. Ahmedi was spent recording a fable about a sheikh who counted his chickens before they were hatched, or, more exactly, his butter before it was churned. Every day, for weeks and weeks afterward, Dara was to give me a new story to work on or translate. When he felt himself to be in danger of running out of stories, he went back to his village and got more from his mother. I realized soon enough what a cheap price I was paying—not just for a punctual, organized tutor who would sit patiently and answer all my questions about Kurdish usage, but for these priceless folk and fairy tales of the Kurds.

I finished with Dara that first day feeling elated, but still afraid that this too would somehow dissolve. We made an appointment for our next meeting, and Dara strode off toward the gate and past the guard, who was staring at him and at me as I stood outside the classroom building. Now it was time to confront the dean about his high-handed behavior.

After a suitable wait in his anteroom, I was shown into his office. The dean glanced at me from behind the tufted black simulated-leather front of his desk, forcing his fierce Mongolian-like features into something that was supposed to appear friendly. Obviously he had no idea why I'd come.

When I told him he knitted his brows.

"We cannot allow teachers of this college to use their time learning languages such as—Turkish," he said carefully.

"Kurdish," I corrected him.

The dean looked impatient. He came from the northeastern part of Iran near Meshed, far from Rezaiyeh and its particular ethnic mix. As an elegant speaker of Persian and a passable speaker of English, he did not have time for distinctions between one non-language and another. And, just as clearly, he had no time for my interest in them.

I told him that I was a linguist and therefore foreign languages were to me what chemicals and the chemistry lab were to the chemist, but he refused to grant my point. As far as he was concerned, I should limit myself to the study of English.

At last he tired of my earnest assertions and parries, saying, with astonishing illogic, "If we allow you to learn Kurdish on college time, then everyone must be allowed to learn this language. It will be a problem for us."

I opened my mouth and shut it, trying to picture all the Persians and Turks rushing to the dean's office, demanding Kurdish classes and study groups.

The dean added pointedly, "I do not ask what you do in your time away from the college."

I knew he was subtly referring to the clause in my contract that specified that I could be fired on the spot for engaging in any other professional activity besides teaching English during the time I was in Iran.

I stood up, and the dean stood also behind his tufted desk front with its vinyl buttons. The meeting was over, and he smoothed his features out of their Genghis Khan look into something that was supposed to be quite pleasant. I smiled too until I left his office.

When I finally saw Mr. Haqzadeh again I apologized for the trouble that his uncle had been put through. Mr. Haq, grinning as always, brushed off my apologies. How could a fifteen-year-old's time be more important than my time or the dean's?

I had wanted to conduct my Kurdish lessons with Mr. Ahmedi at the college because it was more conveniently located for both of us, and it was a more formal setting, suitable for serious study. But most important, it was more decorous. When I met him at the gate for the next appointment and said that we would be going to my house from then on, Mr. Ahmedi accepted the news without comment. Unfortunately no one else was able to accept it.

Every day, except Friday, Mr. Ahmedi would appear at the door to our courtyard. The work of the bricklayers on the new apartment building across the street would abruptly stop as everyone turned to stare at the foreign woman escorting a boy into her apartment when her husband was not present. At last I was justifying the rumors that had no doubt been circulating ever since the neighborhood discovered that a foreign woman was living on the kucheh. In this part of the world men's thoughts about women are so exclusively sexual that even Jared began to get uneasy about Mr. Ahmedi being in the house alone with me. I never heard what the Jaffaris thought of my regular visitor, but I'm sure they took note.

Jared began coming home during the lessons, bursting in through the living-room door, where he would find us seated primly at the dining-room table directly in front of the French doors to the balcony in full view of the whole neighborhood. Then Jared would look around as if he couldn't believe we were sitting, fully clothed, working on Kurdish.

When Jared finally confessed to me that he had all sorts of fantasies about what Mr. Ahmedi and I were up to alone in the house, I was disgusted. Traditionally, in Iran, to be alone with a man is proof that the two of you have had sexual intercourse. There is no possibility of restraint or indifference or mitigating circumstances. Not feeling sympathetic, I let Jared work out his fears on his own while I continued to see Mr. Ahmedi at home. Thanks to the dean there was nowhere else to go.

More and more I began to wonder where Mr. Ahmedi came from. Each day he appeared, a fresh crease in his plaid trousers, as if he had just stepped out of a dry-cleaning shop. When the weather turned cold and rainy, he was still there, always on time, in the same outfit. While I began wearing a sheepskin coat to keep warm, Mr. Ahmedi stuck with his cotton blazer. Several times I overtook him walking in the kucheh as I was rushing back from the college in a taxi in order to be on time for our lesson. I asked him if he always walked or sometimes took a taxi. He replied that he walked, if he had time. I figured it must have been close to two miles from near the bazaar where he lived, but the fifteen-cent fare meant far more to him than it did to me.

Although he had been born in a village, Rezaiyeh was Mr. Ahmedi's town. He knew where and how to walk. He spoke the lingua franca, Turkish, fluently. Rezaiyeh should have been Shehrzad's town even more, but I doubt if she took it for granted the way Mr. Ahmedi did. As a male he didn't require a chador or any other disguise. Because of his excellent Turkish he was not recognized as a Kurd if he didn't want to be. Mr. Ahmedi was on his way up in the world. He was probably the only boy in his village currently attending high school. Yet, Mr. Ahmedi was a long way from renouncing either his Kurdishness or the strict code of behavior he'd been raised with.

On Kurdish grammar he was helpful, but when I tried to talk about other things I found us having absurd conversations that did nothing but make me feel foolish. One day I complained to my tutor about a veiled woman in a bank who had come over and stared at me six inches from my nose.

"Women in chadors must think they're invisible," I said.

"I don't know," Mr. Ahmedi replied noncommittally.

"Do you think chadors are a good idea?" I asked.

"I don't know. . . . Probably not," he said.

"Do you think when you marry your wife will wear a chador?" I pressed.

"Probably."

I gritted my teeth and went back to grammar. Times like these made me more aware than ever of what Ameer had done for us in the days when we didn't know what he was thinking. He had allowed us to let off steam, to criticize, to complain, to get frustrated, and, most important, to get some kind of feedback.

With difficulty, I began to pry out of Mr. Ahmedi a few details of his personal life. When we first began to work together, the most interesting thing I knew about him was that he had a fifty-year-old sister. That intrigued me, although I kept thinking that somehow I'd misunderstood.

Mr. Haqzadeh had originally thought I would like to work with this sister, who was married to Mr. Haqzadeh's grandfather. I was very surprised when he mentioned this—that his grandfather was married to a Kurd—for Mr. Haq was not a Kurd but a Turk, He had not come forward with my other students from Mahabad and the south end of the lake to tell me that he spoke Kurdish. Yet he had shown an interest from the first time he heard my reason for being here . His desire to help seemed peculiar.

Mr. Haqzadeh's own grandmother had been Turkish, so why had his Turkish grandfather taken a Kurd for his third wife?

I discovered that Mr. Haqzadeh belonged to a group of Sunni Turks who live in Azerbaijan. While the overwhelming majority of Azeri Turks, like the majority of all the peoples in Iran, are Shi'e Muslims, there is a small group of Turks who are Sunni. The difference between Sunni and Shi'e is not so much theological as emotional and historical. Nowadays all of the governments in the Muslim world except Iran adhere to Sunnism.

Sunnis accept the order of the caliphate. They follow the laws of Islam without unduly concerning themselves with its brutal early history. But in all of these countries, throughout the growth and spread of Islam, there were dissenters and sects which separated from the main body of believers. Only in Iran were these dissenters numerous and organized enough to establish a ruling dynasty.

The mainstream in Iran became Shi'e while the Kurds, protected and isolated in their mountains, remained Sunni as did the Arabs. Confusingly enough, unlike the Turks of Iran, the majority of the Turks in Turkey also remained Sunni. Kurds were destined to be separate from all the peoples who surround them, by language and culture unrelated to Turks and Arabs and by religion alien to the Iranians.

One of the reasons the Kurds give for hating the Turks is their very Shi'iteness. Kurds almost always call the Turks by a derogatory name, *ajam*, a word borrowed from Arabic, in which it means "barbarian" or "non-Arab." Sunni Turks are not *ajam* to Kurds. I could not help wondering if these Sunni Turks might not be former Kurds who at one time adopted the Turkish language but retained their Sunni faith.

Appropriately enough, Mr. Ahmedi's street was called the Street of the Sunnis. The house in which he stayed belonged to his sister's husband, Mr. Haqzadeh's grandfather, who resided there with his wife and her daughters. Their daily language was Turkish, not Kurdish. In fact the daughters could not speak their mother's language at all.

Mr. Ahmedi's mother, who was younger than the fifty-year-old sister, lived with her own small daughters in a village north of Rezaiyeh where no one spoke anything but Kurdish. Mr. Ahmedi, when he was seven years old, came to the city and began living apart from the rest of his family in order to attend school. At that time there was no school in his village, not even one run by the literacy corps.

Because of his home life Mr. Ahmedi had become completely fluent in Turkish, and because of his schooling he was also very good in Persian. After my search for Kurdish speakers at the college I could really appreciate Mr. Ahmedi's achievement. His native dialect was Kurmanji, northern Kurdish, and he came from a poor village family. Yet with a scholarship at a local high school and good grades he was on his way to college, perhaps in Rezaiyeh. If he went, he would be one of the first Kurdish students from the Rezaiyeh area. Only by dint of determination and hard work, and, of course, maleness, had he managed to overcome barriers that had kept thousands of other northern Kurds out of the high schools and college of their own region.

At Rezaiyeh College, where the proportionately few Kurdish students all came from Kurdish *cities* south of Rezaiyeh, the absence of local, northern Kurds was particularly noticeable. Northern Kurds, unless they are very unusual, like Mr. Ahmedi, or very rich, like Taha, don't have access to high schools.

Mr. Ahmedi's remarkable self-possession made me curious. I wanted to see him in the context of where he came from. But as the snow covered more and more of the mountain slopes ringing the city, the primitive village roads became impassable.

Since I saw no means of getting to his home village, I began to ask him about his sister and the Street of the Sunnis. He answered all of my questions but volunteered little on his own. At last, I pressed him to introduce me to his sister. I said I needed to make tapes of Kurdish women speaking. He took this request as seriously as all my requests for information and soon reported back that I could visit the house on the next Tuesday.

Mr. Ahmedi came to my house first. A taxi took us as far as was possible to the bazaar. After that we had to go on foot, negotiating the mud path that went all the way from the main street to the crude wooden gate that led to the courtyard.

At last I was in the section of Rezaiyeh that resembles the old part of Mahabad, with its maze of muddy kuchehs and hand-formed walls. It was cold and rainy, so Mr. Ahmedi and I did not attract as much notice as we might have on a clear day. I hurried along, clutching an umbrella in one hand and my tape recorder in the other, trying to keep up with Mr. Ahmedi's pace. The people we passed—men in old suits, women in chadors—looked poor. Few had umbrellas or clothing warm enough for the rawness of the air.

I had to stoop low to come in through the hand-hewn doorway of Mr. Haqzadeh's house. Everything except the big console television seemed strange in the little room where I faced Mr. Ahmedi, his elder sister, her two daughters, and one daughter-in-law.

We sat down. Tea was served. Large oranges were brought out and offered, along with store-bought cookies filled with whipped cream. Mr. Ahmedi's elder sister, her two daughters, and the bride of her son smiled, welcomed me over and over, and pushed food on my plate while they ate nothing.

I was all too conscious of the fact that they had not invited me; I had invited myself. I don't think it ever became clear to them what I was doing in their house. Consequently, the anxiety and tension in the air never dissipated in spite of the ritual words of greeting and the smiles of welcome.

It was my show, and Mr. Ahmedi was my manager. So when I suggested to him that his sister could talk about the history of the local Kurdish tribes—particularly the Shikak tribe to which their father belonged—Mr. Ahmedi immediately agreed. The tape recorder was plugged into the waist-high socket that was normally used for the television, and Mr. Ahmedi began to interview his sister about the history of the Rezaiyeh area. Later when I listened carefully to this tape, I was amazed at how little information she had put into her words.

There was a listing of names, vague phrases about the greatness of some tribal leaders. But most of the tape was devoted to praising the present government of Iran, an odd subject for a Kurd. She lauded the shah and the shah's father for making the roads safe, making it possible to travel from one part of West Azerbaijan to another without fear of having your throat slit or being robbed of everything you carried. It was true that the Iranian army and the gendarmerie had made the roads safer, but I had never heard any Kurd mention that the advantages of military personnel posted to Kurdistan outweighed their disadvantages.

At the end of the taping session I thanked the sister for her hospitality, bowed to everyone in the room, and put my shoes on outside the door. Outside, Mr. Ahmedi accompanied me as far as the main street, where I hailed a taxi.

I wished I had somewhere else to go besides the quiet bareness of my apartment. I preferred the coziness of the taxicab with its blue pompoms edging the windows and the scenic postcards the driver had pasted to his dashboard. But all too soon I was back at the head of the kucheh, passing the boy with his pellet gun. Week after week I had to walk by this son of Houshang's friend who continued to hang out on the kucheh with his buddies. The gun never failed to make me nervous.

In the weeks that followed I felt more and more homesick. We celebrated Thanksgiving along with the other Americans at the American army house. In the midst of a huge turkey dinner I had had the sensation of being enclosed in a huge plastic bag. My depression was so palpable that I could not seem to hear what the Americans around me were saying. Had I forgotten my own language?

As Christmas came closer, my homesickness grew more acute. Letters arrived from various family members asking about our Christmas vacation. Jared's brother suggested that we meet him somewhere in Europe over the holiday. Didn't anyone realize, hadn't we made it plain in our letters, that we were not living in a Christian country, that there was no Christmas vacation?

Jared and I made separate trips to the bazaar to try to find the gifts of the magi. After all, we were here in the Middle East, home ground of the kings who followed a star to Bethlehem. We sang the carol "We Three Kings" over and over to get ourselves in the Christmas spirit. But the more we tried, the more we realized how out of tune we were with the place where we were. Jared secretly had a gold ring made for me at the jewelry bazaar, and when I passed by the same shop, the jeweler rushed out and held up the ring to show me how much money my husband had just spent on me before I could look away.

It was unlikely that Jared would discover what I was giving him, but at the rate the Armenian seamstress was going on the embroidery for the shirts I had stolen from Jared's laundry, it was becoming more doubtful that he would see them on Christmas. Back and forth I went between my house and hers, a quarter of a mile away in the courtyard of an Armenian church with fantastic winged creatures painted on the outside walls. It cheered me up to be seeing someone who knew about Christmas, even if she did celebrate it in January instead of December. Because she knew how much it meant to me, she managed to finish in time, even a day early.

That day, a cold, overcast weekday afternoon, I was walking back past the blank walls of the kucheh leading to our house when a light bulb hit my forehead, just missing my right eye. Before I felt the slivers of glass in my hair, I experienced it only as an explosion, thinking that I had finally been shot by the boy with the pellet gun.

I stared at this boy standing in front of me, and felt my face begin to crumple. It was as if someone had taken aim at Christmas itself and shot it out of the sky. I dropped my plastic shopping basket filled with the newspaper-wrapped newly embroidered shirts, and looked around.

The boys were watching me carefully. There were two besides the owner of the pellet gun.

"What was that?" I asked in a shaky voice.

One of them pointed to the glass at my feet and then at the streetlamp overhead.

"Where did it come from?" I asked. The boys looked around and pointed to the left down another kucheh. I felt my forehead and shook my head slowly. The nearest house on that kucheh was many yards away from where I was standing.

Anyway I already knew that the bulb must have come from the right. On this side of the kucheh there was only one house, that of the richest man in the neighborhood, the man for whom all of these kuchehs were named—Mr. Ameerfallah.

As I walked past the boys, tears started streaming down my face. I started running. When I found Jared I sobbed out what had happened, gulping for breath.

For a few minutes we pondered the incident. I was not hurt, but the glass had come very close to my eye. I could have been badly injured. Jared decided to get Houshang's advice.

The first thing our neighbor did was to try to calm us down.

"These things happen," he said. "This is not America. Sometimes people are finished with an electric light bulb and instead of throwing it into the garbage, they throw it out the window. They don't realize that it might hit someone."

"Then why did it happen to hit my head just at the moment I was passing?" I asked. "Why didn't it hit the street?"

We convinced a reluctant Houshang to walk down the street with us to investigate. Houshang rang the bell of Mr. Ameerfallah's house, and after what seemed like a long time a young male servant dressed in baggy pants came to the gate smiling broadly. Houshang asked if his master was at home, and when the servant replied that he was not, Houshang told him why we had come. At that the boy could barely restrain himself. Looking at this snickering servant, I was certain he had thrown the bulb. But, of course, he denied even knowing what we were talking about. Soon we stood facing a closed gate again.

We prevailed upon Houshang, who was growing ever more uncomfortable with this investigation, to ring the bell at the house of his friend, the father of our little see-no-evil witness to the incident. No one answered our ring. In the space of the last ten minutes, the local web of kuchehs had become deserted, unusual for the middle of the afternoon.

Houshang walked back to our house with us.

"Just forget it," he said.

"I can't. Suppose it happens again?"

"Once Shehrzad was walking in the kucheh here with our son and a boy came up and grabbed her around the waist. Our son was very upset, but what could we do?"

"But this was not being grabbed around the waist," Jared pointed out. "This was having a light bulb thrown at your head."

Houshang shrugged.

"I want to get the police," I said.

Houshang turned, a sharp tone in his voice. "You mustn't do that. Mr. Ameerfallah is a good man."

If he was such a good man, I wondered, what did he have to fear from the police? Aloud I said, "His servants can't be allowed to go around throwing light bulbs at people."

"The police will not solve the problem," Houshang replied flatly.

We had reached the front door of Houshang's apartment.

"Thank you for your help," Jared said, shaking hands.

Then Jared and I walked through the still-deserted kucheh once more and hailed a cab to the city police station. We told our story to one sullen-looking policeman who did not seem at all sympathetic. But he went back with us in a taxi to the scene of the crime. The three of us stood outside Ameerfallah's gate waiting for the servant to answer the door. This time there was less outright giggling, but the same denial and the same amused look.

Now that the police had arrived and it was official, a crowd started to gather around us. People were smiling and laughing as they explained to each other what had happened. One teenager came over and volunteered to translate. His English wasn't bad, and unlike everyone else he seemed concerned rather than amused. It was unnerving, all these people laughing and pointing at us. This was Kucheh Ameerfallah, one of the more solidly middle-and upper-class neighborhoods in town. Here it could not be class difference that made us so alien. The people around us laughed as if we were not human.

"Tell me what happened," the policeman ordered us for a second or third time.

At that moment, Houshang's friend, whose son owned the pellet gun, appeared on the edge of the crowd. I went over to him.

"Your son was out here when the light bulb hit me. Maybe he could tell what happened," I said.

"My son knows nothing," the man said coldly.

"What are your names?" the policeman asked Jared and me. We told him.

"What are you doing in Iran?" Again, we answered.

"Yes, but *why* did you come here?"

I exploded to Jared, "He's asking *us* questions instead of any of these other people. The next thing he'll want to know is how much money we make and why we don't have children!"

Just as Jared and I were thinking of leaving this circus, a jeep drove into the kucheh and out stepped Mr. Ameerfallah, the portly, white-haired owner of the house from which the light bulb must have been thrown.

Ameerfallah was quickly informed by a servant what had happened. Stepping over to us, he said he was sorry to learn that we were having trouble, but that he greatly doubted that the trouble could have originated from his house. The policeman, in the presence of this important personage, decided that it was time to wind up the whole affair.

He suggested that Jared and Ameerfallah shake hands. Jared refused, and, seething with anger, we started to walk away from the crowd. This did not suit Mr. Ameerfallah or the policeman, who then ordered us to accompany him and Mr. Ameerfallah in the jeep for another trip to the police station. Our translator came along too.

This time we were met at the station by a lieutenant, who listened intently as we again explained the entire incident.

The lieutenant turned to Ameerfallah and asked him if he was willing to make sure that no one who worked for him would ever do such a thing again. Ameerfallah, without admitting that such an act had ever been committed by an employee of his promised to "twist the ear" of the offending servant boy. I muttered to Jared, "But he's not going to admit guilt. No one's interested in finding out who really did it."

The crime was recorded, and, to the great satisfaction of the Iranians present, Mr. Ameerfallah and Jared shook hands. As a mere woman, Jared's property, I was lost in the shuffle. Afterward we all drove back to our kucheh, where Mr. Ameerfallah again shook Jared's hand.

A day later, on Christmas night, we were sitting in our living room when the doorbell rang. Down in the kucheh six children stood, one of them carrying a cellophane box of roses and carnations, which she thrust into my hands. I invited them upstairs to tea and discovered they were the sisters and brothers of our translator of the previous day. Mr. Ameerfallah's daughter had also come along to wish us a happy holiday. They knew it was Christmas only because I had mentioned it several times during the investigation the day before.

The curly-haired boy who had translated spoke. "My mother wants to know when you will come to dinner at our house."

We thanked them for their flowers and for the invitation.

"But you don't have to invite us to dinner," said Jared.

"My mother wants you to come to dinner," said our translator.

"Are you sure?" I said, hating the hard note of suspicion in my voice, but feeling almost certain that the invitation could not be real. Who *was* their mother? And why had she not invited me herself? No doubt these children were making the kind of polite gesture they had been taught to make.

But, to my surprise, they insisted, so we reluctantly set a date to go to their house. When they left I turned to Jared and asked if he thought the invitation could possibly be real.

"I don't know," he replied.

At that moment I had no desire to accept any invitations. I didn't even want to leave my house.

When we arrived at their house, it was clear that our translator's family was not only expecting us, but looking forward to meeting us. But, in spite of all their smiles and genuine-sounding welcomes, I felt ill at ease among the plastic flowers, gilt gewgaws, and numerous pictures of the shah which decorated their sitting room. I only wished that I had met these people *before* the light bulb had been thrown, or that, better still, the light bulb had never been thrown. I also wished these people had not decorated their house in such a pro-shah style. They seemed to love us for being Americans as much as other people in Rezaiyeh seemed to hate us for the same reason.

The fate of an American teacher at Rezaiyeh College who'd had his throat cut on Christmas Eve six years earlier no longer seemed so remote to us. For the next month, whenever I walked out of the house, I looked behind me. I drastically cut down on the number of times I went downtown alone. Although I had shopped for hours alone in the evenings before Christmas, I was no longer willing to brave the touching, staring crowds of men and boys who filled the sidewalks of downtown Rezaiyeh. I was now more sensitive than ever to the hatred and contempt that lay behind that touching and staring. From the time we had landed in Tehran airport and seen a chador for the first time, I had realized that I was vulnerable as a woman. Now I understood that being a foreigner put me in double jeopardy.

As for the Kurds, they receded from my mind for a time. I wondered that none of the refugees had appeared in the crowd on the kucheh. I continued to put off visiting Maryam's house, and I rarely saw Mr. Khalili in these dark days of winter. The Iranians that I told of this incident were not sympathetic. Houshang and Shehrzad, in particular, voiced their astonishment that we had called the police on Mr. Ameerfallah. "Such a good man," they repeated.

I never even mentioned to Mr. Ahmedi what had happened. Somehow I didn't think he would be at all sympathetic. Later, when an ugly scene developed on his very own kucheh, I knew I had guessed right. To Mr. Ahmedi, almost until the end of my stay in Iran, I was "other." Even when he perceived us as human and as friends, he always believed we were far wealthier than we were, or at least than we felt. His coldness hurt; yet, I could see it was a defense. Mr. Ahmedi acted like an adult when he was still a child.

Mr. Ahmedi and I continued to meet, and I had the sensation of learning a language mechanically. Eventually, I supposed, it would help me to complete a dissertation, but what was the use? The more I got to know both Kurdish and Persian, the more pointless they seemed. Perhaps I would be able to be more polite, or more obfuscatory when people asked me questions, but would I ever get to know anyone better?

New Year's Eve was even bleaker than Christmas. Once the holidays were out of the way, we began to think of getting out of Rezaiyeh for a while. It was midwinter break, heading into the big Shi'e holiday—Moharrem, the period of mourning for the martyred imams, Hassan and Hossein. We decided to fly to Tehran, take the train back to Tabriz, and then the bus to Rezaiyeh.

I went to Tehran bursting with impressions and questions about my first four months in Iran. But I was put off by the American scholars I met in the capital. None of them seemed to have any positive feelings for this place. Most were simply contemptuous of Iran and Iranians. Talking to these people, I knew how easy it would be for me to write off all Iranians as hopelessly xenophobic and misogynistic. Coming back from Tehran with all its noise and traffic, I had a fresh perspective on where I was. There were obviously worse places on earth than this small, clean, quiet, scenic provincial capital. My cynicism disappeared. When I saw Mr. Ahmedi again, I realized that I had learned a lot from him. I was ready to venture out and try speaking Kurdish again.

Mr. Ahmedi in his ancestral village

CHAPTER 9

AISHA AND THE DOCTOR

In Rezaiyeh, it was a rare Kurd who had attended high school, so I wasn't sure I heard right when Mr. Khalili started talking about a famous "doctor," a Kurd with a Ph.D. Not a man who spoke the dialect of the southern cities such as Mahabad or Sanandaj, but a real Kurmanji speaker like Mr. Khalili. And he didn't speak just Kurmanji, but Arabic, Persian, Turkish—both Istanbuli and Azeri—Russian, English, and perhaps some German. It seemed incredible that such a man who had no association with the college, the only institution in town presumably connected with higher learning, was living in Rezaiyeh.

Mr. Khalili mentioned him only in passing, with great caution, the way he said most things to me. "There is a Kurdish doctor," he remarked tentatively in response to my continual queries about finding Kurdish women. This was in the days before he finally deposited me on Maryam's doorstep. In those days he would always plead innocent of knowing any Kurdish women. Although the doctor was a very important man, if I was very, very lucky he might consent to help me with my Kurdish.

It was simply impossible for Mr. Khalili to believe that I was really looking for ordinary Kurdish women. Perhaps I was so exotic—an overeducated Western woman researching Kurdish grammar—that he felt I merited at least as exotic a teacher. The fact that this doctor knew English would be, in Mr. Khalili's eyes, a great advantage to me. Mr. Khalili did not have the patience or the time to teach me Kurdish. But he thought that I wasn't making enough progress because of our language barrier, not for any lack of practice and instruction. To Mr. Khalili's way of thinking, translation would solve the whole problem and I would be able to learn Kurdish in a snap.

There was no lack of doubts in my mind that anyone who had a Ph.D. was going to speak the typical village language that I wanted to study. More than Mr. Khalili, such a person was bound to be influenced by other non-Kurdish sources. But even if I didn't think I needed a teacher who spoke English I wanted to meet this mysterious doctor, and, as I assured Mr. Khalili, I especially wanted to meet his wife. My unshakable Western assumptions led me to imagine that she also would speak Russian and English.

Just when my hopes were aroused to match my curiosity, Mr. Khalili was becoming vaguer and vaguer about the idea of the doctor's teaching me Kurdish, until he never brought it up again. Was the doctor too busy to meet me? Was he too suspicious? Had Mr. Khalili ever even mentioned me to him? Now that I was aware of a Kurdish doctor I couldn't just forget about him, Mr. Khalili had mentioned that he had studied at a Russian university, and I wondered endlessly what subject his degree had been in.

Several times, in Mr. Khalili's company, I had unknowingly passed the house of this very same doctor. A couple of men cleaning the Land Rover outside had greeted Mr. Khalili and stared at me in a curious but not unfriendly fashion. They worked in front of the same magical house that I had noticed during my first weeks in town—the one behind the blue metal doors. In front of these doors usually stood the long Land Rover and the two khaki-outfitted men with turbans who now looked at me surreptitiously after they saw me in the company of Mr. Khalili.

A week later we again were walking by together when Mr. Khalili excused himself to go in and pay his respects to the doctor. Finally, he had been forced to divulge whose house it was. But he did not invite me to come inside with him.

Several days after our return from Tehran I was inspecting oranges at a fruit stand on Pahlavi Street when a woman in a black chador appeared at my elbow. Thinking that she was only there to stare, I started to turn away, but she grasped my hand and gave me a hearty salaam. Looking at the full, glittery dress under her black lace chador, I realized she was a Kurd. Her pink face seemed very familiar, but I could not remember if I had met her.

"Where have you been, Khanim?" she asked. "Our hearts were narrow for you."

I started to feel embarrassed that I could not place this woman. Then it came to me that she was the maidservant who had greeted me at the door the first time I had gone to Maryam's house.

I smiled, grateful for her friendliness.

"When are you coming to see us again?" She was still holding onto my hand, long after the shake had ended.

My first impulse was to be vague. It was a reflex I had finally acquired in response to such questions put to me in Persian. But then I caught myself. Wasn't this woman being especially warm and friendly, and wasn't she speaking Kurdish, not Persian? Besides, I had promised myself that I would go back to Maryam's house this very week.

"This afternoon I will come," I answered impulsively. "Is it all right?"

"Very good," she said. "We will see you then."

As I watched her walking away down the street at the unhurried pace of the chador wearer I wondered if I had made a mistake. Suppose she had only meant the invitation as *ta'arof*? Suppose there was no one at the house on Pahlavi Street who wanted to see me? Suppose she wasn't going to tell them that I was coming?

A few hours later when I rang the doorbell, my fears were instantly allayed. Khadija herself stood in the doorway, grinning and shaking my hand and asking me where I had been all this time. I explained I had gone to Tehran, but inwardly I felt guilty because I had been in Tehran for only a week but away from Maryam's house for over a month. Khadija told me she had been in the village for only a couple of weeks and when she returned had been waiting and waiting for me. In one hand she carried my handbag, and in the other in she grasped my hand as she led me past the doves up the stairs to the bedroom. As soon as I seated myself on the rug, she sat down next to me.

"Margaret, you have such a beautiful name!" she exclaimed.

I smiled.

"Do you know the other Margaret?" she asked.

I shook my head. I had thought that Margaret was strictly a Christian name in Iran, limited to Assyrians and Armenians. Was there a Kurdish Margaret?

"I will show you." Khadija jumped up and went to the closet. From its depths she extracted a large book with a plastic cover— the family photograph album.

We began at the beginning, flipping through pages of photographs of unsmiling Kurds, all members of Haji Ismail's and Maryam's family, all lined up in the same style as in the photographs Shireen and Parweneh had shown me in Mawana.

Toward the middle of the album, on a page by herself, was the professional photograph of a small dark Assyrian girl named Margaret. I had seen this picture before in a book on the Kurdish war of the 1960s. This Margaret had fought with the Kurdish revolutionaries in Iraq. Although she was Christian, she and other Assyrians fought with their neighbors, the Kurds, against the oppressive policies of the Arab government in Iraq.

"You are Margaret just like her," said Khadija. I was curious to hear more about this other Margaret, but Khadija seemed to know about as much as I knew about her—perhaps less. To Khadija she was Kurdish, not Assyrian. Although I did not have any immediate plans to take up arms with the Kurds, I was glad to be identified with someone who had.

Farther on in the album we came to a picture of a bride. This was Aisha, the same Aisha I had met on the day Maryam went to her village.

"Aisha's husband studied in your country, Margaret," Khadija informed me. "He is a doctor."

Suddenly what I had learned when I first met the regal-looking Aisha and what Khadija was now telling me clicked with that long-ago description from Mr. Khalili, Could there be two Kurdish doctors in Rezaiyeh—one who had studied in America and one who had studied in Russia? I thought it was more likely that Khadija's vague sense of geography had combined the U.S. and the USSR into one equally remote place.

"Are you sure he didn't study in Russia?" I asked her.

She looked puzzled. "Your country, I think it was your country, Margaret," she said uncomfortably.

One of the most delightful things about Khadija was her country ways, her hearty manner, the way she would slap your knees or grab your breast. Khadija would hang out the window of Maryam's house and hold long conversations with the neighbors across the alley. Such activity was hardly seemly for urban ladies, but Khadija was a raw newcomer to the city when I first met her. She had married only a few months before, and this was the first time she had ever been to Rezaiyeh. She had never gone to school, never learned to read or write. Later I saw her discomfort when her illiteracy was pointed out once in my presence by her sister-in-law. That Khadija didn't know where the countries of the world were was no fault of her own. Her brothers, only a few years younger, were being sent to high school in Rezaiyeh. But Khadija was ashamed of her lack of learning, as though she were to blame. I did not continue to question her about the place where Aisha's husband had studied. Ebullient Khadija was not someone I wanted to make uncomfortable.

Before I left she asked me if I had gone to see Aisha. "She is waiting for you, Margaret."

I felt a twinge of regret and shame. All this time I had been assuming that it was only important to me whether I went to these women's houses.

It had never crossed my mind that they could be sitting around wondering why I didn't come. That they could be looking forward to my arrival.

On my way downstairs, I felt like kissing the orange-kerchiefed pink-faced servant. Khadija stood in the first-floor hallway, looking into my eyes.

"You are like my sister, Margaret," she said. "Come to our house again soon."

I was so fascinated by her husband that, in the beginning, I did not appreciate how extraordinary Aisha was in her own right—more extraordinary perhaps, for she had not had the advantages of being male. She had not been educated at officers' college in Baghdad, nor had she traveled to the Soviet Union and studied Kurdish history. Her father had not allowed any of his female children to go to school, limiting them to the most cursory lessons at home by mullahs.

Aisha's house, when I first went to it, felt completely different from Maryam's. It seemed much larger and airier, in part because there were fewer people in it—Aisha was childless—and in part because it had clean floors and high ceilings. The sitting room where she received me on the second floor was covered by two large, exquisite Persian carpets with animals and flowers woven into their sylvan design. Crowded along the long ledge below the floor-to-ceiling windows that stretched across the whole front of the house were potted plants of all sizes and varieties. At one end was a tree bearing lemons, and at the other end was a fragile-looking fuchsia. Framed tapestries were hung on the wall, and in the corner stood a console television with a stuffed weasel on top. The most unusual thing in the room was a large wood glassed-in bookcase. Even the Jaffaris, modern as they were, had no bookshelves in their over-furnished house.

As soon as I was face-to-face with Aisha in a metal folding chair placed uncomfortably near her in the vastness of the sitting room, I had the sense of someone observing me, judging me in a way I had not felt with Maryam and Khadija. Aisha did not take my refusal of a chair seriously. Nor did she fail to supply me with a spoon when she ordered tea brought for me.

Aisha herself did not drink tea; instead she drank hot water, which was offered politely when I asked her what it was. Now we sat staring at each other, our chairs so close that our knees were almost touching. Aisha seemed to be waiting for me to start a conversation, I had always thought my dearest desire was to be alone with a Kurdish woman without an audience to distract me, but now I wasn't so sure. Aisha looked at me with such an amused, almost sarcastic smile playing on her lips.

"Do you want me to teach you English?" I asked her, not knowing what else to say.

"Yes," she replied, sounding far less enthusiastic than she had when I had asked the same question at Maryam's house.

I tried giving her words and phrases, but she seemed halfhearted and embarrassed about repeating them, so I stopped.

"Margaret, don't you miss your family?" she asked me, apropos of nothing.

"Yes, I miss them, but not so much. Iran is very interesting and I am happy to be here," I elaborated.

Suddenly, she broke out in peals of laughter. I stared at her uncomfortably. *What* had I said?

"Your Kurdish is so funny," she commented, wiping her eyes.

After that our conversation went awkwardly. Being constantly afraid that she would again find my Kurdish ridiculous, I spoke slowly and sparsely. She continued to scrutinize me relentlessly.

After a while, a rotund, apple-checked woman came into the room and sat down on the floor while Aisha and I remained on the chairs. She and Aisha spoke rapidly and in a slightly different dialect that I couldn't understand. But Aisha didn't forget about me and included me in the conversation as much as she could.

Even before I saw the tall man in the doorway I noticed that Aisha and her friend were suddenly on their feet. I stood too. Was this bearlike man at the door of the sitting room the famous doctor? He came forward, his blue eyes twinkling.

"How do you do, Miss Margaret," he said in very careful English. "Welcome to our house."

I nodded and made some reply, awed not only by his size—his chest was enormous and he was very tall—but by his English and the way these women, including his own wife, were standing silent and respectful in his presence. He seemed to sense the discomfort he was causing, for he soon bowed out of the room, wishing me a pleasant stay in Iran.

I wondered if I would ever see him again. He acted as if he were a visitor in this house. But surely he lived here. I looked around the sitting room at the closed doors leading off to other rooms and wished I could see all of them. When Aisha disappeared from the room for ten minutes without telling me where she was going, I wondered if she was hinting that I should leave. Perhaps she was too busy and didn't want to tell me. When, at last, she returned, I stood up quickly and said I had to go.

If Aisha's laughter at my Kurdish coupled with her peculiarly unexplained absence from the room had happened before my visit with Khadija, I would have been tempted to avoid her house in the future, thinking she did not really want to see me. But somehow I believed that she did want to see me, that she found me as interesting as I found her. She invited me to come again soon, whenever I liked. The fact that she was childless, like me, and that her house was relatively empty made me feel more comfortable about dropping by.

The next time I came to her house I discovered what Aisha had been doing when she disappeared so suddenly during my first visit. This time she prayed in front of me, going off to a corner of the sitting room, where she stepped out of her long pantaloons, leaving them in a little pile next to her. I had never seen any non-Kurdish Muslim women step out of their underpants before praying, but the rest of the ritual—chanting, bowing, and then prostrating herself toward the southwest in the direction of Mecca —was an exact replicate of an act repeated five times daily all over the Middle East. She did all of this in the presence of me and the apple-checked roly-poly woman who seemed to be her constant companion.

The two of us sat in silence as I studied the machine-made tapestry hanging near the book cabinet. On it two men in pith helmets were depicted standing next to some black folds looking into a black ellipse. At the same time I realized that this must represent the Kaaba, the innermost recess of the shrine at Mecca, I also perceived an unmistakable resemblance to female genitals. Having seen the tapestry once from this point of view I could never undo the image, and afternoons at Aisha's were always enlivened by staring at this rather curious wall-hanging.

After finding these types of "tableaus" in more than one Kurdish house it struck me that Kurds tend to hang garish machine-made tapestries on the wall while leaving ordinary priceless handmade carpets on the floor. Wealthy urban Iranians who had limitless access to shops overflowing with manufactured goods were beginning to appreciate the old handicrafts more and more, while Kurds, isolated in their villages, still regarded the new products of Iran's Plastic Age as beautiful.

After I began visiting Aisha regularly, a relationship developed between us that soon went much further than my relationship with the women at Maryam's house. Aisha only asked me once, instead of every time I came to visit, whether I liked Iran or America more. After that she inquired in detail about my family, my life, my reactions to my work at the college, American politics. She wanted to know why my parents had been satisfied with only two daughters and no sons; what my mother did now that her children were no longer at home; why Richard Nixon had left office (Iranian newspapers had said it was because the Jews had forced him out); she wanted to know what Americans thought about drugs. I never would have believed that the conversations I had with Aisha were possible—both because I did not think I knew the language well enough and because I had naïvely not suspected that she could know about and be interested in things outside Kurdish society.

It was also Aisha's style to make moral judgments. Not until three years later did I hear from some members of her family that Aisha had right off pronounced me to be a person of good character. But it didn't take me three years to find out how highly some of these other women valued Aisha's opinions or to hear Aisha tell me things about her family that no one else wanted to reveal.

Who was Aisha's family? I still wasn't sure. She seemed to be related to Maryam, but for a while I did not understand exactly how. One day she asked me if I had been to her father's house recently.

"Your father's house?" I repeated, puzzled. *Who* was Aisha's father?

"The house on Pahlavi Street," she added.

"Maryam's house," I corrected her.

"Yes, Maryam's house," she said tolerantly.

It must have been an effort for Aisha to accept my misconception that the house was Maryam's. But Aisha understood much better than her sisters and sisters-in-law that I was a foreigner who knew nothing of Kurdish customs.

Aisha herself had lived in countries where people knew nothing of Kurds. She realized that it might never have occurred to me that she had been raised to dislike Maryam and to feel envy for what was given to Maryam and Maryam's children. Only gradually did I figure out that Aisha's mother and Maryam were co-wives of Aisha's father. Aisha was the second-eldest of all of her father's many, many children. She was also close in age to Maryam's sons. While Aisha's mother had had only girls, Maryam had borne the haji four boys.

This could not have made the ordinary rivalry between the two wives any easier for Aisha's mother to bear. But the sons, although of great advantage to Maryam, did not make her the proprietor of the house on Pahlavi Street any more than Aisha's mother was. Owning was reserved for the haji.

Aisha was special to me because of her wit and her sensitivity. But she was special to many other people because of her position, not just her personality. Until I understood this, I wondered why she dressed more magnificently and wore more gold than any other Kurdish woman I knew, why she spoke Persian so much better, and why she alone had traveled to England and Europe.

When Aisha was eighteen years old she had been given in marriage to Maryam's brother, her father's first cousin, the Kurdish doctor, Sheikh Avdilah. After this, Maryam was not only Aisha's stepmother, but her sister-in-law as well. Since her marriage, a marriage that Aisha told me she had dreaded and railed against and had never forgiven her mother for allowing to take place, Aisha had been elevated to a position that she could never have enjoyed otherwise, despite the importance of her father, a large landowner and well-known sheikh in greater Kurdistan.

Her father had shown no interest in his daughters beyond guaranteeing their virginity. He had kept Aisha confined to the village, where no one besides her female family even knew her. Now she was the wife of a man older and more important than her father, a man who, as it turned out to both their sorrow, did not give her any children.

Aisha's position as Sheikh Avdila's wife, without children at her skirts, without co-wives to compete with, living in a fine house with many servants and jewels, made her a real princess. She had money at her disposal and, in comparison to her mother, stepmothers, and sisters, a surprising amount of freedom. Her husband was an educated man, and it was clear from talking to Aisha that he had spent some time educating his young bride. I wondered if she had always been as proud and as self-confident as she seemed to me now.

I had occasion to see Aisha in the role of gracious hostess to the Iraqi Kurdish refugees who frequented their house. One day, in order to amuse a mother and daughter who were visiting, Aisha took down an impressive scroll with Sheikh Avdila's family tree inscribed on it. The root of the tree was the Prophet Mohammed himself. Because of this, the family enjoys the right to the title "Sayid." All the family members on the tree were represented by neatly drawn green circles with names in beautiful calligraphy inscribed inside. The trunk grew upward through Sheikh Abdel-Qader, a founder of a Sufi order in twelfth-century Baghdad, and branched out through nodes containing circles with the names of many of the major revolutionary figures in nineteenth- and twentieth-century Kurdistan.

There was Obeidullah, the sheikh who had threatened to bring most of the Rezaiyeh area under Kurdish control until he was tricked by an American missionary and subsequently exiled to Mecca, where he died. There was Aisha's husband himself, Sheikh Avdila, a man who had written a scholarly history of the Kurdish Revolution in Russian.

"But where are you? Where is your name?" I asked Aisha.

"There are no women here," she answered, looking at me as if I were slightly crazy.

By now, I was dying to see Sheikh Avdila again, but he never seemed visible when I was visiting his wife. Her upstairs sitting room was reserved for female guests. Although I never saw them, I assumed that the men who had come with these women stayed downstairs with the sheikh.

I wondered about all these Iraqis who visited. I knew that the sheikh had lived part of his life in Iraq, but I didn't know when or under what circumstances. Maryam, his sister, had also lived in Iraq and was able to read Arabic quite well. But she had been living in Iran for a long time, as had the sheikh's father. Why had Aisha's husband stayed in Iraq so much longer, I wondered, and why did the refugees come to see him?

One day I spied a new addition to Aisha's decor. On the wall near the television I saw a calendar with the title "Calendar of the Iraqi Kurdish Revolution" printed in English, Kurdish, and Arabic. The current month—January—was illustrated with a picture of General Mulla Mustafa Barzani, his face done impressionistically in shades of blue with a red turban. Flipping through the other months, I studied brightly colored lithographs of weeping women, soldiers, a dove with a bleeding wound, and a girl hanging from a scaffold with the caption "Layla."

On each month many historic dates in the Kurdish nationalist struggle were noted—the execution of various leaders, the major Kurdish victories and defeats in Iran, Iraq, and Turkey over the last century, the date of the Treaty of Sevres, and the date of the subsequent Treaty of Lausanne, in which all mention of a possible Kurdish state had been dropped.

In answer to my questions, Aisha said she did not know where to find another one. I admired the calendar several times, and before I left she presented it to me. This was not *ta'arof*, but a genuine gift. I knew that because Aisha had previously cut through my *ta'arof*-like demurrals to give me several other presents, exquisite handmade things from a suitcase of treasures she kept in a corner.

Khadija too had given me pairs of handmade Kurdish socks. Gradually I came to understand that if you admired something in a Kurdish household you would find yourself being presented with it. This was no Iranian-style *peesh kesh* when the owner of a thing was heavily obliged to virtually offer it to you and you were obliged to ritually refuse it.

Later I learned not to admire things I saw in Kurdistan. But for now, like an ingenuous child, I hugged the calendar to my chest as I rushed home to tack it up on our wall. Aisha had urged me to hold it so that no one on the street would know what it was.

I took to dropping by Aisha's house on my way home from the college in order to discuss the day's events with her. Once I came at midday and she invited me to lunch. I declined her offer and left quickly, afraid that I had somehow invited myself. The lessons of Iranian *ta'arof* died hard. But the next time she invited me and urged that I call Jared to come also, I accepted. Without realizing it, I was about to have the opportunity I had been waiting weeks for.

"Would you like to eat with your husband or upstairs with me?" Aisha asked me when Jared arrived.

We were down in the sheikh's sitting room, because the kitchen was also downstairs and Aisha was alternating in her roles as chef and hostess. Sheikh Avdila was leaning back in one of the enormous easy chairs which lined the walls of his sitting room, making small talk in slightly too formal English.

When Jared came to the doorway of the room I looked from him to Sheikh Avdila and back to Aisha. Here was Jared, getting to meet Sheikh Avdila on his first visit to this house, a chance I had waited weeks for. But if I chose to stay with the men, what would Aisha do? She would have to eat alone. Craftily, I appealed to Sheikh's Western sensibilities.

"Can't we all eat together?" I asked.

"Of course," he said genially, and he instructed Aisha to eat with us. For Sheikh Avdila it was simple. But for Aisha, I saw it was not so easy. She barely touched her food, and I felt badly that my curiosity had outweighed my feelings of consideration for her. But I could not be really sorry.

At this meal I finally learned why so many Iraqis came to visit Sheikh Avdila. Finally, the articles and chapters on Kurdish history I had read in the United States and the green circles and names inscribed on the family tree took on a human face. Here was a living legend of the Kurdish Revolution.

Sheikh Avdila had been born in Turkey more than half century earlier. As a young child he had watched his uncles and grandfathers being hanged by the Turkish government in punishment for one of the uprisings of the Kurds following the rise of Mustafa Kemal Ataturk. Avdila's family, one of the foremost families of Kurdistan, did not have to give up everything they owned in order to flee the continuous repression by the new Turkish government. They simply went and resettled in another country where they owned land. Their villages might be confiscated by the government, but there were many other villages they owned in Iraq and Iran.

Avdila was raised in Iraq. In spite of being a Kurd, as the scion of a great family, Avdila was given the privilege of attending officers' college in Baghdad. Upon graduation he was made an officer in the Iraqi army. For reasons that were not clear to me, his father, a venerated sheikh with a large following, came to settle in Iran while Avdila stayed in Iraq. Then, when Iraq got too hot for freedom-minded Kurds, the young Avdila followed Mulla Mustafa Barzani to Mahabad, where he became part of the army that defended that republic.

At the fall of the republic, when Barzani fled to Russia, Avdila and others went with him. The Kurdish refugees that accompanied Barzani were soon scattered across the Soviet Union, doomed to suffer the murderous purges and internment Stalin visited not only on his own people but foreigners who had been invited into Russia.

Avdila himself spent two years in Siberia, part of it on a hunger strike. For a while he worked in a factory in one of the eastern provinces, where he took a Russian wife and had a daughter by her. Finally, as he had been promised years earlier by Soviet agents in Iranian Azerbaijan, he was able to study at the University of Leningrad.

Eleven years after their arrival in the USSR, events in Iraq once again seemed propitious for Avdila and the other Kurds. In 1958, Abdel Karim Qassem staged a coup in Baghdad and invited the Kurds to take their rightful share of economic and political power. Mulla Mustafa Barzani made a triumphal return from the USSR as a new day of progress and inter-ethnic amity was supposed to dawn in Iraq. Avdila, leaving his Russian wife and daughter behind, soon followed Barzani's men back to Baghdad.

By 1961 Iraq was again in chaos. Communists were fighting Arab nationalists. No one, except the Kurds, was interested in the question of Kurdish autonomy. When it appeared that Qassem was not going to abide by his promises to the Kurds, Kurdish guerrillas began fighting in the mountains. Qassem responded with all-out war. Under this new challenge to their rights, the Kurds began to build a united movement. Mulla Mustafa, strong man of the Barzani tribe and general from the days of Mahabad, was undisputed military leader.

There were also other political leaders in the KDP. The letters originally stood for Kurdish Democratic Party, until the name was changed to Kurdistan Democratic Party to represent all oppressed groups in Iraqi Kurdistan, including Assyrians, Turkomans, and Arabs as well as Kurds. The Kurdish army expanded from the Barzani irregulars to the Pesh Merga, literally the "Death Facers," the name by which the Kurdish army has been known ever since.

The 1961 offensive, like other wars against Kurds, was not popular with the common Iraqi soldier. The Kurds got many weapons from deserters as well as on the black market. Many Kurdish officers left their posts in the Iraqi army and joined Mulla Mustafa.

The Iraqis strafed, machine-gunned, dropped napalm, and fired rockets at Kurdish villages. The countryside was laid waste, and many villagers fled to the hills and caves for shelter. Despite this onslaught the Kurds were still not able to stay politically united. Some Kurds allied themselves with the Iraqi government and fought against their fellow Kurds. The traditional tribal enemies of the Barzanis, such as the Zibari, were quickly recruited by the Arabs to fight the insurrection. Then the Kurdish leaders began arguing among themselves. The KDP was split between the old tribal feudal interests represented by Barzani and the new left socialist elements who were with Jalal Talabani.

Sheikh Avdila's family background made him a landlord, but, with his Soviet education, he was to the left of Barzani. Perhaps Barzani feared him because he could have brought together these two factions. On the basis of aristocratic lineage alone Avdila could have challenged Barzani's right to rule Kurdistan. His forebears were famous Kurdish revolutionaries as well as revered şheikhs. Barzani had no family tree which went back to the Prophet.

Sheikh Avdila referred to Barzani contemptuously as a *diktatór*, with the accent on the last syllable. According to the sheikh, after Barzani imprisoned him in the mountains, he was released only through the intervention of SAVAK agents dispatched from Iran at the request of his father.

I wondered at the latter part of the story—the implications of Avdila's father's involvement with the Iranian secret police. Perhaps it was only a matter of expediency to Avdila—he had to get out of Iraq. Several years later Barzani would purge suspected Communists from the KDP. But Avdila, son of a famous Muslim sheikh, was no more Communist than most of the people who disagreed with Barzani. He saw that even if the Kurds did manage to win their autonomy from the Iraqi government, most Kurds would still be oppressed; they would still owe their work and their crops to landlords. Avdila and other Kurdish intellectuals doubted that Barzani could win, given his out-of-date methods and loyalties. The main leader of the opposition, Jalal Talabani, fled from Iraq, leaving the reins of the KDP solely in the hands of Mulla Mustafa Barzani.

Although Qassem was deposed after only a few years in power, the Kurdish War went on for nine more years. In the beginning there was a ceasefire, but the new government under the leadership of the Baath Party only mouthed support of Kurdish aims. Not long after they consolidated their control over Iraq, it became apparent that the Baathists were more violently anti-Kurdish than anyone who had preceded them. As Pan-Arabists these rulers of Iraq had no sympathy for Assyrians, Turkomans, Kurds, Jews, or even the Shi'e Arabs in the south of Iraq. The Baathists and their agents made life difficult for anyone who was not both Sunni and Arab. But the Kurds contributed to the instability that plagued Iraqi governments. From 1963 on the Baath Party leadership underwent countless purges reminiscent of the Stalin era in the USSR.

In 1970 the Kurds and the Baathists signed a fifteen-article Peace Agreement. A census was supposed to be carried out in northern Iraq to determine which areas had a majority of Kurds. Those regions would then be declared self-governing. But the census was never taken. In fact, the Iraqis began forcibly deporting Kurds away from their own lands. Besides guaranteeing the Kurds their linguistic and cultural rights, the Baathist agreement was supposed to economically rehabilitate the areas devastated by the nine-year war.

According to the Kurds, nothing was done to improve life in Kurdistan. In 1974 it was easy for the shah and the American CIA to encourage the Kurds to begin fighting once more. At the time the Kurds thought that the concessions offered by the Baathists did not fulfill the original terms of their agreement. But if they had known they would subsequently lose the right even to speak Kurdish in their own schools, they would never have gone to war at all.

When Avdila returned to Iran a decade before the start of the next Iraqi Kurdish War, he found the family fortune still large, although depleted. In the 1960s the shah had implemented a land-reform scheme, the key part of what he grandiosely referred to as his "White Revolution." Under this law, no landlord was allowed to retain more than one village. The rest had to be given up. Despite all the evidence that points to a grossly uneven enforcement of this law in Iran, in Kurdistan it seems to have been applied, at least in this one stipulation of one *khan*, one village. I never met a Kurdish landlord, no matter how rich or influential, who in fact had more than one village. Turks on the other hand seemed to have fared better, at least some of them. Ameerfallah, the rich man at the head of our kucheh, was reputed to still own six villages.

Following the land reform, Sheikh Avdila's father bought back one of the family's villages from the government, and it was in this village that Avdila later came to invest his money and his future. He had arrived in Iran on the edge of old age, at an untimely break in a political career that had seemed to promise much and had certainly involved great preparation and suffering on Avdila's part.

Avdila had hardly rested on inherited riches or on the position of his family. While his cousin Haji Ismail stayed in his ancestral village and married five women, Avdila had been educated, had fought in Iraq and Iran, had worked in a factory, and lived in Siberia. When he came to Iran, after all those years, he had nothing, not even a wife.

A wife was easily found from within his own family, but the rest was up to Sheikh Avdila. He could not follow in his father's footsteps, because a decade in Russia was not the sort of preparation appropriate for being a practicing Sufi sheikh with followers. Neither could Sheikh Avdila make use of his considerable education. In Iran, Soviet degrees are not highly regarded, since anyone who has lived even temporarily in Russia is viewed with suspicion.

Whatever Sheikh Avdila did do with his time—and that was never entirely clear to me—it was plain from the way that he spoke that he felt SAVAK's eye was always on him. When I asked why he did not write his memoirs he said, smiling as if it were a joke, that it was utterly unthinkable. Even to *write* them, without attempting to publish, would be dangerous.

Despite Sheikh Avdila's non-personhood in Iran and the constraints that bound him to a backward provincial city and a small village, it was obvious that in Kurdistan he was somebody. This was why the refugees came to visit, why, when I later went to his village, I saw a steady stream of local mullahs and leaders waiting to ask his advice. I wondered whether this small bit of homage and respect compensated at all for what he had lost.

Sitting in Avdila's salon, eating thistle-shoot stew with rice and yogurt, I tried to get some feeling for how Sheikh Avdila felt about his past. I looked curiously at the photograph hanging on the wall which showed his father bowing to the shah. Such photographs were *de rigueur* in any house where people could "boast" of any personal contact with the shah.

What did it mean to Avdila, a man with a Ph.D. from Leningrad, a man who had fled the collapse of the Mahabad Republic, to have to hang such a picture in his room? I watched Aisha bending uncomfortably over her plate as she sat on a stiff chair instead of the floor she was used to. Had Avdila wanted to marry an uneducated village girl? There was no sense of tragedy or drama in this room, no feeling about what the sheikh had just told us. In front of me I saw just a husband and his wife decorously eating a meal with two foreign friends. Sheikh Avdila's story was new to me, but it was very old to him.

After the meal, Jared remained behind with the sheikh while Aisha led me back upstairs for tea in her sitting room. As we drank our tea I looked at the pictures in a large photograph album which she had taken down from the bookshelf. They were all black-and-white photographs of Avdila and his friends in Russia—informal picnic scenes and bathing suits that would have been unthinkable in Kurdistan with or without a camera. I saw the Russian wife with Slavic cheekbones and the Russian daughter with long blond braids and Avdila's strangely shaped blue eyes.

"I have written to her and asked her to come and live with us," Aisha told me earnestly.

"Who?" I asked, imagining she meant the daughter.

"My husband's wife."

I was astonished. Didn't Aisha enjoy her status as only wife?

"But she cannot come," said Aisha sadly.

Aisha and Avdila were not typical Kurds, but, then, the more Kurds I got to know, the more I realized that none of the ones I met could have been typical. Mr. Ahmedi was certainly not, nor was Maryam. Even Khadija, with her provincial manner, was not typical. All of them reacted to me in different ways, but only Aisha and Avdila seemed to see past my Westernness, my foreign looks and manners. With others I often felt that they could never understand what I was really like, but Aisha seemed to know.

On my second visit to Iran, Aisha pointedly referred to the fact that Jared and I had no doubt lived together before we were married, a fact which I had *never* mentioned to any Kurd. When I feebly tried to deny it, she laughed, as if to say she knew better. Such sophistication and especially such tolerance were extremely unusual for a Kurdish woman, or, indeed, for any woman in Iran. I have heard urban Iranian ladies with sons studying in the United States refer confidently to the fact that all American girls are whores.

What future did Sheikh Avdila and Aisha see for themselves? Would they ever leave Iran? Could Avdila resume his former activity in the Kurdish nationalist movement?

In the months that Barzani's army seemed to be gaining ground in Iraq, these questions did not occur to me. To me, it seemed that Avdila had been a threat to Barzani. He had lost; Barzani had won.

If Barzani could lead the Iraqi Kurds to victory, it would be the greatest triumph of his career.

Later, when everything changed, I recalled Avdila's word, *diktatór*, spoken with more emotion than he had used when discussing SAVAK and the Iranian government. Still, Sheikh Avdila was a true patriot. I don't believe he was glad for a moment about what happened to the Kurds in spite of the blow dealt to Barzani. But Avdila did have harsh words for the leaders of this revolution, men who had sold their revolution to the Iranian government and SAVAK and filled their pockets with gold. After ten years in Iran, Sheikh Avdila was in a better position than most to appreciate what Iran's true motives were in its support of the Kurdish nationalist cause.

CHAPTER 10

KURDS FROM IRAQ

The memory of the Kurdish refugees I met at the refugee school haunted me. I can still see them sitting in their circle in the teachers' break room. These men and women were an entirely different set of Kurds from the ones I interacted with in Rezaiyeh. These were highly educated, urban Iraqi Kurds. They dressed as I did or even more fashionably. I could imagine them in any elementary school in the United States. That they were in Iran, that many of them were doomed to face torture and death, was only chance. Not only were these people like me, but I made the mistake of trying to involve myself in their fate.

Jamal's face was the most vivid, as I read over the names of those executed in Iraq. The soft jaw and the softer brown eyes of this man whose career was teaching first-grade children. I was one of his first-graders, to whom he showed the same degree of caring and patience that he showed to all of us—whether we were twenty-five years old or seven.

I had never seen a Kurdish man like this, never imagined that any could exist. Perhaps they didn't under the harsh, brutalizing conditions of Iran, but in Iraqi Kurdistan, a whole generation of Kurds had grown up, schooled in their own language, trained at their own university in Suleimaniya, armed with their own primers and textbooks, all in Kurdish. It was hard for me to believe that these too were Kurds. The dialect they spoke and wrote was so different from that of the Rezaiyeh Kurds that I could hardly follow it.

I came to the refugee school under the auspices of the enemy. The Iranian government under the aegis of the Red Lion and Sun Society, was in charge dispensing aid for the refugees. Although Barzani and his advisers had decided to let the Iranians take over the Kurdish Revolution, ordinary Kurds did not trust the Iranians. It wasn't only that they remembered Mahabad; they also hated living in Iran. In Iraq they had known the freedom to be Kurds and to take up arms when they felt they were oppressed. Iran with its shah whose picture and whose secret police were ubiquitous was more than they could stomach.

I had been watching the refugees for a long time before I met any of them. Most of the non-Kurdish inhabitants of Rezaiyeh referred to refugees as "Barzanis"—as if they were all from Mulla Mustafa Barzani's tribe. But this name was only appropriate for the soldiers with red turbans, a fraction of all the refugees.

Kurds from everywhere had come to participate in the Kurdish Revolution of 1974. Professionals from Baghdad had given up their jobs to join. Some Kurds from abroad even left their comfortable lives and came to Barzani, confident that their dedication to this concerted effort for Kurdish autonomy would not be in vain.

From talking with Ameer I had learned that there was a two-tiered hierarchy of refugees. The great mass of refugees were housed in large camps on the outskirts of the city. One camp had been set up due west past Band, while several others were to the south. Ordinary villagers and tribesmen as well as poor townspeople from Iraq were registered in these camps. They were people who had picked up their children and fled the ceaseless bombing with little else but the clothes on their backs.

Even the wealthier Kurds who had managed to bring gold and one or two of their servants out of Iraq had suffered hardship and terror on the back mountain roads that led to Iran, One family with many children had started out in their car, but, for fear of being visible to the pilots, they had ended up on foot. A wealthy doctor's wife, unused to physical exertion of any kind, had come alone without her husband on the back of a donkey. But the plight of the villagers was the saddest. Because they didn't live in Rezaiyeh, at first I didn't see their faces, blackened by sun and dirt, dulled by fear and deprivation – two constants of war unleashed on a civilian population. Not until nearly the end of my stay in Iran did I witness the suffering of these people when a group of them arrived unexpectedly in the village of Haji Ismail.

In late winter most of the permanent refugees were women and children. The men came only periodically on leave from the fighting. Then we would see the lucky ones who had passes from the Iranian government on trips into town. They visited the bazaar and then piled into their battered jeeps for the drive back to the camps.

The refugees allowed to lived in town were a small, elite group. These were the families of the leaders of the Kurdish Democratic Party and officers of the Pesh Merga, or "Death Facers." The Red Lion and Sun, fronting for SAVAK, paid their living expenses while the men went back and forth across the border to direct the war effort.

The refugees in town were far wealthier and usually more educated than their counterparts in the camps. On the street they tended to wear Western dress, although the official uniform of Barzani's army consisted of khaki *shalwar* with a tight-fitting jacket and a turban, exactly like the clothes worn by Sheikh Avdila's two servants. Despite their wealth and the relative ease of town life, these families were prisoners too. They could not go anywhere outside Rezaiyeh without passes.

Part of Iran's support of the Iraqi Kurdish war effort included personal tours for a number of Western reporters who came through Rezaiyeh to visit the refugee camps and then crossed over to Iraq to view the battles. I decided to use my only connection to see if I too could visit a refugee camp. I was especially interested in seeing the school there; the only schools in Iran conducted in Kurdish.

My contact was the man we had met on our first day in Rezaiyeh, or, rather, on the plane before we'd even landed. As the director of the Rezaiyeh branch of the Red Lion and Sun he had been made responsible for the management of all the camps. I had seen him and his wife on several social occasions since we began living in Rezaiyeh, and he knew I was studying Kurdish. Since he and his wife had both been friendly to me I was fairly confident that he would at least listen to me.

When I arrived at his office and stated my request, I was relieved that he seemed amenable, as if there were nothing remarkable in my wanting to see one of these camps. There was only one catch—he had to call SAVAK and have his decision approved by them. No one was allowed in the camps without SAVAK's approval.

I spent the entire morning in his office waiting for SAVAK to get back to him. At last they did, with a negative answer. However, there was an interesting twist. I had been worried for months that SAVAK was monitoring my activities in Rezaiyeh, but, far from knowing what I was up to, it seemed that SAVAK didn't even know who I was.

According to the director of the Red Lion and Sun they had me pegged as another American woman in town who was married to an Iranian and had previously spent time in Iran serving in the Peace Corps. When I denied this identity, the director, who ought to have known better, looked at me as if he were sure I was lying. It seemed clear that though it didn't matter exactly who I was, SAVAK was not about to allow any foreign women without press credentials into the refugee camps.

Having read the clippings about the camps and the war that relatives in America sent to us from *The New York Times*, I could see SAVAK's point. A person with no knowledge of Persian or Kurdish on a one-week jaunt through the area from a regular post in Tehran or Beirut or Paris missed a lot of the real story. Most of these journalists didn't even know what SAVAK represented in Iran. But then SAVAK might have looked a lot different to me if I too had been a journalist who was being entertained on orders to make the Kurdish War a *cause célèbre*.

When the director of the Red Lion and Sun Society saw how disappointed I was, he made me a counteroffer. Without SAVAK's approval he couldn't allow me to visit the camp, but he could, on his own say-so, send me to the local refugee school in town.

I immediately assented to the suggestion that I come back to the Red Lion and Sun headquarters in two days and be chauffeured there. The director of the Red Lion smiled, obviously pleased that he had been able to do something for me. I smiled too, glad I wouldn't have to spend any more time sitting in his office watching the stream of supplicants who came before him begging for favors.

When I returned two days later, not yet knowing where the authority of the Iranian Red Lion and Sun ended and Kurdish authority began, I couldn't tell if the black-haired man with the battered American Buick was a Kurd or an Iranian. We rode in silence to the school, which was really just an old house behind a high wall on one of the main streets in town. Upstairs in the faculty room the teachers sat in a circle of metal chairs. They all stopped talking and looked at me when the man, the driver, who turned out to be a Kurd, led me in.

I tried to explain in awkward Kurdish why I had come. The expressions of curiosity turned to puzzlement. I stopped and started and then stopped. As far as they were concerned I was speaking gibberish. One teacher asked in fluent English if I had come there to learn Kurdish. I nodded.

"Ah, she has come to learn Kurdish," they said to each other, smiling.

But I was sure they were thinking about how I had come from the office of the head of the Red Lion and Sun, right from SAVAK. Did it make any sense to trust a person like me?

Whether or not they trusted me, they took me in. They gave me one of the primers that had been smuggled across the border by the Kurdish army.

They let me sit while they aired their worries and apprehensions about the fate of neighbors and family who were still in Iraq.

Jamal enthusiastically accepted me as a student in his first-grade class. After my first day of school I wondered how I had ever been able to stand first grade. It was so boring and so confining. I wriggled in my seat just like my classmates who sat near me on narrow wooden benches with narrow desks placed in front of them. The first-graders, all of whom were immaculately dressed in colorful Western-style children's clothes, stared and giggled at their huge visitor. One by one we were all called to the board to perform. The children were also strictly disciplined, but fortunately Jamal did not chastise me when my attention wandered.

My Iraqi Kurdish classmates at the refugee school

Breaks were announced by a bell every forty minutes, and I spent them in the teachers' room. There were mathematics, English, Arabic, geography, physics, and a physical-education teacher, specialists for most of the subjects that needed to be taught from the first through the twelfth grade. I was impressed, not only by the fact that the council of the Kurdish Revolution had moved to set up this school as soon as the refugees came into the area, but also because the teachers seemed so dedicated.

I taught in a college, not a high school, in Iran, but there the teachers seemed cynical and uninterested not only in the students, but in the subject matter as well. Every Iranian elementary school text had full-page pictures of the shah, his wife, and the crown prince at the front of the book. None of the Kurdish books had any such pictures. Iranian high school English texts were rife with mistakes. The Iraqi English teachers in this school, both of them, had studied in English-speaking countries, and the English texts they used were accurate, if old-fashioned.

The headmistress at the Kurdish school urged me to come every day, but that was impossible. I still had my classes at the college, and I knew how impressed the dean would be to hear I was attending first grade at the local refugee school. Besides, I could only stand so much of first grade. I decided, having mastered first-grade arithmetic terms in Kurdish, to skip the math portions of the class. The pace of even the reading portions went very slowly, the instruction consisting of rote recitation and memorization. What I enjoyed most was sitting in the teachers' room, listening to the Kurdish and the Arabic of the teachers.

I sat in the no-person's land where the semicircle of women teachers met the semicircle of men. In the first part of the year there were about equal numbers of men and women, but they talked together across the circle rather than sit next to each other. Jamal often came over and took my notebook full of homework to show another teacher.

"Isn't her handwriting beautiful?" he would ask the physics teacher.

I would blush, thinking that everyone did not necessarily judge by first-grade standards. But, despite my embarrassment, I was pleased at the praise.

The teachers shared whatever they had with me—the precious textbooks in Kurdish, the food that was routinely handed out by the Iranian government to all schoolchildren. There were oranges and pistachios, tea and milk. One of the other teachers braved no-person's land to come and talk to me regularly. She was Mary, the physical-education teacher. I had been watching her for a long time. She was very tall, with a lithe, athletic body. Her dark hair was long and pushed back from her narrow, sallow face. I kept hearing her say, "*Yallah, yallah,*" to the students as she hurried them down the stairs and outside to play at recess. *Yallah* means "hurry up" in Arabic. Later I realized that although all of the teachers occasionally used Arabic to each other, she spoke to the students exclusively in Arabic.

The first time she ventured over to talk to me, she had a stack of black-and-white photographs in her hand to show me. These were her wedding pictures. I stared at them, surprised at her short skirt and floppy hat. Then I realized that they were all taken at a church in Rezaiyeh.

"Are you Kurdish?" I asked her.

"No," she answered, laughing. "We are Assyrian."

Mary had many younger brothers and sisters who attended the school, but none of them spoke Kurdish. Still, they had to read from textbooks written in that language.

Another one of the teachers was an Iraqi Turkoman who spoke her native Turkish at home and Arabic at school, just as Mary spoke Aramaic to her brothers and sisters and reserved Arabic for the Kurds. At first it seemed very odd to find non-Kurds in the Kurdish refugee school, where the emphasis was all on using the Kurdish language as a medium of instruction. But, in the context of the Middle East, perhaps it was not remarkable. Other groups had joined the struggle of the Kurds because all of them had been denied their rights under the Baathists' racist government, which favored Sunni Arabs above all other people in Iraq. The centuries of enmity between the Kurds and the Assyrians had been dissolved in the face of a modern-day government which wanted to wipe out both groups.

If I had known that the days of this school were numbered, I might have come more often; but I didn't. I had my work at the college, and I saw Mr. Ahmedi regularly as well as the Kurdish women in town. All the same, I felt I should come, just to sit in the teachers' room. Something besides my busyness and boredom at the first-grade curriculum held me back in spite of my admiration for the conscientiousness of these teachers and their determination to teach their own language in the midst of an uprooting and terrible war.

Partly it was the aura of depression. Some days I would have such a sense of what these refugees had gone through that I did not want to be in the same room with them. One of the little girls in first grade spent much of the day hiding under her desk. Jamal yelled at her constantly to behave, but I couldn't help wondering how all of these children were marked by the bombing. The teachers ran nervously to the window whenever a plane flew by overhead. I noticed that Iranian army pilots enjoyed scaring the local inhabitants by flying as close as they could to the roofs of the houses.

After awhile I got used to them, but it would be years before these Kurds overcame the reflex of fear. To them, every plane was an Iraqi MiG.

It was not only their depression that kept me away, but also their suspicion. Every once in a while when I would be straining particularly hard to follow a conversation, someone would ask me sharply, "Do you understand? Do you understand what we are saying?"

When I replied, "Not really," as I usually did, they seemed satisfied and often did not even try to explain to me what had been discussed. They had not wanted me to understand. They shared their grief and their fear with each other. I was not an Iranian, but by then, some of them knew that for Kurds and Kurdish interests, America was no better than Iran.

One day, as I was sitting in first grade, a great commotion broke out in the hall and my heart stopped momentarily. What had happened? Perhaps a bomb had gone off after all. The door flew open and an older student imparted the news to Jamal. "A cease-fire."

Everyone streamed out of the classroom into the hall, where teachers were embracing each other. A cease-fire. Peace. The words rang out. People smiled at me and I smiled back. There had been rumors that Iran and Iraq would come to terms, and it had finally happened in Algeria under the self-protective interests of OPEC. But what of the self-interests of the Kurds? What would Iran do for them now that they no longer needed them to needle Iraq?

I wanted to ask the teachers. What did they know that I didn't know? Later, on my way home, I realized the answer. They knew the bombing, only the bombing. They were not soldiers. Day in and day out they had feared for the lives of those left behind in Iraq. Now the bombing had stopped and so had their fears, for a day or two. They did not think of what would happen afterward. That turned out to be far worse than anything they could have imagined.

A few days later the school was forced to close. The refugees had been offered an ultimatum—go back to Iraq right now or the border will be closed forever and you and your children will have to stay in Iran. Uniformly they did not want to stay in Iran. Iran had never even established their official status as refugees and so had never allowed the Red Cross to inspect the camps. It had played with the Kurds, and now, with no more use for them, it seemed as if the playing would get rougher.

Some of the teachers went back across the border in the next few days. I heard that the father of one of the English teachers was immediately executed. Iraq had declared an amnesty for all returning refugees, but everyone knew there was a death list.

Mary's father and the father of the children who lived behind our house would never return. They had already spent time in Iraqi prisons and were well known by the government. Kurdish Pesh Merga, trapped and frantic in the mountains, tried to continue fighting. Some officers vowed they would not quit despite Barzani's acquiescence to a cease-fire. Iranian guns positioned on the border and elsewhere which had been there in support of the Kurds were now ordered turned on Kurdish soldiers who would not comply with the cease-fire. Iraqi forces were having a field day mopping up Kurds, cordoning them off in the snow-filled mountain passes, where many starved to death.

The refugees in Rezaiyeh held meeting after meeting. Stay or go? The school reopened and then closed again. At the request of the remaining teachers I taught English for a while to the high school students, but no one had their minds on studying anymore.

Jamal told me he would like to come to America, and my immediate thought was how to help him. It happened that the American consul was on a tour through Rezaiyeh, one of his many tours, which also took him farther south and west, close to the Iraqi border. I wondered what *his* role in the Kurdish War was. But I didn't wonder enough as I set up a meeting between him and Jamal.

I just assumed it was the consul's job to see people who wanted to come to America and to give them a fair hearing. It simply did not occur to me that the consul might have different priorities with regard to Kurdish refugees.

The consul arrived at our house with Mr. Khesheni, a short, powerfully built man with fleshy features and a brusqueness that was very unusual for an Iranian. I knew that Mr. Khesheni, a teacher at the college, spent a great deal of time entertaining the American army experts living in Rezaiyeh. Knowing his capacity for rudeness and his feelings about Iranian minorities, I wondered what he was doing at my house. What information about the United States was Khesheni going to impart to Jamal?

The meeting between Jamal and the two men did not proceed at all as I had expected or wanted. They began interrogating him. Since Jamal didn't know English, Mr. Khesheni put question after question to him in Persian, questions that had nothing to do with the matter at hand—whether or not it was possible or advisable for Jamal to emigrate to America. I had heard that a waiting list was being prepared and that two hundred Kurds would be allowed to go to the United States, a number that was to seem pitifully small in the light of later information. But the consul was cagy about this list. He waited to hear what Jamal would say in answer to Khesheni's questions, which Jamal couldn't really understand, because he didn't speak Persian much better than he spoke English. I tried to translate into Kurdish, but Khesheni cut me off.

"Let him speak Persian. He knows Persian, don't you? Jamal, did you say your name was?"

They were playing with him, trying to find out what Jamal's role and feelings in the Kurdish struggle were, trying to find out what he thought about Iran. What were the consul and Khesheni up to? Khesheni had long been a suspicious figure to both the Americans and Iranians in town. He was too nosy, too friendly with the American army, much too influential with all the wrong people.

As for the consul, I was surprised. He had always seemed human, even compassionate, before this. But, of course, before I had seen him only in the company of Americans. His behavior with Kurds seemed to bear no resemblance to the gracious friendliness I had formerly attributed to him. Did he really need to promote this kind of harassing of Kurdish refugees? Surely he could see that Jamal was just a teacher and that even if he knew something more, he wasn't going to tell them.

What was the point of the humiliation? Maybe it was intended as a lesson to me, one misguided American bleeding heart. As Henry Kissinger would comment later in response to accusations about the callousness of American involvement in the Kurdish tragedy, "Covert action should not be confused with missionary work."

To cap off the evening, Khesheni stared pointedly down at his watch and asked Jamal, who was looking more and more downcast, if it wasn't getting late. This cue of dismissal was so blatant that it took my breath away. Jamal got up instantly and left. My other two guests stayed longer, making small talk as if nothing had happened. I could barely bring myself speak to them.

The next day when I went to Jamal's house and apologized, he looked at me smiling and said there was nothing to apologize for. A few days later

I heard that he had taken his family back to Iraq. Mary told me that he had been a minor official in the Kurdish revolutionary government prior to the war.

One refugee who did not share the fate of Jamal was an English-speaking doctor. He too spoke to the consul at the house of another American living in Rezaiyeh. But he had wisely stipulated that no one was to be present at his meeting besides himself and the consul. Several days later this doctor invited us to his house.

After an awkward hour or so during which the doctor bragged about his association with Barzani and with Iranian SAVAK agents, we stood up to leave, deciding we had heard enough. However, the doctor insisted that we stay and have a drink with him. We sat down again and watched as he quickly downed half a bottle of Iranian-made "Cognac."

You know, I hate America," he confided in us.

"No, I didn't know," I replied drily. "I thought you were trying to go there."

"Yes, yes. Under the circumstances it is the only place I may go. But the Kurds will never forget what America has done to us. You are responsible for the fate of the Kurdish War. You told us to begin the war. We would never have started if the Americans hadn't promised us arms. Promised no matter what," he said accusingly.

"Who promised you?" I asked. "Richard Helms? Kissinger? Nixon?"

"I am not going to tell you who," said the doctor secretively. "I was there. I heard what the CIA had to say. Maybe you don't know, but I know."

I was as repelled by this doctor as I had been by Khesheni. But one man had the excuse of being in a precarious position and being forced to do everything he could to save his skin. The doctor was not as prudent as Khesheni. He drank too much. I felt in my bones that what he said was true. What exactly had been happening here in Rezaiyeh right under our noses? Who had authorized the American army to be here, and how closely were they working with the Kurds? Why did the consul make so many trips to the border? The consul's callousness, like Kissinger's, smacked of guilt.

Here we were in our own private Vietnam that hadn't even made the news yet, and never would except in the most peripheral way. Here we were witnessing firsthand the Kissinger approach to geopolitics, realpolitik. The army officers, the consul, and other Americans in town kept putting off our questions, denying our observations. We were getting so used to double-talk in Iran that we constantly asked ourselves if we weren't imagining things.

But there was more to our discomfort than this. Barzani and his generals had looked so righteous, so pure, from a distance. William O. Douglas, in his reminiscences of a trip through Kurdistan twenty years earlier, had compared Kurdish patriots to American patriots of the Revolutionary War. Here, he said, was a pure cause and a brave people whom no one could question. But it wasn't that clear-cut.

There were too many doctors, and well-heeled revolutionaries in town spreading their gold around while the people in the camps scrabbled in the dust. There was too much cooperation with SAVAK and too much talk about giving away Kurdistan's oil to America.

The doctor's accusations were not that different from what I had heard from Iranians who blamed everything that was wrong with their country on America. One woman, a strong supporter of the shah, had even told me that the reason Iranian machine-manufactured clothes tended to fall apart was that Western nations sold Iran inferior thread.

With the Kurdish refugees it was worse to hear and half-hear these accusations. I had imagined meeting and befriending the refugees, the Kurds who said they had no friends. I had thought the only restraint would be legal or physical, coming from the government. I had not expected their distrust and my eventual resentment. I had not expected the ostentatious wealth of revolutionary leaders in exile—men whose wives wore gold and ruby necklaces, who served expensive caviar at dinner parties.

I had been reading Kurdish Democratic Party propaganda for so long that I expected to find Iraqi Kurdish women more liberated and relations between people more egalitarian. Instead I found the usual landlord-vassal, master-servant pattern just as in Iranian villages. In refugee households, younger sister waited on older sister. Sister waited on brother and wife waited on husband as wealthy refugees tried in vain to adjust to the acute reduction in the number of servants available to them. There was polygamy and ostentation among the privileged refugees of Rezaiyeh in spite of the assertions from the Kurdish Democratic Party that polygamy was dead among educated Kurds.

The refugees often told me how much better life had been in Iraq than in Iran. But the more I talked with them, the more I understood that they had lived under a reign of terror in Iraq. Iran was only intensifying that terror.

The doctor was the first Iraqi refugee who was allowed to emigrate to the United States. Before he left I accidentally saw a brown paper bag full of machine-gun bullets in the front seat of his Land Rover. Since all refugee Kurds had been routinely disarmed at the border I could only assume that he had been given these by the Iranian authorities. It was only fitting, I supposed, that the American government would welcome a wealthy doctor who had collaborated with SAVAK, and that they would ridicule and turn away a poor elementary school teacher.

CHAPTER 11

THE KURDISTAN OF TURKEY

Kurdish nationalism in Turkey, the country in which Kurds are more numerous than anywhere else, is a much older story than that of the revolutionary Kurds in Iraq. Turkish nationalism solidified early, and, consequently, the Kurdish question, like the Armenian question, was dealt with far more thoroughly.

The Turks have a fearful reputation throughout the Middle East, where they are often thought of as marauding nomads who stormed in from the east like the Mongols, oppressing and slaughtering the settled people in their path. As far as the Kurds are concerned, there is nothing more despicable than a Turk. As far as the Turks are concerned, "the only good Kurd is a dead Kurd." As one veteran of a Kurdish uprising in Turkey put it, "Turkish soldiers were ordered to bayonet Kurds rather than waste bullets on them."

A year before I came to Iran I had found a Kurmanji teacher in the United States who was the servant of a Turkish professor teaching at an American university. The fact that Musa, the servant, was a Kurd was only remarked upon by a friend of mine who is a professor of Iranian languages. As far as Musa's employer and Musa himself were concerned, Musa's Kurdishness was a most peripheral fact.

Musa had been brought to the United States in order to speak Turkish to the children, and he did that very well, better, I later discovered, than he could now speak Kurdish, his first language. Close to half his life had been spent in Istanbul, where he had been doing his best to forget the unhappy memory of his childhood in a small town outside Diyarbakir in the bleak poverty of eastern Turkey.

As soon as I knew I was on my way to Kurdistan I had peppered my teacher with questions: What is life like in the small town you come from? What do people wear? What do they think? What should I wear when I go to Iran?

In America, all of my knowledge was theoretical, vague, based on secondary reports. Musa, shy and ashamed of his rural background, told me things I didn't believe. He asserted that any of my clothes, including sundresses, would be acceptable in eastern Turkey, that people would not care whether or not Jared and I were married. As far as he was concerned attitudes and mores in Turkish Kurdistan were hardly different from those in Boston. But even in Boston, Musa could not forget the stigma of being Kurdish.

Once at a party I gave, Musa cornered a friend of mine, a Turk, and asked why I made such a point of his Kurdish identity. He was glad to earn extra money for teaching me the language, but the way I focused on his culture disturbed him.

"Doesn't she realize that I am Turkish?" he demanded of my friend.

Kurds who want to succeed or even survive in the regime established by Mustafa Kemal Ataturk, "Father of the Turks," must themselves become Turks. For, as the Turkish government has been trying to prove to the rest of the world for years, there are only Turks living in Turkey.

Across the border in Iran there were Kurds, Armenians, Assyrians, and Jews. Presumably this same mixture of nationalities and religions dwelt together at one time in the towns and villages of eastern Turkey. The Kurds were used by the Ottomans and then by the Turkish Republic to help eliminate the non-Muslim peoples.

Kurds played a significant role in the massacre of the Armenians. But once that happened they themselves became targets. No longer by massacres. In the beginning the Turkish government used Kurdish rebellions as an excuse to massacre. But once that stopped the methods became more political.

There *were* no Kurds in Turkey, Ankara alleged; only "mountain Turks." There was no Kurdish language, just a mixture of about three hundred words of Persian, Turkish, and Arabic ancestry spoken by some ignorant villagers. Even the most sophisticated, most educated Turks believed this. The overwhelming majority of the Turks have never even admitted the massacre of Armenians that took place in their country. Turkey is a land of the Turks. It will never make the mistake of Iran, which is always under threat of being torn asunder by its warring nationalities.

Turkey is where the majority of Kurds live and speak the Kurdish dialect least studied in modern times, but my attempts to go there to study that language went nowhere. The government of Turkey was not like the shah's government in Iran. It might accept arms from the Americans, but it does not hesitate to throw Americans out of the country or imprison them if it thinks they are actual or potential nuisances.

I knew of people who had been arrested on far less serious charges than trying to write a grammar of an outlawed language. So I turned my sights toward the northern end of West Azerbaijan and the dialect that was most closely related to the Kurdish spoken in Turkey. But I never gave up my plan to visit Turkey.

For five months I had watched the mountains that formed the border. In the fall, when we arrived in Iran, they were dusty beige with tints of pale orange and purple. Until winter, the dirt on the ground was utterly without green or moisture. Leaves had begun to fall from the trees in early August, but the slopes of the Zagros range were barren. Deforestation and erosion had helped to bare them over a century ago. It was hard to believe that only a month before we had arrived, a big harvest had taken place in the valleys and plains of the Rezaiyeh area. The moisture of the snows of last winter and the rains of last spring had evaporated without a trace. What remained were eroded, treeless slopes and rocky, dusty plains.

Having lived most of my life near the ocean, I needed time to get used to the closeness. Little by little the Zagros Range became my mental horizon. Looking west and northwest, I saw the mountains that faced onto Turkey. To the south and southwest was Iraq. Most of the adult Kurds of my acquaintance had been over the mountains to Iraq or Turkey at some time or other—fleeing wars or just going hunting.

The Kurds liked to think that Kurdistan was all theirs, in spite of the national borders. Their knowledge of the terrain and their mountain skills made it possible for them to go where they pleased. But increased patrolling of the borders with sophisticated weaponry and equipment was encroaching on this Kurdish right. However, young Kurdish boys still boast of their trips to Turkey. Kurds I met were always whetting my appetite to see more of Kurdistan.

"Ah, the Kurdistan of Iraq. That is the *real* Kurdistan," said one woman. "There the mountains are green."

"But what about Turkey?" I asked another Kurd.

"The Turks are dogs," he replied.

Kurdish nationalists from Iraq and Iran shake their heads when they speak of the Kurds in Turkey. "Are they still Kurds?" one sophisticated

Iraqi Kurd wondered aloud to me. "They obey the government that calls them 'mountain Turks.' They speak Turkish. They don't dress like Kurds. They have become Turks."

The Turkish consul in Rezaiyeh was happy to give us travel information on Turkey. Over superbly prepared Turkish coffee he rhapsodized about the varied cuisine, the excellent taxi service, and the fine cultural activities we would find in Turkey—in Istanbul, to be exact.

Western Turkey was a part of Europe, whereas eastern Turkey resembled Iran in pre-petroleum days. For travelers, this was a crucial difference. I couldn't resist mentioning that I would love to be living in Turkey rather than Iran.

"Well, why not?" said the consul, beaming. "We certainly need people like you to teach there. I'm sure you could get a position in Istanbul or Ankara."

His smile faded when I added, "Actually I was thinking of living in Anatolia, where I could study Kurdish."

"We have no such institutes in Turkey," he commented, flustered.

The conversation moved quickly back to our travel plans. A quarter of an hour later we gathered up the beautiful travel brochures he had given us and walked home in the winter sleet that had been falling on Rezaiyeh for two days.

Since the train from Tabriz to Istanbul had been fully booked long before we thought to buy tickets, we were going to have to take our chances with local buses. This made the choice of a border crossing particularly critical.

As March 21, the date of the Iranian New Year, moved closer, we began a detailed consideration of how and where we ought to cross the border. The closest official customs point was Serow, only an hour from Rezaiyeh and 200 kilometers from Van, which had an airport.

The route over the mountains at Serow would take us through part of Turkish Kurdistan. The only other border station with Turkey, Bazirgan, farther north and west of Tabriz, was located on the main road from Europe to India. The nearest Turkish airport to that point was Erzerum, the old center of Turkish Armenia. The advantage of Serow was mainly its proximity, but Bazirgan might offer a greater possibility of public transportation.

Our Kurdish friends in Rezaiyeh recommended that we take the Serow route. "More comfortable," they explained. Upon later reflection I wondered whether this wasn't from the point of view of crossing illegally. There were probably fewer patrols at Serow. Most Kurds I knew had never purchased an Iranian passport.

Once we had decided to go by Serow, the next hurdle was to figure how we were going to get there from Rezaiyeh. At the time we owned no car, although even if we had, it would have been foolhardy to drive it to eastern Turkey. We would have had to leave it sitting for three weeks while we flew west. I wouldn't have expected to see so much as a windshield wiper on my return. Since we weren't going by car, we were obviously going to have to rely on public transport. There was one bus a day from Rezaiyeh to Serow.

"Don't bother taking the bus," said a Peace Corps volunteer who had made the trip the year before.

"Why not?" we asked.

"Because the bus will get you to Turkey too late to get the bus from Yuksekova to Van on the same day."

"Yuksekova?" we said blankly. We consulted our Fodor's guide, which described Yuksekova as the perfect jumping-off spot for your mountain-climbing expedition in eastern Turkey.

"Yes, Yuksekova," the volunteer said emphatically. "I'll never forget it. Full of ugly shaved-headed little boys. The townspeople will never let you out of their sight. It's got one horribly infested hotel. I don't recommend it, especially not for women.'

The Turkey of the consul's brochures was fading. What seemed to be emerging was a Turkey that was likely to be even poorer and more hostile than rural Iran.

"Don't ever tell them that you have different last names in Turkey," the volunteer cautioned. "They'll immediately assume you aren't married and that Margy is for sale."

This sounded even worse than Iran, where no one had yet questioned whether or not we were married. I decided it would be prudent to wear a scarf on my head, but I didn't know what else I could do to make myself less visible. Unlike Iran, where many women still wear the chador, in Turkey the veil has been strictly outlawed for years.

Mr. Khalili offered to accompany me to the center of town near Dara Ahmedi's house to select a rural taxi that could take us to the border. Since he often had occasion to travel near the border, he felt confident that one of the taxi drivers he knew would take us for a reasonable rate. What happened after we alighted at the line of battered blue-and-white Volgas seemed like an omen of what was to come in Yuksekova.

As our friend moved down the line, questioning first one driver and then the next as to whether they could take his friends, the Americans, to the border at six in the morning next Friday, a crowd of poorly dressed young men gathered around us. When Mr. Khalili noticed them in the course of his queries, he asked them to leave. But my mild-mannered friend was no match for this crowd, which grew larger and more unfriendly by the minute. Mr. Khalili was looking extremely harried.

"No one will agree to a fair price," he whispered to me. "Also they say six in the morning is too early. They think you ought to go in your own car."

Finally we reached the end of the line. Not one driver was willing to take us to Serow. The crowd surrounding us had grown large enough to obstruct traffic on one the widest streets in Rezaiyeh. I had the feeling Mr. Khalili wished he had never offered to help. Extricating myself from the mob, I ran to the other side of the street. An orange cab pulled up almost immediately, and as I got in I waved goodbye to Mr. Khalili, still on the other side of the street. As the taxi driver whisked me away to (relative) safety in my own middle-class neighborhood, he inquired about the crowd.

Even with my sketchy explanation, the driver seemed to know exactly what I was talking about. Wasn't it obvious that where there were foreign women, there would also be crowds of Iranian men? You only had to look at the male-packed entrances to Iranian cinemas showing soft-core Italian films to know that.

In desperation Jared and I began asking some of our Iranian friends with cars if they would mind driving us to the border. The Americans flatly refused and the Iranians hemmed and hawed. The Jaffaris told us *inshallah* (God willing) they would take us. At last a solution was generously offered by a U.S. Army colonel. An Iranian officer would take us in a U.S. Army car to the border.

In the early-morning light of the day of our departure we walked the six blocks to the army house to meet our driver. The huge American car floated up and down the hills and around the hairpin turns of the Serow road. The air was spring-like, but snow still lay on the mountains all around us. We arrived in less than an hour, got out of the car, and began walking, since the officer was not allowed to take us right up to the border. Looking back at the car we clutched our bags nervously. All around us we heard the chirping of birds and the thawing sounds of the river, Ahead of us lay the Iranian border station. Beyond that, in the distance, we could not make out a Turkish facility.

The Iranian border station, when we reached it, resembled a large U.S.-Canadian border area with a well-lit parking lot and a large, modern, centrally heated building. All this for the two or three cars or trucks that crossed in a typical day. It took an hour for the Iranian customs officer to be awakened and come to his post. By the time we were processed through it was nearly nine o'clock.

We grasped our stamped passports, shook hands, and said *khoda hafez*. Suddenly Iran seemed wonderfully familiar and safe. What lay immediately ahead was a mystery. The Iranian customs people had not been able to answer *any* of our questions about what went on half a kilometer away on the Turkish side.

The paved road and parking lot of Iran immediately changed to dirt. As we walked alongside the river running through the mountain pass, we glanced up on the mountainside and saw two shingled houses that could have been lifted from a 1940s American housing development. In Iran most dwellings are made of brick with walled courtyards, but this was Turkey, the Western republic created by Ataturk, where walls and presumably veils are relics of an unenlightened past.

Turkish army patrols stood at their posts, wearing white helmets with chin straps and white spats, looking more like toy soldiers than the ruthless killers the Kurds had described. They directed us to a cement-walled warehouse. Inside we found a bare concrete floor, one tiny wood-burning stove, and two short stocky men with Asian features, ferocious expressions, and two huge cloth sacks slung over their shoulders. The men claimed to be from Pakistan but were able to converse in Persian. We saw a couple of other men who didn't appear to be transients, but seemed too poorly dressed to be customs officials.

After some inquiries we learned that the Turkish customs officer was still asleep. The large wall clock showed seven-thirty, two and a half hours earlier than when we had left Iran several hundred meters away. Both Iran and Turkey, although wide countries from east to west, have one time zone apiece.

At last a small wiry man with blue eyes arrived. Our encounter was neither as smooth nor as friendly as it had been on the Iranian side. Our suitcases were thoroughly checked, and then, after some questioning, we were waved out of the little office at the back of the warehouse.

"Where do we get the bus to Yuksekova?" we asked the official as we left the room.

"Speak to those men over there." He pointed in the direction of the non-Asians we had seen earlier. We walked over to them and they stuck their palms out.

"Taxi, taxi. Money, money," they said in a mixture of languages.

So the rumors we had heard in Rezaiyeh were true. No bus was ever going to arrive to ferry us to the next town, Yuksekova. Instead we would have to hire a taxi to take us the ten kilometers. The price would be ten dollars, robbery by Iranian or Turkish rural taxi rates. Furthermore, the fee was payable in advance only; otherwise no taxi would materialize. The customs official had come out of his office and was observing these proceedings with equanimity.

Stalling for time, Jared and I walked to the front of the warehouse and looked out the window. No vehicles were in sight. If we were extremely lucky we might be able to hitch a ride with a friendly Iranian or European, perhaps in the next week. We decided to hand over the ten dollars. I held out the Turkish money, wondering what would stop the men from simply pocketing the money without supplying the taxi.

As we were standing around uneasily, one of the border guards, who seemed to be on friendly terms with the taxi men, walked over and gestured for us to follow him to another building. Over in the guardhouse we watched as one of the taxi men cranked up the telephone to call Yuksekova. At least they were making a pretense of ordering a car.

At some point, during the taxi negotiations, I became aware that I was hearing Kurdish, not Turkish, being spoken around me. Now, inside the guard's room, I began to converse with our host in Kurdish. His eyes widened a little but he made no comment. However, he did quickly turn off his radio, which had been tuned in to the station of the Kurdish Democratic Party in Iraq.

As we warmed ourselves by his wood-burning stove, we began to feel more relaxed. Our host immediately poured us glasses of grassy-tasting

Turkish tea accompanied by huge lumps of *qand*. He showed us the books he was using to teach himself Persian, a project he had begun to pass the time in this lonely outpost.

After an hour, the minibus taxi arrived from Yuksekova. As we got into the second seat of the bus, the guard who had served us tea was whispering to the driver and his assistant.

"She speaks Kurdish," I heard him say.

The driver immediately asked me if I knew Haji Ismail. I replied that I knew his daughter.

"Aha," they remarked to each other. "That is where she learned Kurdish."

As we drove out of the border area, my apprehension returned. I peered out the dusty windows of the van to compare Turkish Kurdistan to the Kurdistan of Iran. The eroded dirt road seemed to wind through a more remote place than we had ever been in Iran, but then we had never traveled without a guide in the countryside around Rezaiyeh. Here we were alone. Although our driver was impressed that I knew Haji Ismail's family, I doubted that this was going to go a long way toward protecting us in the wilds of eastern Turkey.

The driver stopped a number of times to fill the leaking radiator with water from the ditch. At the first village, set high on a hillside, the bus stopped to take on bowls of fresh yogurt. I saw some women in the distance who were dressed in the traditional many-skirted Kurdish costume, but the men were garbed in a fashion quite unlike any Iranian Kurds.

They wore flat-crowned brimmed caps and ancient wool jackets and trousers. The whole outfit, both in style and condition, could have dated from Britain in the 1930s. To complete the picture, they carried walking sticks. We assumed that this must be the official Western costume introduced by Ataturk in the 1920s and '30s to replace the outlawed Kurdish *shalwar* and turbans.

After a half hour of jolting over the ruts in the road, skirting deposits from avalanches, and adding water to the leaking radiator, we arrived in downtown Yuksekova. As we dismounted from the high seat of the minibus, the white mist rising off the snow-covered ground reminded us of Fodor's description of the place. But we didn't see any tourists or mountain climbers. Instead we were immediately confronted by a throng of ill-clad men and boys who appeared to be the inhabitants of a filthy bare room which the taxi driver indicated was the bus station.

I stepped over to the low wooden table that served as a counter. Behind the table sat a tall, handsome man with curly red hair and a red mustache. His blue eyes twinkled as he watched me get out the necessary Kurdish.

"We want to buy tickets to Van," I began.

The red-haired man gazed briefly out the window. The rest of the males present watched the ensuing interaction closely.

"You are too late," he told me. "The bus has gone for the day."

I looked at my watch. It was not yet ten o'clock, and our American friend had told us the bus from Yuksekova to Van didn't leave until eleven.

"It couldn't have left. It's too early," I said.

"Yes, but it *is* gone," he told me, looking pleased. I glanced behind me, where Jared was standing by our suitcases, straining to understand what was going on.

The red-haired man added, in response to my anxious look, "What is your hurry? You must stay and see our town."

I translated this to Jared, who was looking apprehensive and uncomfortable. He was not used to being incommunicado. In Iran, nearly all the Kurds we met knew some Persian, but now, since he knew neither Kurdish nor Turkish, Jared was left out in the cold. The audience soon sensed this fact, and the men were intrigued by it.

"Who is he?" asked the red-haired man gesturing toward Jared.

"My husband," I answered.

"He doesn't speak Kurdish. Why do you hang around with him?"

If I hadn't been in eastern Turkey, I might have enjoyed this turnabout from the time Jared had been offered another wife in Mawana. But here in Yuksekova I was in no position to laugh. I was very glad Jared was with me, and I didn't want these men to think otherwise. I had heard that two American women who went over the Iranian-Turkish border alone in their car were gang-raped.

I scanned the walls and table of the bus station for any schedule that might tell me when the bus really left. Then I asked the red-haired man again, but he kept assuring me that the bus had left at eight o'clock that morning and that if I would only stop worrying I could spend the night in Yuksekova and get the bus the next day. Well, perhaps the schedule had changed since last year, I thought to myself. After our experience at the border, it didn't seem too unlikely that all bus service for foreigners had been abolished in eastern Turkey.

"Well, if there's no bus, is there a taxi?" I asked the man. "We must get to Van today."

"A taxi?" he echoed, grinning. "Of course, of course. But first we must go and have tea together. Then you can go to Van. I know a truck that will take you there."

"Are you sure?" I asked.

"Of course. Do you think I would lie to you? You are just like a sister to me." In the course of the next hour he repeated this last remark many times, often accompanied by invitations to his house. Although at the border station I had begun to feel confident that my knowledge of the language would endear us to the locals, or at least make us a little less alien, that idea was quickly turning sour. My knowledge of Kurdish was simply helping them to better communicate their lechery.

I told Jared that we were going to the teahouse. Since the red-haired man seemed to be in charge, I decided we'd better humor him for a while. Despite my reservations, I was half-charmed by this handsome, exuberant Kurd. We hesitantly set our suitcases down on the floor in a corner of the waiting room. Would they still be there when we returned? The crowd of men and boys leered at us, and we were too intimidated to act as if we didn't trust them.

As we walked out of the room and down the main street, our self-appointed guide showed us a large red truck that was sitting on the street.

"That will take you to Van," he told me.

"Really?" I asked. "When?"

"Soon, soon," our guide replied patiently. "But first we must have tea."

We entered the teahouse, which, with its small square tables, was indistinguishable from the teahouses of Iran. No women were present. As I entered with the red-haired man and Jared, all heads turned. For the first few minutes we sat there I enjoyed the aura of suspense and excitement. Each time I spoke the room became so quiet you could have heard the crunch of a sugar lump. Then the walls buzzed as men relayed what I had said to their friends in the remoter alcoves.

Television hadn't yet reached the teahouses of Yuksekova, but the next best thing—a foreign woman speaking Kurdish—had. As I talked, the sweat was trickling down my back underneath my blouse, wool sweater, and heavy raincoat. More and more I was wondering how we were going to get out of here. The red-haired man acted as if he would like to go on showing me off to his teahouse buddies forever.

As we were being served our second *finjan* of tea, out of the corner of my eye, through the window, I saw the red truck that was supposed to carry us to Van rounding a corner on its way out of town. Panic-stricken, I relayed this information to Jared.

"Speak Kurdish. We don't know English," the red-haired man ordered.

I stared at him and then abruptly stood up. Jared followed. Our host went after us out of the teahouse with many hurt protests that we had not even finished our tea. A number of other teahouse patrons also chose this moment to leave, and the crowd swirled around us as we made our way back up the street to where our suitcases remained intact, although not untouched.

After a hasty conference with Jared, I turned and addressed the red-haired man.

"I always thought Kurds were good honest people, famous for their hospitality," I said. Everyone smiled. "But I don't think you are telling the truth. You knew that truck wasn't going to take us to Van. Why did you try to trick us?" The smiles went away and people started murmuring.

The red-haired man was aghast. No matter how true an accusation might be, in Kurdistan grave insults are rarely uttered aloud. These people had not been treating me as a guest, but rather as a passing female tourist to have fun with. Although we were at their mercy, they didn't want to be accused of bad manners.

This paradox is very real among Kurds, who have a fable that rather resembles this situation. A hunter falls into a bear pit during a snowstorm and, to the man's relief, the bear does not kill him, but lets him stay in the den for the remainder of the winter. Whenever the man is hungry or thirsty, the bear gives him a foot to lick. This proves so repulsive that the man permanently loses his appetite. When spring comes, the bear helps the man climb out of his pit. Before he goes away, his "host" asks him, "Did I treat you well, brother?"

The man answers truthfully, "Yes, but your feet really stank."

The bear then begs the hunter to stab him in the back. The man hesitates, but at last, at the bear's insistence, he complies.

After returning to his village, the man remembers the bear and tells his family that he wants to bring him a couple of sheep in thanks for keeping him all winter. When the man returns to the bear's pit he sees that the bear's knife wound has healed. He hands the sheep to the bear.

The bear refuses it. "I don't want your presents. See, the wound from your knife has healed without the help of doctors or medicine. But the wound from your ungrateful words will never heal."

Eastern Turkey has been opened to tourists only in the last six or seven years. Before that, robbery and armed uprising were common. Although I thought at the time that my accusations had cut them to the quick, maybe it was the red-haired man's knowledge of the bus schedule that prompted him to accede to my request.

A battered taxi complete with driver materialized and we bargained on the fare. Although the price was higher than it should have been, the fifteen dollars for the three-hour trip to Van was a far better deal than the ten dollars we had paid for the half-hour trip from the border. Two locals squeezed into the front seat with the driver for what was no doubt a free ride.

All of the men crowded around our car to say goodbye while the red-haired man leaned through the window.

"Do you still think Kurds are bad people?" he asked.

"No," I answered, just glad to be leaving Yuksekova.

"Good," he said. "Don't forget us. Remember you are my sister. Come back and visit me."

"Thank you very much," I replied from the safety of the car. Several people came forward and shook my hand through the car window.

That's when I saw my first and last woman of Yuksekova. She passed like a specter, about fifty feet away, across the snowy field. Over her head was a densely woven black cloth that reached her knees, and below that were bare calves and ankles encased in white socks inside flat black shoes, She seemed to be staring in my direction, but I wondered how she could see through the cloth. I should have known better than to think that the veil, in all its cruder forms, had been abolished in Turkey.

As we pulled out of the center of town, a bus rounded the corner and sped past, but not so fast that we couldn't read "Lake Van" written on the outside. I glanced at my watch. A few minutes before eleven, just as the Peace Corps volunteer had told us.

The countryside of the Hakkari district in Turkey seemed greener, but less populated than West Azerbaijan. The roads were in much poorer condition. As we wound through the mountains we saw shepherds with large dogs. A few of the men wore Kurdish turbans and wide trousers, but most were dressed in the 1930s British style. After several hours, we pulled into Boshqaleh, a very old Kurdish town with cobblestone streets set on the side of a mountain. Here we ate lunch with the driver and his other passengers. I remarked on the fact that they paid for us, but Jared pointed out grumpily that they could well afford to be generous with the money they had robbed from us.

After lunch the road turned due north toward Van, and we began climbing into the higher reaches of the Zagros. The sun disappeared behind clouds, and the pale-green grass of early spring was replaced by ice and snow. At the highest point of our journey we drove into a small blizzard, and the car started to slither as we negotiated hairpin turns. I shut my eyes, trying not to think about how the car probably didn't have much tread on its tires, let alone chains. At last we began descending.

As we came down the mountain we gazed up at the edge of the cliff and saw the ruined facade of an ancient fortress. I was glad that it was no longer inhabited. Because of the commanding position it had over the road, anyone in that fortress could have extracted what he liked as tribute from passersby. The Kurds, even without such fortresses, had ruled over the mountain passes of eastern Turkey until the army dispatched from Ankara had stopped them.

Gradually we left the mountains and began traversing fields. On the outskirts of Van, housing similar to the buildings we had seen at the border had been constructed, again with no walled courtyards. A boulevard led to the center of town as we hurriedly scanned our guidebook for the name of a hotel.

Our driver agreed with our choice, the Besh Kardesh. As he pulled up in front of a tacky-looking court spread with pebbles and pink statuary, one of the passengers, with whom I had had a friendly conversation, scrawled his name and his village on a scrap of paper and handed it to me.

"When you come back to the border, be sure to visit me," he said.

I thanked him, and Jared, his spirits revived by the fact that we had made it to Van after all, joined me in a cordial goodbye.

We entered the hotel lobby and walked past some seedy stuffed chairs and a dusty fish tank.

"Do you understand Kurdish?" I asked the dapper young desk clerk,

Taking his silence for assent, I said, in Kurdish, that we wanted a room. He smiled, saying nothing, and handed us forms to fill out and then a key. We took our baggage upstairs and inspected the room. For eight dollars it was tiny and not very clean. The toilet across the hall was worse.

A few minutes later we went out to the main street to change money at a bank, buy our airplane tickets for Istanbul, and eat dinner. On our way back from the restaurant we were accosted in a dark alley.

After greeting us as if he might know us, the stranger said, "Where do you live?"

"In Iran," I answered, since he was speaking Kurdish.

"Oh, really? In what city?"

"In Rezaiyeh," I answered.

"Rezaiyeh. I know many people there. Do you know Mr. Feilani?"

I couldn't quite make out the name he uttered, but five months in Iran had finally made me wise to this sort of encounter. I had also been warned that eastern Turkey is crawling with secret police agents. I muttered something at this stranger and then we fled. He did not pursue us.

Back at the hotel we seated ourselves in the lobby next to the fish tank and ordered glasses of tea, which we had seen being served to everyone around us. A great deal of business seemed to be carried on in this lobby, but I wasn't able to discover what it was right away.

The next day, on the street in the early morning, I got a better idea of Van's layout. Set near a large salt lake and surrounded by mountains, Van greatly resembled Rezaiyeh. However, since Turkey lacked an oil boom and Iraqi refugees (the border with Iraq being mined to keep out Kurds), the population of Van was about a third of Rezaiyeh's. Van's foreign community, if it existed, was not apparent. In spite of this, we were hardly stared at—a great relief from Iran, where no matter how many times the local men saw me, it was as if they had never seen me before.

A few women were out wearing the sort of makeshift veil we had seen in Yuksekova, but, in general, women seemed to have solved the problem of veils being forbidden by not appearing on the streets at all. Schoolgirls wearing short Western dresses with long pants underneath and scarves on their heads walked arm in arm.

Jared and I found a teahouse and had sat down to enjoy our glasses of tea when I noticed a man watching us closely from a nearby table. There was something about his stare that I didn't like. We hurriedly finished our tea and went outside, down a hill, and around the corner to finish up our breakfast at a pastry shop. We were sitting there waiting for some of the mouth-watering *börek* when the door opened and the same man entered and sat down nearby.

Back in the hotel lobby, where the man did not follow us, I seated myself next to a group of men. I was sure that most of the people in Van were Kurds, but I had overheard some people in town speaking Turkish to their children.

In contrast to Yuksekova, the people here seemed reluctant to speak to me in Kurdish. Considering the speed at which I had been placed under surveillance, that did not seem surprising. The hotel lobby, however, was full of rustic types who resembled the Yuksekovites. They were all speaking Kurdish to each other.

I turned to the man sitting next to me and said hello and asked his health. His response was friendly, and soon I was having a conversation with a whole group of Kurdish smugglers.

"What do you smuggle?" I asked them.

The men looked around and then answered openly, "Sheep, cars, anything."

"Sheep?" I repeated.

"Oh, yes. You can get a much better price for sheep in Iran than you can here," they assured me. "You come from Rezaiyeh?" they asked.

"Yes, do you know where it is?"

"Of course. We have been there many times." Their weathered faces split in amused grins. "Do you know Haji Ismail?"

"Yes," I answered, surprised at how far the haji's fame reached.

The airport at Van was to the airport in Rezaiyeh what the Turkish border station near Serow was to the Iranian side. Considering that both Rezaiyeh and Van only offered thrice-weekly flights to the capitals of their respective countries, the construction of the Van airport was far more cost-efficient. The building contained no nightclub, glass display cases, or fake marble. When we grew bored with the portrait of Ataturk hanging in the manager's office, we wandered outside into the sunny but chilly air to watch the plane arrive from Istanbul.

After the passengers had disembarked, a plain wooden coffin was carried down the stairs from the plane, and a number of men wearing

Kurdish headdress moved forward to receive it. At no other time in eastern Turkey did we ever see a group of people so easily identifiable as Kurds. The men picked up the coffin and carried it away to a larger group of men who were waiting and crying behind the gates.

Finally airborne, we looked down on the terrain of eastern Turkey, creased and folded upon itself. In the next year and a half, two earthquakes would strike here. Iraqi Kurds published reports of the terrible suffering that followed these quakes, and that much of the international aid sent was reputed never to have reached the victims. "After all, they are only Kurds," the Iraqi Kurdish newspaper reported Turkish officials as saying.

Six hours later we reached Istanbul. It seemed more like six centuries later. Istanbul was a graceful city, full of commerce and industry, with the contrast of beautiful ancient and modern buildings. In Van the only ancient buildings were the Armenian churches which had been desecrated decades ago. Since then, the government has built little of beauty or substance. Why should they bother? Only Kurds lived there.

In Istanbul the 50,000 or so Kurdish residents come to find work were lost in the crowd. As we walked around the streets and alleys I couldn't help listening for Kurdish. Musa, my Kurdish teacher from , had come back there with the family he was still working for. He kindly offered to show us the sights. I was shocked when I discovered he would no longer speak Kurdish with me. Now, after all my practice in Iran, when I could speak his language better than ever, Musa preferred broken English.

I asked him if he would go with me to the bazaar to look for Kurdish books and records, which, despite government pressure, have appeared from time to time in Turkey.

"No, Margaret, I don't think so," he replied gently but firmly.

"Do you think I will be able to find any such books?"

"Perhaps. I don't know," he said cautiously.

The next day we made our way from bookseller to bookseller in the bazaar and later up a narrow, steplike street leading to Taksim Square. I managed to acquire two copies of a Kurdish-Turkish dictionary and four 45-rpm records of Kurdish music. The dealers gave me piercing looks, and I wondered if they had been waiting for a foreigner to take these illegal books off their hands. Or maybe they had back rooms stacked with Kurdish materials, but, because they didn't trust me, they didn't offer to sell them.

After a week in Turkey we went on to Egypt, and in the Cairo newspapers we read more about the end of the Kurdish Revolution. One article said that General Barzani was asking for asylum in the United States. I thought of the teachers in the refugee school. How differently the war had ended from their expectations! They had believed that a Kurdish victory was possible, and I had hoped for a chance to visit Iraqi Kurdistan. I wondered if the refugees would still be in Rezaiyeh when we returned.

From Cairo we flew to Beirut, then to Ankara, and finally to Erzerum, an ancient town of dark stone houses, stone walls, and stone streets. The Armenians were long since gone—murdered in the massacres of the early 1900s or dispersed to foreign lands. I didn't find anyone in Erzerum who would speak Kurdish to me. All diversity seemed to have vanished. Everyone dressed in the same sort of drab Western clothing, and, of course, everyone spoke Turkish.

After a long, dusty, and dangerous bus ride from Erzerum we finally reached the Iranian border, passing through first Bazirgan, then Maku, and finally arriving in Tabriz. Even with the maddening mob scene at Bazirgan, Iran looked sweet to us. Here at least the secret police had seen us before and didn't bother to accost us in dark alleys. Here Kurds talked and dressed like Kurds. Here was diversity instead of order.

Perhaps we should have gone away sooner to find out that Iran was our home. I couldn't wait to get to Kurdistan. In Turkey I had heard the name of Haji Ismail on the lips of every sheep smuggler. I used to think that real Kurds lived somewhere else—in Turkey, in Iraq, in Mahabad, but not in Rezaiyeh. I used to think the Azeri Turks were stopping me, that SAVAK would expel me for exploring Kurdistan. I had to go to Van, where Kurdish children spoke Turkish, in order to find out that I lived in Kurdistan and that Haji Ismail had been waiting for us all this time.

CHAPTER 12

A CHARISMATIC SHEIKH

A tall, spare, black-suited figure with a pale face and deep-set blue eyes was standing in the doorway of the large sitting room. He was speaking to Maryam as she sat among her female family members on her last day in the city. He appeared for only a moment and then he was gone, to where I did not know. In those days the whole first floor of the house, except for the hallway, did not exist for me. Later, when I returned to Pahlavi Street to see Khadija, I was occasionally aware of this man's presence, but only in the most peripheral, out-of-the-corner-of-my-eye way. He never walked into the room where I was sitting or gave any indication that he knew of my existence. I wondered if the women had even told him of my visits.

By the time spring came I was acutely aware that a very powerful man controlled the lives of these women I spent so much time with. They always spoke of him in near-whispers or half-giggles. "The haji said this" or "The sheikh wants us to do that." Although he had still not been formally introduced to me, I had already pinned the name "haji" on that mysterious tall figure I had glimpsed in the fall.

By strange coincidence, the day that the haji and I came face-to-face was also the day I chose to show off the Kurdish clothes Jared had ordered made at the bazaar for me. I stood alone in front of our tiny bathroom mirror, trying to adjust the orange scarf so it would not slip off my head, pinning the plum-red sateen *fistan* with a large safety pin, Kurdish-style, over the white, red, green, and gold *kiras*.

Although I had worn Kurdish dresses in Mawana and in Mr. Sheikhzadeh's village, I had not dressed myself before. Now I had to struggle to put the *kiras* over my head, wrap the sash of this underdress around my waist, and draw the long pointed sleeve endings out so that when I put on the fistan I could tie the *kiras* sleeve ends and throw them over my head, where they would tie on my back.

The *fistan*, which was open down the front, fastened with a large safety pin. Looking down at my outfit, I realized that my shape was not as full as that of most Kurdish women, but I was not about to wear two *fistans* the way Khadija did. The cotton dress that was called a slip would have been covering enough for me without the *kiras*, *fistan*, and vest that went over it. Underneath all this the red satin bloomers felt as if they were slipping off my waist from the sheer weight of so much gathered fabric.

I wondered how far I would be able to walk on the street before they crashed down around my ankles. It was hopeless. I wanted to sit down and forget the whole thing, but I was afraid to crush my new dresses. I stood in a quandary. Wasn't I being an exhibitionist, wanting to wear Kurdish clothes on the street?

Suppose the local Turks recognized *me*, their favorite amusement, all got up in Kurdish clothes? It would be too much for them. I could imagine them crowding around, following me. Only the thought of surprising Khadija and the other women propelled me out the door. If I had known that Haji Ismail would be there waiting for me, I would probably never have gathered my courage and my skirts together and stepped cautiously down the stairs to the courtyard.

On the landing Shehrzad's mother popped out the door and looked me over, up and down. I had thrown a black lace chador over the whole outfit, but the Kurdish clothes showed through plainly.

"*Mobarak*," she muttered drily, congratulating me either on my new set of finery or, more likely, on my nerve at wearing it.

I swished out across the courtyard and opened the gate. Because I had never seen a woman in a chador wearing eyeglasses, I had put mine in my purse. I only hoped I could find my way out of the kuchehs to the main street without bumping into anything. Fortunately, the weight of my clothes gave me a momentum that sent me forward in spite of myself. My veil seemed to billow around me, and everything seemed to be slipping, slipping. So this is what a chador does, I thought. It keeps a woman totally occupied with holding it on. The more serious veils of Arabia have their advantages; at least they stay on by themselves.

A boy rode by on a bicycle, and I squinted at him. He continued on without even a glance in my direction. I knew he never looked back because I did, in astonishment. What was wrong? For the past five months no boy had ever passed me on a bicycle without staring back. It was almost impossible to reconcile my overwhelming feeling of conspicuousness with my newly inconspicuous appearance. I would have reached Khadija's door completely unremarked if I hadn't made one fatal mistake. I stared the greengrocer in the eye as I passed. No woman in a chador ever stares any man on the street in the eye. The grocer's mouth fell open as he recognized me. I hurriedly sought out the doorbell next door, hoping that Khadija would answer before he spoke.

Khadija congratulated me loudly when she saw my clothes, and upstairs all the women gathered around to admire. All the Kurds I ever met were genuinely proud of their clothes, truly thought they were superior to Western clothes, and delighted in seeing others dressed the same. This is a living tradition, and the Kurds are proud of it. They do not have the self-doubt necessary to see themselves as the Turks and Persians see them.

Zeinab came over to me chuckling and undid the big safety pin and lifted the *fistan* off my back.

"Margaret, not like this," she corrected, unzipping the *kiras* underneath, lifting it up, and turning it around so that the zipper would be at the front, not at the back. Zippers and safety pins might be thought of as ugly in the West, but the safety pin is more than a functional object in Kurdistan. Safety pins, I later discovered, are quite useful for warding off *khilbileeks*, those evil Kurdish spirits that appear at sundown in the guise of real people and wreak havoc on their victims. I didn't know if zippers had any magical properties, but they were certainly not considered unsightly.

Zeinab also adjusted my headscarf, which was already half off my head, showing my hair, not a thing to be revealed by any virtuous woman. Just as the rearrangements and the oohs and aahs were tapering off, the tall, gaunt man appeared in the same black suit in the doorway. He was grinning impishly as he slipped off his shoes. I stood up immediately, looking at him and then at the other women. My excited anticipation turned to shock. It was as if a blight had come over the room, as if Medusa had come to the door instead of a mischievously smiling man. Their faces were ashen; their voices were silent; they seemed to have turned to statues as they stood unmoving. I stopped smiling, but as Haji Ismail strode into the room and held out his hand to give me a firm shake, I couldn't resist smiling again.

"Sit down, sit down," he kept saying to me, but I continued to stand. I wasn't going to sit down when all the women around me were frozen upright. "Why doesn't she sit down?" he appealed to Zeinab.

Zeinab, her eyes downcast, replied, "She knows our customs."

Haji Ismail hastily lowered himself to the floor. I followed, and the other women seemed to deflate, rather than actively sit down. The haji ordered Zeinab to bring a large bowl of fruit, and she jumped up, went hurriedly out, and reappeared a minute or two later with a cut-glass platter of bananas. Haji Ismael then served me and took some fruit for himself.

The women still did not move.

"Tea, have you given her tea?" he asked Zeinab, who silently rose again to bring tea at her husband's command.

Then I caught sight of Khadija, who looked as if she were experiencing an earthquake. She was not even sitting, but crouching on the cold linoleum beyond the edge of the carpet near the door. Her kerchief was drawn up over her face, which was turned toward the wall.

Haji Ismail was still talking to me, as if nothing at all were amiss, so I tried to ignore the plague that had afflicted all the women around me. After so many visits in exclusively female company, there seemed to be something very wrong, even to me, in having a tête-à-tête with a man in this house.

"Well, they tell me that you are learning our language," said the haji, smiling.

I nodded.

"What have you learned so far? What have they taught you?" he asked, looking at the statue-like women.

I didn't know what to reply, but the haji soon spotted the little blue notebook that I carried everywhere with me.

"What words have you written down?" he asked. "Read them to me."

I opened the notebook, feeling exactly as if I were about to take my first examination in Kurdish. Slowly, I read over my entries. Haji Ismail asked me to define each word, and when he didn't agree with what I said, he chided his women.

"You must teach her correctly," he admonished them. "She is writing a book."

I felt bad that they were being called to account for my mistakes, but neither Zeinab nor Khadija showed any sign of protesting this unfair blame. They were far beyond showing any sign of anything.

Haji Ismail kept looking at me and breaking into a grin. He seemed to be delighted that he had finally caught up with me, and his delight was quite contagious. I felt excited to be learning Kurdish and glad to be talking to him. If only the women didn't look as if they had all gone into shock. After about twenty minutes, Haji Ismail excused himself to go into the next room to pray. As soon as he left the women came back to life.

"What is the matter, Khadija?" I asked, relieved to see her looking normally animated again.

My friend laughed gaily. She knew exactly what I was talking about. "It is our custom, Margaret. A woman must have shame in the presence of her father-in-law." She moved quickly through the doorway.

"Where are you going, Khadija?" I called after her.

"To do some work," she called back, obviously relieved to be able to escape.

Now I was afraid that I would be left alone with the charismatic haji. Some of the women's fear had infected me. Khadija's servant girl was also gone by the time the haji came back. Only Zeinab stayed in the room with us.

Haji Ismail had just listened to the news on the radio, and he wanted to know all about what I thought of the *Mayaguez* incident when the Khmer Rouge seized a United States Merchant vessel in the last official battle of the Vietnam War. Being poorly informed about most international events during my stay in Iran, I didn't know what to say, but Haji Ismail sat grinning at me as if anything I said would fascinate him.

Somehow I managed to struggle through another half hour of conversation. The man's energy, as well as the strain of being the only other person in the room making conversation, was wearing me down. I felt that my Kurdish was on trial, and I chose my words carefully, fearing to make mistakes. At last I decided that I had reached the end of my ability to perform for one day, especially clothed in a mass of sweat-drenched synthetic material. I told the haji that I had to leave, but this time, unlike that first long-ago afternoon with Maryam, I managed to phrase my announcement politely.

"Do I have your permission to leave?"

He looked at me smiling, refusing to answer such a question.

I tried my old tack. "I have to go home and make dinner."

"You must stay and have dinner with us."

I was charmed and alarmed at the same time. How could I stay and eat dinner? He and I would be the only people in the room eating.

"My husband is waiting for me," I added.

"Your husband?" he repeated, looking at Zeinab for confirmation. "She has a husband? Ask him to come here."

I was so intrigued by the haji that I decided I wanted to share him with Jared. Zeinab showed me into the haji's bedroom, where I called our house and invited Jared to pick me up. Actually I was relieved that I would not have to negotiate the way home alone in my Kurdish outfit.

As soon as Jared walked into the room, Haji Ismail ordered a metal folding chair to be brought for him. The two men shook hands. Then Jared sat in his chair while Haji Ismail and I sat on the floor. The haji, beaming all the while, invited us to come out to his village, Dustan, for the weekend.

Jared and I looked at each other. What should we say? Three months earlier we would have instantly accepted. But we no longer instantly accepted anything in Iran.

"Thank you, but we can't," I said.

"Why not?" asked the haji.

"We have to teach classes the day after tomorrow," said Jared.

"I'll drive you back to your classes," the haji promised.

"That would be too much trouble," I answered.

"But I want you to come," the haji said earnestly.

I looked at Jared inquiringly, but Jared shook his head. No, we would not accept. Haji Ismail did not give up right away, but when he saw we were firm, there was an unfathomable expression in his eyes.

Later, as Jared and I walked home together, the Kurdish lady and the foreign man drawing some strange looks, we asked ourselves if we had done the right thing in refusing the haji's invitation. When I returned to the house several days later to see Khadija, she told me the haji had been very hurt at our refusal. Zeinab repeated the same information, adding that the haji liked us very much. I was filled with regret. But how were we supposed to have known that *this* invitation was real? Would he ask us again? Maybe he was so annoyed that he wouldn't.

Now that I had actually seen Haji Ismail, actually talked with him, he became very real. I discussed him with Mr. Khalili, who had some fairly sarcastic comments.

"Oh, Haji Ismail. He has five wives, you know. Five wives. Imagine that!" And he snickered.

Five wives? I had only seen and heard of three. Five was one more than the Quran allows. How was it possible that a religious man like the haji who prayed five times every day had five wives?

One day a woman with sharp features and a pale-blue tattoo on her pointed little chin was sitting among the women at the house on Pahlavi Street. I looked at her curiously. The only Kurdish woman I knew with a blue tattoo on her face was an Iraqi refugee. Tattoos and nose rings which women in other parts of the Muslim world used to adorn themselves are considered old-fashioned among many Kurds today. Later I asked Khadija who the tattooed woman was.

"She is the mother of one of Haji Ismail's wives," Khadija told me. "No one likes her."

"Why not?" I asked.

Khadija shrugged.

I wondered about all these wives. Where did they live? Did they have separate houses? Did Haji Ismail spend equal time with each one as the Quran prescribes? It was all quite fantastic to me.

The wives lived in the village, except for Zeinab, who had been assigned to care for the haji's sons old enough to attend school in the city. In the city, everyone seemed like an individual to me. Maryam appeared to have little to do with Ismail.

Now I realized what a huge joke it had been to say that her husband would look around for another wife if she left the city. He had already taken three wives after her, and even that turned out not to be enough for him. In the city Zeinab alone seemed to act like his wife, sleeping in his bedroom with him. The other three wives were total mysteries to me. Even Aisha's mother, whom I had met once, but could hardly remember.

Haji Ismail might be famous throughout Kurdistan for his marital excesses, but I couldn't readily see this aspect of his character. He had been nothing but polite and friendly to me, and he was never anything but respectful through all the time I knew him.

His relationship with his women was something else. Only once did I come into direct conflict with him over it. I had asked Khadija and Zeinab along with the haji's small sons to come on a picnic near the lake, and Zeinab had replied, giggling nervously, that I had to ask the haji for permission for them. I did this, and the haji, of course, refused, a glimmer of annoyance in his voice.

"What for? Why do you want to go to the lake? If you want to go somewhere, then come to the village. That is the only place I want them to go," he replied.

Khadija told me I should never have asked directly, that she would have found a way to get around him. Her husband, Taha, the haji's eldest son, wasn't nearly so strict. Later she was as good as her word in defying the haji's rule. But Zeinab refused to budge and would never allow herself ever to be photographed, saying it was the Haji's will. When I asked him directly about the no-photo rule, he said *he* had no objection. What was the real story?

Haji Ismail, husband to five disgruntled wives, father to several dozen children, was a delightful man. There was no doubt about his energy or intelligence, but it took me a long time to understand what a privileged relationship we had with him.

One day as Jared and I were sitting with Taha and his cousin Raheem in his father's guest room I noticed that twenty-four-year-old Taha and twenty-year-old Raheem were whispering together like schoolboys. They had not turned to stone as the women had in the haji's presence, but neither did they presume to have a direct conversation with their father and uncle.

Haji Ismail's word was law to at least several hundred armed Kurdish men. He was famous throughout Kurdistan. Yet, there came a time when even the haji went too far with his power. As far as his sons and supporters were concerned, Haji Ismail could flout Iranian laws as much as he liked. They were with him to the end. But when he tried to flout Muslim law, endangering the honor and well-being of his own family, Taha stopped whispering in his presence.

When we returned to Kurdistan three years after we left I sensed that all was not well with Haji Ismail's family. Although our hosts' concern about us and whether we were having a good time never flagged for a moment, the longer we stayed the harder it became for them to hide the fact that something was going on, something that was making Maryam unbelievably cranky, something people stopped talking about when I entered the room.

One morning I saw Maryam carefully writing a letter on a piece of paper torn from her youngest son's school notebook. It is an unusual occurrence for a village woman to write a letter, so I watched as Maryam folded the paper and handed it to Taha, asking him to take it up to Haji Ismail's house. As she gave Taha the letter I heard her say something about "shame" and "too many children," but I could not piece together this mystery that was beginning to make me uneasy.

Days later I was sitting in town among the women of the family when I heard a strange discussion that did not quite make sense. Someone was about to be married, and the women heartily disapproved. Who could it be?

I assumed it was the bride that Zeinab, the haji's third wife, was about to bring for her eldest son. As far as I knew, no one else in the village was about to bring a bride. But the women did not want me to know what they were talking about. They kept speaking more and more elliptically. Finally they dropped the subject.

Later Aisha, who had been present, brought it up with me alone. Had I understood what they were saying? I stumbled over my suppositions, watching Aisha's face signal me that I was wrong. She was emphatic in her correction. There was nothing wrong with the girl Zeinab wanted as her bride. She was a good girl and no one had anything against her. What, then, was the problem? I wanted to know.

Now Aisha studied my face. "My father wants to take another wife."

I almost gasped. This I had not thought of.

"A sixth wife?" I managed.

"Yes, he wants to take as his wife the younger sister of his last wife."

Now a lot of things clicked into place. I could only guess at the dislocation and rancor Haji Ismail's plan was causing. It nettled Maryam and the other two elder wives that Haji Ismail had taken his fourth and then fifth wives, both of whom were regarded as servants and the last of whom was forbidden by the Quran as over the four allotted to any one man. What could be their reaction to a sixth, especially as she was the sister of the fifth, adding the one sin to the other that the haji would be committing in the eyes of Allah?

Sheikh Avdila sat on the other side of Aisha. His only comment was: "Haji Ismail has so many children he doesn't know their names."

"Yes, my father has some kind of sickness. It is terrible," Aisha added.

I sat, lost in thought, trying to understand. A picture I had recently seen came before my eyes. It was Haji Ismail's mother in a group photograph taken in Turkey before the family had fled for their lives. Haji Ismail had been a small boy at the time, and this old photograph from eastern Turkey showed his mother to be a strikingly beautiful, delicate-featured woman, more beautiful than anyone I had seen in Dustan.

One night, a man came by to visit Maryam and we learned from him that he was the son of Haji Ismail's old wet nurse, who had been employed by the haji's mother over half a century ago in eastern Turkey.

"She was an incredible woman—the haji's mother," said the wet nurse's son. "No man ever saw her face."

So that is the definition of an incredible woman, I thought silently. Did this man know she had been photographed, no doubt by a man?

Before Haji Ismail was ten, both his father and his grandfather had been hanged by the Turks. His father had had two wives. One went to Istanbul and raised a son who now speaks not a word of Kurdish. Although he and Haji Ismail regard each other as brothers and have visited together, they cannot easily communicate. Haji Ismail and his sister were raised in Iran, as Kurds, under the protection of some unknown male figure who must have stepped into the place of both father and grandfather.

What was the source of Haji Ismail's "sickness"? No doubt that source was also the source of his life energy, the aliveness that made him a Sufi, a seeker, a lover of foreigners. Haji Ismail was an attractive man, but I could not but feel saddened and repelled by his treatment of his wives and children. Why, when he seemed so devoted to Islam, did he ignore its marriage laws?

The question of whether the haji would indeed take another wife built up slowly and reached its climax just before our departure. Aisha had told me that the family of the girl he wanted was frantically trying to marry her off to someone else before the haji could get her. They did find a more suitable bridegroom, but not before the haji's older sons had taken the desperate step of going to their father one night and threatening to kill him if he went through with it.

We would not have known anything about this if Aisha had not told me. On that fateful night Taha left us in Rezaiyeh, merely saying he had some business in the village. The next day he came back tired, telling us he had been up the whole night doing some work or other. I just assumed it had to do with the harvest, which was going on at the time.

Because I came to know Haji Ismail as a person I could never totally condemn him for oppressing the women in his power. Perhaps this was because he treated me so generously. Generations of Haji Ismails have fascinated European travelers who found themselves in Kurdistan.

In the nineteenth century, missionaries from the West came to ease the hardships of the lives of Assyrian Christians. These Christians were constantly being terrorized by the less-settled Kurdish tribes in the Rezaiyeh area, and some of the missionaries were "martyred" when they got caught in the middle of this conflict. Yet, many of the Westerners reported their attraction to the proud, independent Kurds. Even though there was little hope of winning Muslims to Christianity, the missionaries studied Kurdish and wrote grammars of the language. One woman missionary—a nurse—married a Kurd and stayed in Mahabad when her fellows left. Women in the West might wonder how she could choose such a life, but they have not been to Kurdistan.

CHAPTER 13

PICNIC FOLLIES OR "KEYFA TE"

In America, the more I replayed the tapes I had made back in Rezaiyeh and the villages, the more I realized what was special about the voices of Kurdish women: a low throatiness, and a richness that is utterly unlike what many languages prescribe as the ideal pitch and quality for a feminine voice. There is nothing thin or high about these voices. The sound emerges full-bodied. It's not at all like the high, nasal singsong of Persian or the girlish whisper of some American women. These are the voices of women who have known hardship. These voices speak of experience and self-control. They speak of births and deaths, of old legends, of recent events, and of marriage.

I have listened to the tape of Khadija describing her wedding to Taha over and over. Yet I never listen without wishing I were there and had been there, both in the nearer past when I taped her account and in the more distant past before I ever met her.

In Haji Ismail's house, where the recording was made, the clinking of tea glasses and the whisperings of Zeinab's little boys are heard throughout. But it is Khadija who fills the tape with her magnificent warbling voice, her laughter, her embarrassment at being asked about her wedding and her pleasure at recalling the grandeur of it.

Khadija's maid begins by correcting her mistress when she says that fifty vehicles showed up at the start of the festivities.

"One hundred cars," she says. "Three hundred guests."

The party goes on for ten days and ten nights. For all of this time, according to Khadija, her maid, and the little boys, no one does any work. They just dance and dance.

"Men and women together? Or separate?" I ask.

"Men and women together," they reply.

A picture of fantastic revelry emerges in my mind. These Kurds whom I have never seen either singing or dancing are winging on a wild orgy. The bride is brought in from her village, and the young bridegroom goes up on the roof of his house and shoots off his rifle to mark her arrival.

"*Tak, tak, tak,*" says the maid.

But wait. There is more to the story that is of special importance to Khadija. For it turns out that she is not part of the party. She is only the cause of it. She has been brought many kilometers under a red veil to Haji Ismail's village from her parents' house in the mountains near the Iraqi border.

According to custom her parents cry bitterly as their daughter is taken from them. They do not accompany her to the wedding. Khadija herself is crying. She has never seen Taha, not even a picture. Yet, because one of her male relatives has already married a girl in Haji Ismail's family, she has been promised to the eldest son of the great haji.

Khadija is proud of the fact that she never saw Taha before she was brought to the village. She is proud of the thousands and thousands of dollars Maryam settled on her, both for the religious ceremony in front of the mullah where the sum of money that must be returned to her if the marriage is dissolved is set, and for the bride price that was paid to her father, money that represents the cost of feeding one girl child until she comes of age to be married.

For Khadija, the fear and pain of being taken blindfolded and handed over to lose her virginity to a strange man in a village she had never seen before were offset by all the glory that accompanied it. The bride price was enormous; the guest list illustrious; the family she was marrying into old and powerful.

Only later did I find out that it was the family of the enemy. That Khadija, unlike many Kurdish girls, did not marry her cousin. Instead she married the heir of a great clan that had been actively at war with her own tribe as little as ten years earlier.

Why was Khadija so happy, surrounded as she was by people she had never known before? She had been thrust ceremoniously but abruptly into the midst of a foreign environment with a mother-in-law to serve and a husband she had not chosen. I wondered a lot about Khadija's exuberance and ease in the midst of all these people.

Undoubtedly she was good-natured and easygoing to begin with. She had also been raised to expect no more than a marriage such as this. But there was a third, more interesting reason for Khadija's content. She was now living in Rezaiyeh, surrounded by all the comforts and diversions of city life that she had only dreamed of in the village. It didn't matter that much to her that the refrigerator in Haji Ismail's house was always broken. There were stores full of food only a few steps away from her front door.

Who cared if the naked bulb hanging in the middle of each room was only a dim, ugly forty watts? The difference between oil lamps and electricity made any wattage a miracle. For Khadija there were no more grimy dark kitchens with pits of fire to squat over. No more dust and insects. And, most important, no more boring isolation.

Perhaps part of the affinity that Khadija and I felt for each other was related to the fact that this was a special year for both of us. For me, it was the realization of a dream that took years of preparation. For Khadija, it was the chance to live in a city. Both for Khadija and for me the specialness of the year was not the fact of our recent marriages, but rather the lives they had brought us.

My marriage had given me a passport to the far corner of a distant land that I would not have ventured to alone. Khadija's marriage had brought a reprieve from the village she had known all her life. This was Khadija's year of freedom, of exploration, of authority over a houseful of children and visiting villagers. This was the year she went to Indian movies at the local cinema, talked out the windows to her neighbors, went to the public baths, and traveled around the countryside in a car with one determined American woman.

I did not know how fleeting this time would be for Khadija or what she had escaped from in the past and what she would be faced with in the future. For now, it was a splendid moratorium for her, an adventure and challenge for both of us.

Most of my time with Khadija was spent in the sitting room or the bedroom she and Taha shared on the second floor of Haji Ismail's house. That gorgeous, overstuffed rainbow of a bedroom I had first sat in with Haji Ismail's women was all Khadija's. She had lovingly decorated it, had crocheted the colorful doilies that covered every surface, had been given the tapestries that hung on the wall.

As the weather grew warmer, more and more of the inhabitants of this house and other houses of Kurds fortunate enough to have city residences drifted out toward the village. I was relieved that Khadija was spending the summer in the city. Her twenty-four-year-old husband was still a sophomore in high school and had secured a summer job in Rezaiyeh.

When Zeinab left with the children and Haji Ismail became more and more occupied with his crops, Khadija remained in the house on Pahlavi Street, attended by her maid, Asma. The three of us would sit laughing and talking and drinking tea for hours. Khadija spoke to me as naturally and unselfconsciously as if she had known me for years. No subject seemed to faze her. She talked about birth control and the fact that she and Taha had decided not to have a baby right away because Taha was still in school. This was in spite of the fact that many people in the family were pressuring them to have a baby, according to tradition.

Then she asked me slyly, "Margaret, how many times a week do you wash your head?"

"I don't know, once or twice," I answered unsuspectingly.

"I wash mine every day," she said, looking mischievous.

I was puzzled, because I had forgotten what my Peace Corps friends from Mahabad had told me. Since they had had no bath in their house, they had gone to the public *hammam* in that city. After a while they realized that the local populace was paying an inordinate amount of attention to the number of times the Americans went to the baths.

Khadija reminded me of what they had learned. "We must wash our heads every time we go near our husbands," she said. "It's a bad business, isn't it, having your husband do these things?"

Her broad smile seemed to indicate that it wasn't bad at all; quite the opposite.

One day, when another woman from the village was visiting, Khadija suggested we should all go to the bazaar. Glad to get out of the house for once, I immediately agreed to accompany them on a shopping expedition so that the village woman could get some shoes. The Kurds adjusted their chadors in front of the mirror as I waited, already prepared for the street (I thought) in my lemon-yellow corduroy trousers and matching yellow turtleneck.

Outside on the street we didn't see any taxis, so we began to walk. But Khadija started fretting that I would get too tired. I assured her that I would not, but she continued to worry, and soon enough I saw what the problem was. It was exactly the same one as the day Nazi had abandoned me. I was being ogled and heckled by all the men we passed, and the Kurdish women, used to the anonymity of their chadors, felt uncomfortable. Unlike Nazi they did not abandon me. We quickened our pace and quickened it again so that we reached the bazaar in very short time. All the way there

Khadija looked nervously from side to side, commenting on how all the men were staring at me.

The attention directed at the two chadored Kurdish women and the yellow-clad foreign woman with her uncovered hair increased inside the vaulted roof of the bazaar. People clustered around to stare; sellers came out of their stalls no doubt hoping to make a killing. Khadija sized up the situation in one shrewd glance. We took a few desultory looks around, and Khadija insisted on buying me a coarse bath mitt as a memento of the occasion. Then she led us to a waiting taxi. Days later she commented on the fact that "all the men on the street were staring at Margaret," but the statement was one of wonder rather than censure.

Khadija's freedom was only relative. Compared to the freedom most Western women take for granted she operated under severe limits. She did not go outside without the proper chaperone or the right excuse. I never correlated the haji's comings and goings with Khadija's expeditions, but no doubt her visits to my house corresponded to his absences. In any case, much to my delight, she took to inviting herself to my house. Sometimes she would telephone in advance, usually at about six in the morning, her favorite hour for calling, or sometimes she would just show up, with whomever was in attendance at the haji's house that day.

While Asma, her maid, seemed nervous that my husband or some other dangerous creature would unexpectedly show up, Khadija was very much at ease. Asma drew her chador more tightly around herself than she did on the street, while Khadija let hers slip off. But then Asma was not yet married, while Khadija's virginity had been sold, once and forever.

For a while Gulnam, Khadija's charming little five-year-old sister, accompanied her to these tea parties at my house. Khadija told me that her family sent Gulnam down from the village to keep her company in the city. They were worried that their elder daughter, so used to being surrounded by family and other human beings in the village, would pine away in the summer emptiness of Haji Ismail's city house. I asked Khadija if her parents ever came to visit her, and she replied that they did not. As a new bride she was not allowed to return to her village and see her parents until at least one year was up and her husband gave his blessing. Without that, she could spend the rest of her life without ever going home again.

As I came to spend more and more time with Khadija, I naturally bumped into her husband, Taha, who, like his wife, usually seemed to be in a remarkably good mood. After my conversation with Haji Ismail when he refused to allow me to take his women on a picnic, I formally asked Taha's permission to take his wife places. Mimicking my formality with a twinkle in his eye, Taha immediately assented.

Taha was a charmer, like his father. He lacked his father's nervous energy and his old-fashioned strictness. I suppose that in comparison to Haji Ismail's, Taha's life had been easy. Although, with a father as capricious as I later understood Haji Ismail to be, perhaps ease was not everything. Still, Taha enjoyed many privileges as eldest son.

A fortune had been spent in acquiring a bride for him. He and Khadija had a bedroom all to themselves, which no one else but the great haji could boast of in this house of portable bedding. Taha's only problem was how to grow up. Because of army service and a late start in school he was still a high school sophomore, but even if he had not been a high school student, there seemed to be no way, in Kurdish society, for him to free himself from his parents.

When Jared and I finally broke down and bought our own car—a brand-new Iranian-made two-cylinder Citroen—it was to Haji Ismail's house that we went to celebrate. We knew that one of Taha's dearest wishes was to have his own car. He came right out to inspect and admire it as Khadija beamed from the doorway. From that time on Khadija was full of plans as to where we should go each weekend.

Our first trip was to a valley south of Rezaiyeh where people who did not relish the crush or the proximity of Band often went for picnics. Jared and I supplied the picnic and the car, while Khadija and Taha supplied the company. This was one of our first tests at entertaining Kurds, and, sad to say, we failed.

Our first mistake was to imagine that Khadija and Taha would come alone. We had invited them alone. We had discussed the expedition as a foursome. But when Friday morning came, Khadija's brother, a high school student to whom I took an instant dislike, was there climbing into our two-cylinder car, making our comfortable back seat crowded and causing the engine to strain mightily up the slopes of the mountains we needed to cross.

Our second mistake only compounded the first. We bought enough sandwiches and soft drinks for exactly four people—no more. Somehow we had not yet appreciated the lesson we had learned from all those groaning tables of food at Iranian dinner parties. No one in Iran worthy of the title "host" serves exactly the amount of food necessary to fill the number of guests invited. Two, three times the amount that everyone could eat was not only appropriate, it was obligatory.

Our final mistake, which we probably could not have avoided, was not knowing the first thing about guest-host protocol in Kurdistan. Thus, from the time we got into the car until the time we returned to the city, we found ourselves caught in this circular conversation:

"Shall we ——— [stop here, eat now, go there, etc.]?" we would ask.

"*Keyfa te*," our guests would reply.

Soon enough we too learned to say *keyfa te*, which translates as "it's your choice." The result of this particular politeness was that decisions were postponed as long as possible, usually until we were all forced into a choice that no one much relished.

We drove around the countryside, visited a spring where a venerated sheikh was supposed to be buried, and then went to a small Kurdish town called Shinou where Khadija purchased a pair of pale-lavender plastic sandals at the bazaar. Then the trouble started.

We started to get hungry, so we suggested to our guests that they should

choose where to eat. As we drove by a number of lovely deserted spots I began to get the feeling that these did not meet some hidden standard. Their *keyfa te* to each place I suggested was totally lacking in enthusiasm.

When we came to the first crowded place with dozens of parked cars the *keyfa te* took on a longing quality. Jared parked. We got out and started walking. The place was so crowded and so littered with trash that we had to go quite a long way before we found a spot. But when we sat down we were unaccountably assailed by the odor of feces. Again, we went through the round of *keyfa te* before we were able to make a group decision to leave.

When lunch was finally served everyone was so starved that the meagerness of our assortment of sandwiches was even more noticeable than it might have otherwise been. Everyone's throat was so parched and dusty that all the bottles of Coke and orange soda that we had brought could not begin to quench our thirst.

Khadija and I went in search of a spring. Khadija's brother joined us, and when we saw a flock of sheep on the side of the mountain we were climbing, he insisted that I take a picture of the animals as he held one of them.

"This will be really interesting in America," he announced.

"They've seen sheep in America before," I snapped.

After Khadija started to tease me about the possible presence of snakes I decided to wait while they went to the spring at the top of the hill. When they returned, Khadija described the meal of kebab and beer that she had seen a group of *ajam* eating. Even the *ajam* had eaten better than we had.

In spite of our deficient hospitality, Taha and Khadija and Khadija's brother seemed to want our expedition to go on and on. But all Jared and I could think of was shedding the unwelcome brother back in the city and retiring for the remainder of the afternoon to our house, where there was plenty of clean running water.

We could not seem to get enough to drink. On our way back to the city we stopped at one of the primitive roadside refreshment houses that dot the countryside and bought orange sodas for everyone, but these were too sweet for me.

Even after this failure, Khadija and Taha's appetite for joyrides in our new Citroen did not wane. So the next Friday we drove out to the lake. The air was breezy, but warm. Of course no one was swimming, because the season would not start for several months. Khadija and I started talking about going in the water, while Jared and Taha sat on the rocks drinking the beer we had brought.

Khadija declined to touch the alcohol, and I only had one taste under Taha's amused but shocked glance. Most of the village Kurds we knew did not drink, but those few who did were all male. The men assured us that they would follow us into the water, so Khadija and I went around the bend and began undressing behind some rocks. When we were down to our underwear, a car suddenly pulled up on the bluff overlooking our stony beach and a couple with two children got out and started walking toward the lake. Even before I realized that they were people I knew from the college I started to look around desperately for shelter on this barren shore. There was only one large rock, which did not provide much cover from the vantage of the cliff. I imagined that Khadija was panicking, but when I looked at her she acted excited rather than scared. In fact, she seemed far less flustered than I felt. When she heard that the woman on the cliff was an American, she became so curious that she seemed to forget all about her state of undress.

The distance was great enough that I wasn't sure whether the couple could see our faces, but they were obviously aware of our presence, because they hurriedly went back to their car and drove away. Only much later, after I had experienced the lake in full action, did I realize how lucky we were that these modest people and not some Turks had come upon us.

When we were alone again, I came out from crouching near the rock and eased my body into the warm salt water. It felt delicious until I splashed some in my eye. Khadija and I floated in shallow water for about twenty minutes and then got out. As I was picking up my clothes to get dressed, I noticed Khadija looking at my crotch.

"Margaret, don't you want to take off your underpants? They're wet," she said.

This query, unlike the question about the frequency of my showers, did not catch me off guard. I saw that she wasn't taking off *her* underpants. I decided to address the object of her curiosity directly.

"It's the custom for women to shave their hair here, isn't it?" I asked.

"Yes, it's a sin not to."

"But that's not our custom," I replied.

"Really?" she said innocently, as if she had never heard of such a thing.

But I was sure she had heard that Western women don't generally shave their pubic hair just as I had heard that Iranian women routinely shave theirs.

"How could it be a sin not to shave it when God makes it grow in the first place?" I asked.

"I don't know," Khadija replied thoughtfully.

The salt was drying white and caked on our hair and skin as we went back around the bend, where we found the men still fully clothed. They had never had any intention of going in, it seemed. We couldn't drive home fast enough to suit me. I felt as if my pores were going to suffocate. Khadija, as she and Taha got out at Haji Ismail's house, made one last attempt to see my pubic hair.

"Wouldn't you like to come in and take a shower with me?" she asked.

"No thank you," I replied.

Khadija showed the full extent of her daring on a day when she agreed to go to the lake alone with me—or rather as alone as she could ever get. Taha did not come. Only her maid, Asma, and Maraz, an old Assyrian woman who had taken to hanging around Haji Ismail's house, accompanied us.

This time we bathed in the salt water, washed off with a bottle of tap water I had brought along in the car, and then headed back to the city. As we pulled up in front of Haji Ismail's house, Khadija began cowering in her seat.

"Drive on, Margaret, drive on," she whispered frantically.

As we passed the house, Khadija looked back and sighed loudly with relief when she saw that the Land Rover that had pulled up behind us was not Haji Ismail's.

"I would have been so ashamed if the sheikh had seen me," she whispered.

The fact that Khadija did not keep her fears and thoughts and opinions to herself was of great benefit to me. Where others would keep silent out of politeness or embarrassment, Khadija spoke out. Thanks to her I learned a great deal about what was appropriate among Kurds.

One day I learned what the Jaffaris thought of my Kurdish women guests when Khadija spoke contemptuously of how my neighbors slammed their inside door shut every time they saw her coming up the steps. On another day I learned why the group of women at the house on Pahlavi

Street were staring overly long at a photograph of Jared and me I had shown them.

"Her husband's arm isn't really around Margaret's waist," I heard Khadija defend me to the others. "Margaret wouldn't do *that*."

Early on I had made the terrible gaffe of turning a large porcelain teacup completely upside down instead of on its side. All the other women in the room regarded me with amused horror, refusing to tell me why it was wrong. Only Khadija let me know that this was a signal that the hostess was a bad woman.

With Khadija I was protected from being an outsider. The other women remarked on it. "Khadija really likes Margaret. She tells her everything," Khadija's sister-in-law said in wonder.

All the times I went to Haji Ismail's house I was aware of the village, Dustan. A variety of strange-looking characters came and went from that mysterious place. Once I met toothless Gulbehar, the old midwife who had attended the births of many of Haji Ismail's children. Another time I was introduced to Hajer, a woman in her early thirties who came to the city in order to have all her rotting teeth pulled and be fitted for a set of false teeth. There was the woman with the blue tattoo who was the mother of the Haji's fifth wife, as well as a number of other women who were never identified. On another level altogether were people like Nadia, Maryam's other bride, and Nasreen, Maryam's only daughter.

These women came for a few days to see a doctor or to go on some crucial errand and then they were obliged to return to the village, where their real life was. Khadija's life, it seemed, was not quite real. That was why Zeinab and Nadia had laughed so hard that winter about Khadija being dragged out to the village to work.

I often thought of Haji Ismail's invitation to Dustan. Since that day I had not seen him to talk to again. But Khadija and Taha were so friendly that I felt the haji could not be angry. Still, no one said anything about going to Dustan.

Then, on a Friday afternoon after Taha and Khadija had eaten dinner at our house, Taha raised the subject.

"When are you coming to Dustan?"

"I don't know," I said. "Whenever you say."

"How about next week? I will try to borrow a Land Rover and we can all go Thursday afternoon."

"I'd like that very much," I replied. Jared said nothing.

After our guests left I said to Jared, "Isn't it great? We're finally going to go there. I'll see Maryam and Haji Ismail. Everyone. Now that it's spring the mountains will be *kesk o sheen*." I twirled around happily at the thought of it.

Jared regarded me unsmiling. "Don't count on it," he cautioned. "Maybe Taha will forget. Maybe he won't be able to borrow the Land Rover. Maybe he was just being polite. Anything could come up between now and next Thursday."

At first I wouldn't let Jared dampen my spirits. He didn't know Khadija, how forthright she was. As far as I could see she didn't deal in *ta'arof*. Jared, who was always more sensitive about invitations than I am, had suffered a bad case of *ta'arof* burn. He was loath to believe anyone.

As the day grew closer Jared grew protectively more skeptical. I felt the doubt growing in my own mind. I was not yet sure enough of these relationships to fight it. One minute I would be dreaming about the village, about what I would wear there, whom I would talk to. The next minute I would tell myself not to get so excited.

One reason for Jared's pessimism was that he knew how important this trip was to me. This was no one-day fling in Mawana. The female members of Haji Ismail's family had become not only my best Kurdish contacts, but my best friends in Iran. If they didn't mean this invitation, what was there in Iran for me to look forward to?

In the end, on the day that Taha had promised to come and pick us up, I got ready half-heartedly, without really allowing enough time. Jared was lying down taking a nap, overcome by the fear of yet another rejection. Were we about to go for our first overnight stay in a Kurdish village, or not? Our apartment was bare and silent as we waited for the loud buzz of the downstairs bell.

PART THREE

INSIDE KURDISTAN

CHAPTER 14

THE HEART-WARMING HOSPITALITY OF HAJI ISMAIL

"*This* is Kurdistan, Margaret," said Nasreen, Taha's sister, Maryam's only daughter.

With my eyes, I followed the arc that her arm described as Nasreen flung it out to encompass the whole of the circular valley. The floor of the bowl-like valley and the mountains that form its rim were both covered in soft green. It was spring, the favorite season of Kurds, the season of Newroz, the New Year, when the mountains are at their greenest and the flocks are swollen with newborn.

"*They* call this West Azerbaijan. What does *that* mean?" Nasreen asked contemptuously. "This is *Kurdistan*."

In a land where people do not speak openly of their oppression, Nasreen's words moved me deeply. I did not yet know how freely the Kurds of the village, especially the women, spoke their minds. What Nasreen said to me was so true I wondered that no one had said it before. The Tehran government called one small province in Iran "Kordestan." It lay well south of Mahabad. The real Iranian Kurdistan began miles south of "Kordestan" province and ran far north of Mahabad—all the way to the Russian border.

Taha had come after all to bring us to his father's village. To our embarrassment he had arrived early and found us not ready. But, being Taha, he waited good-humoredly in our bare hall as we rushed around. By the time the

Land Rover along with our driver, Khadija, Gulnam, Taha's cousin Raheem, Taha, Jared, and I reached the village, it was mid-afternoon.

The first thing I noticed was the silence. Then Maryam appeared, welcoming Jared and me formally and hugging Taha. As usual, she was dressed all in blue. I was turned over to Nasreen, a stocky girl with a long pointed chin and the blue, blue eyes of her mother. Before I knew what had happened to her, Khadija had disappeared around the back of the house, not to be seen again until late that evening.

Jared and I were quickly plunged into the main activities for guests—drinking tea, sitting, talking, and touring, in approximately that order. While Jared went with the men, Nasreen was in charge of all my tours. First we walked out in front of her mother's house which sat at the head of the village, thus commanding a good view of the valley. We strolled among the sheep and lambs, goats and kids scattered across the large pasture. Constantly worrying aloud that she was tiring me out, Nasreen soon led me back to the house for more tea. I don't think an hour passed without at least one glass of tea. We looked at Maryam's photograph album and drank tea. Talked and drank tea. Sat silently staring at one another and drank tea.

Later in the day, as the shadows lengthened, Nasreen took me on another walk that led to the village proper, a warren of dirt alleys and mud walls. At the beginning of the lane that wound past the dwellings, we came face-to-face with Haji Ismail, a strangely foreboding figure in the twilight with his black suit and tall, gaunt frame. But there was nothing foreboding in his eyes, which lit up with pleasure when he saw us.

"Welcome, welcome," he said to me. "This is *your* village. Come here whenever you like."

I thanked him, overwhelmed by the intensity he put into his words. When the haji left, Nasreen bubbled over about what a propitious meeting this was. Later she repeated his words to her mother, sister, and cousin. I got the impression that she rarely talked to Haji Ismail and regarded him with awe, as if he were a king rather than just her father.

Slowly we made our way up the road that led into the heart of the village, about a quarter mile away from Maryam's house. Haji Ismail's house had been built on a slope, also at a distance from the houses of common villagers. It was not until I experienced the attentions of ordinary, poor Kurdish villagers that I appreciated the splendid isolation of the aristocrats of Dustan. Our hosts were not only the richest people in a relatively prosperous village; they were also some of the richest people in all of Kurdistan.

As I stared into narrow crooked passageways between mud walls surrounding mud houses, the half-light of dusk made everything seem shabbier and darker than it already was. Perhaps it was the time of day, but suddenly I felt depressed and alien, like a visitor from the future witnessing the avoidable filth of the Dark Ages.

A group of women, children clinging to their skirts, saluted Nasreen, who stood out in this mud-dark atmosphere like a star in her cerise taffeta *fistan*. Nasreen called to the women gaily in answer to their more subdued, formal greeting. One by one the women silently approached Nasreen, grasped her hand, kissed the back of it, and bowed, touching her hand to their foreheads. I watched in fascination as the women then backed away. One woman glanced at me, as if wondering whether I too were worthy of this obeisance, and then, evidently, decided against. But about a month later, when I appeared in Dustan in Kurdish dress, my hand too was seized and kissed.

That first afternoon passed swiftly in a blur of endless conversation, of smiles and questions, of tea served on a fine new red Persian carpet where we sat facing whitewashed walls and neat metal-framed windows. I had not thought very much about where the servants in Maryam's house lived or who actually cared for that extensive flock spread across the pasture. I was also worn out from Nasreen's exuberance. She had taken on the role of hostess with enough energy to shepherd at least ten women around her village. I kept wondering what had happened to Khadija. I knew that Jared was spending time with Taha and some other sons and cousins of the village. Why wasn't Khadija here with Nasreen and me?

I was relieved when at last Nasreen led me away from the dark village and back toward her mother's house, where I could see the twinkle of lights from the pressurized lanterns which had just been lit. As I walked into the guest room where I had spent a lot of the afternoon, Nasreen went off somewhere else. The room was now full of men and boys—Jared, Taha, two of Taha's brothers, and Taha's cousin Raheem. I was the only female.

As I sat talking and drinking tea, I realized how exhausted I felt. When Nasreen had accused me of being tired, I had protested. But it was true. I *was* tired. We had not even been here for one day and the walks I had taken with Nasreen had been quite leisurely. The clothes Nasreen wore were hardly made for running. Perhaps it was the language that was making me tired. Even now, sitting with Jared, I was, of course, speaking Kurdish. But more than the strain of speaking Kurdish was the strain of just being here, taking in all the dark contrasts, always wondering what was expected.

Now that it was night, the remoteness of the village pressed in on me. The company that surrounded us seemed smaller and more fragile, likely to disappear in a flicker of the oil lamp. The mountains on the horizon loomed larger. Looking through the windows of the room, I could see no lights out on the plain. The road we had traveled to get here was plunged into darkness and silence. The village at night is a refuge, a gathering of human beings for comfort, warmth, and light. But I was too new to the village to draw sustenance from it. To me, it was only a little less alien than the dark silence of the plain.

Suddenly a group of men appeared in the doorway, throwing their shadows across the floor. Everyone rose as Haji Ismail and his male entourage entered the room. The haji was smiling and eagerly shaking our hands. As we all sat down, I noticed his men studiously trying not to stare at me. The haji seemed to be running in high gear, as usual, and he was full of questions and comments for us. One of his major concerns was to find out why we were not *his* guests. At first I didn't understand what he was talking about. Dustan was *his* village. Maryam was his wife and Taha was his son. In the chain of ownership, we were surely *his* guests as well.

"My house has electricity," he said pointedly. "The next time you come to Dustan you must stay with me."

I nodded politely, wondering why only his house had electricity, and wondering even more why there was such a separation of guests. I had not realized we belonged to Maryam. Nor did I yet realize what a great mark of interest it was that the haji had come here after us to Maryam's house. Ordinarily traffic between the two houses went up to the haji on the hill, not down to Maryam on the edge of the plain.

It was not long before Jared's Persian petered out as he lapsed into an exhausted glaze. I was forced to keep up a conversation with Haji Ismail, who was admiring my command of Kurdish as I stumbled along wearily trying to follow what he was talking about. The haji wanted to show me how he had taught himself to write the Kurdish language in the Latin alphabet used in Turkey. He copied the words off his pack of American-made cigarettes and promised me that when I went back to the United States he would write me in my own alphabet. While the haji was talking, no one else said anything, throwing the burden of half the conversation on me. But this time, unlike the time at his city house, I hardly noticed. I was too far gone with fatigue.

At last Maryam came to the doorway. She wanted to know whether I would eat dinner with the men or with the women. When she saw that I was incapable of answering this simple question, she simply led me around to the other side of her house. Although there were only four rooms altogether, two on each side with storerooms at the back, the two halves of the house did not connect from the inside. I was led into another bedroom, where Maryam, Khadija, Nasreen, and Nadia all watched as I consumed food from a huge tray set in front of me, Despite my protests, none of them would eat until I had finished.

After dinner they attempted to show me how to dance Kurdish-style, as they put on a tape cassette and formed a line in the narrow space between the double bed and the wall. I could hardly keep my eyes open.

"Margaret is tired," observed Maryam, and she hustled the girls out of the bedroom and over to the other side of the house, where Haji Ismail and his retinue had recently departed. A large shotgun was hurriedly extracted from underneath Maryam's mattress, and then the double bed was freshly made up. Khadija set a platter of fruit, two small serving plates with paring knives, a pitcher of water and two glasses, and a cassette player with a crocheted bag of cassettes on the windowsill near the bed. As soon as everything was assembled to their satisfaction our hostesses bid us goodnight and closed the door.

Jared and I were left alone to ponder the events of the day and the presence of that shotgun. Since this was our first overnight stay in a village it made relatively little impression on us. We knew Haji Ismail and his son were avid hunters, and it did not immediately hit us that this gun was *Maryam's*. She did not go hunting.

Later, after my stay in Kurdistan was finished, I realized that I had not walked ten steps in a village without being escorted and, more important, we had not slept one night without having a guard watching over us. Theoretically Iranian Kurds were not armed, but the prevalence of blood feuds and murder made that a moot point. Whatever the law was, it was clear that many Kurds possessed firearms.

I looked at the large battery-operated clock on the wall; it was nine-thirty. All of a sudden I didn't feel tired at all. On the other side of the house I heard talk and laughter, and I looked out our window at the pool of light that fell from the windows of Nadia's bedroom. The bed wasn't long enough for Jared to stretch out at full length, and the whole thing sagged like a hammock. Knowing how tired I would be through the next day, I tried to go to sleep—waking and sleeping, waking and sleeping and waking at last to a cool green misty dawn that stretched away to the rim of the mountains.

My drowsiness vanished when I heard the sound of the birds through the open window. A maid soon arrived at the door with a huge round aluminum tray full of breakfast—fresh-baked whole-wheat flat bread, white cheese, yogurt, honey, and glasses of steaming hot milk. Raheem came too to keep us company, and soon the day was beginning again. After breakfast Nasreen arrived to take me to meet her sister, Amina.

After a quarter-mile walk up the hill we approached the house from the rear, going around the back of the harem. This first time I didn't see the twenty-foot wall separating the harem from Haji Ismail's *diwankhaneh*, the long dark sitting room set aside for men visiting the village. This time I saw only a poorly dressed servant woman struggling with a pile of greasy-looking metal pots at the spigot at the back of the house. Nasreen and I climbed the concrete stairs at the entrance to the harem and stepped over the cucumber and orange peels and a monstrous sheepdog in the dark hall. Nasreen then let go of my hand as we both paused to take off our shoes in front of a metal door.

Half a dozen women were standing as we entered the room. Only the heavy-set woman I vaguely remembered from that long-ago day at Maryam's remained sitting with a blanket spread under her and a cane at her side. Nasreen greeted the older woman first, and she craned her neck up at me, a smile creasing the folds of her face. At last I understood that this woman with the cane was Susin Khanim, Aisha's mother. Amina, the tall, black-haired, gray-eyed girl that Nasreen was introducing me to, was Aisha's youngest sister, and Nasreen's sister as well since the Kurdish language makes no distinction between full sister and half sister.

As soon as everyone was seated, the women started asking whether I liked the village—a question that had been much on Nasreen's lips as she had shown me around the previous day. Tea was served by the woman with the blue tattoo on her chin, whom Khadija had pointed out as the mother of one of Haji Ismail's other wives. I wondered where those other wives were.

After a mere half hour in their company I began to feel mesmerized by the slow pace of life. I imagined them sitting around day after day in this dark, dingy room where flies hovered over bits of food ground into the carpet. There seemed to be no topic of conversation other than the question of whether or not I liked the village better than the city. From the way their eyes were glued on me I understood that it was a relief for them just to have a fresh face to stare at.

I would never have guessed from this meeting with Susin Khanim, Haji Ismail's eldest wife, that long ago she had been involved in scandal and adventure. Now, as far as I could tell, she sat from one day to the next fingering her prayer beads, her mind filled with God knew what regrets and thoughts— of her stroke four years earlier, of the other wives she had to put up with, of her four daughters.

Nasreen, who did not seem affected by the languor of the room, began chattering away about me as if I wasn't there. She told them of my job at the college, the types of food I prepared for dinner, how I had decorated my house. Most of this information was secondhand at least. The women asked about my husband, and Nasreen announced that he was quite tall, and, most important, young. I was silent, feeling a little like Nasreen's pet bear. Amina occasionally tried to get in a word or two, but failed. Alal, Haji Ismail's giddy-looking niece, kept giggling, gold already glinting in her fifteen-year-old mouth. I could see that Nasreen was used to holding court up in Susin's sitting room and I wondered how her younger half sister and cousin felt about her.

Later, when she came to Rezaiyeh for a visit, Nasreen announced to me that she had no friends in the village.

"What do you mean?" I asked, thinking of all the time she spent with Amina and Alal. "What about your sister and cousin?"

"Oh, them," she replied scornfully. "They're not my friends. How could Amina be my friend?"

But on my first visit to Dustan I could not easily discern this tension. For now, the only hostility I sensed was a competition for proprietorship of me, the visitor. Nasreen had already won that contest hands down. For it was clear to everyone that I was Maryam's guest, not the guest of Haji Ismail's harem. When Susin pleaded with us, a little pathetically, to stay for the noon meal, Nasreen was almost peremptory about the way she stood up and took me down the hill to her mother's house.

I wondered if Nasreen's sense of importance stemmed partially from the fact that she was Maryam's daughter. Maryam, for the last couple of years, had lived apart from the tedious harem. At the time of our visit a lot of building seemed to be going on in Dustan. Gelawezh, Haji Ismail's sister, was moving out of the communal women's quarters that summer. I felt sure that Susin would have liked to leave also, but she was too old and sick. Since she had no sons and thus no brides, she was dependent on the young wives to cook for her. Only women with grown sons like Maryam could feasibly live alone.

Although I had heard we were going to be taken on an expedition to a nearby hot spring, no one seemed in any hurry to get started. First, an abundant dinner was served. Then everyone drowsed. Finally it looked as if we might be about to get into the Land Rover. Since I had eaten dinner with the men and boys I had not seen the women for a while. When I bumped into Khadija at the side of the house I asked her conversationally if she was going to the hot spring.

"I don't think so, Margaret," she replied, smiling.

"But why not?" died on my lips as she disappeared again behind the house where I presumed the kitchen was.

When the time came, it was clear that only Jared, Taha, Raheem, one of Taha's younger brothers, Amina, Nasreen, and I were going. Taha took his engraved shotgun and strung a bandolier across his chest. Nasreen was practically jumping up and down for joy as we set out, following the road and the electric line toward the Iraqi border. I wondered aloud if Haji Ismail's electricity came from this wire, but the answer, from Taha, was that no village was allowed to tap this power. It was strictly for the use of the army at the border. Haji Ismail's electricity was supplied by his own private oil-driven generator.

For two or three hours before we left, Nasreen and Amina had talked of this outing as if it were their one outing of the year. They gushed and bubbled to each other and to me about how wonderful it was going to be. I was doubtful. But Dermanawa, literally "Medicine Water," was far more spectacular than I had imagined.

Part of the beauty lay in the fact that it was almost untouched. No wonder. We had to cross an open sea of mud in order to reach this gorge cut by a river running through solid rock. The Land Rover barely made it. But the view alone was worth the ride. The color of the river was pale green, just a little paler than the surrounding vegetation. When I climbed down the rocky bluff to put my hand in one of the bubbling pools, the water felt deliciously warm.

Nasreen and Amina led me around by the hand, constantly worrying that I was getting too tired. I might have thought this was the result of our retiring so early the previous night except that Nasreen had been suggesting that I must be tired almost from the moment I had arrived in Dustan. Perhaps that was why I got so tired. It seemed to be a Kurdish custom—speculating on how tired your guest must be because she is unused to the mountains.

While the men went on ahead, I adjusted my pace to Nasreen and Amina's, stopping with them while they talked with a family that seemed to be camped out under a rock along the bluff. These were people in Western clothes who wore gold jewelry like the Kurds. I imagined they were Iraqi refugees not registered with the local authorities, but when I asked my hostesses about them I was told that they were *ajam*. I thought it was strange that *ajam* spoke Kurdish, but I did not pursue the subject.

Two other men—both clearly Kurds in baggy *shalwar* and turbans—were perched on another rock smoking cigarettes and watching us. I wondered how and when these other people had arrived. Our Land Rover was the only vehicle in sight.

Now Taha was hunting in earnest, and the shots rang out. The girls hurried to watch as Taha's younger brother Hossein waded out in the middle of the river to retrieve the corpses. Hossein had stripped off his imported jeans, and I was interested to see that his underpants were long muslin *shalwar*, gathered at the ankle. While the girls were swaddled from head to foot with traditional Kurdish clothing, all three males were dressed in a more comfortable and practical Western style. Only language and underwear identified them as Kurds.

Before we actually caught up with the hunting party, Nasreen and Amina begged me to ask Taha to take us all to Zeweh, the refugee camp. On our way to Dermanawa when we had turned off the main road onto the muddy field, we had seen the metal roofs of the camp barracks glittering in the distance, next to the snow-topped mountain peaks. I too had wanted to see the camp but I had not thought it was possible.

"Why don't you ask him yourselves?" I said curiously,

"He won't go for our sake, but if you ask him, Margaret, I'm sure he'll take us."

The morning and the day before Nasreen had been mooning around about riding to Iraq on the back of a "Barzani horse," being pastured right in Dustan.

With dreams like that, what could be more exciting than seeing some refugee men interned at the camp?

Hossein presented the dead partridges to Taha, who then put them on the ground. He smiled in response to the many compliments from his sisters.

"What shall we do now?" he asked. "Maybe I should get a few more birds?"

I was glad that Nasreen had given me an excuse to propose the end of this hunting.

"Do you think we could drive past Zeweh and have a look at the camp?" I asked.

"Of course, if that's what you want to do," said Taha. Nasreen and Amina were grinning.

We walked slowly back to the car, Nasreen enjoying the privilege of carrying the dead birds. When we reached the main road Taha headed toward the metal roofs. I could hear Amina and Nasreen whispering excitedly to each other in the back of the Land Rover.

After all of SAVAK's deliberation about whether I should be allowed to visit Zeweh, I couldn't believe that we were actually entering the camp this easily. There were no fences and no guards. We simply crossed a concrete bridge and found ourselves on a road with rows of narrow barracks on one side and army tents on the other. Women and children in Kurdish dress stood next to the barracks, while a throng of men were gathered in front of what appeared to be a teashop. I started taking pictures out of the window, much to Taha's amusement. He didn't seem to be at all afraid of SAVAK.

A man in Kurdish clothes came over and greeted him through the window. Finally, after a few minutes, a soldier approached and asked Taha what we were doing. I hurriedly put my camera away, and Taha replied that we were merely passing by. The road that went through the camp was the main north-south artery in Kurdish West Azerbaijan. The soldier waved us on. As I looked back, the roofs of the barracks again glinted in the sun. But up close the camp had appeared dusty and dreary.

The rest of the afternoon passed quickly, with more tea and talk at Maryam's house. When it was finally time to go, Khadija appeared at last from behind the house. She had spent the entire weekend cooking and doing chores for her mother-in-law. The rest of our party assembled as Haji Ismail came bumping down the hill in his Land Rover to take us all back to the city. Just after we got on the government highway a policeman from the gendarme post near Dustan stepped into the road and motioned us to stop.

"Who are these?" he asked, pointing to us.

"My guests," said Haji Ismail. The gendarme nodded and stepped back. We continued on our way.

The light on the road was fading, and the haji seemed tired. He kept blinking and then opening his eyes wide as if he couldn't see. Beginning at Band the road was choked with the cars of city people who had spent the day near each other's vehicles and, incidentally it seemed, the green outdoors. Just beyond Band there was space enough for everyone to spread out, but, as Nasreen had reminded me, that space was Kurdistan, no place for *ajam*.

Being well acquainted with the proper *ta'arof* for this occasion, Jared and I begged Haji Ismail to let us off several blocks before we arrived at our house. Time and time again we had seen Iranians practically leap from moving cars in an effort to save a driver the effort of taking them all the way home. But the haji was clearly not going to stop until he was sure we were in front of our house. Reluctantly we directed him to our courtyard door, where he got out of his car in order to shake our hands.

Taha was then ordered to present us with two of the partridges he had shot. But when he held them out to us, we refused to take the tiny birds, not out of *ta'arof*, but because we genuinely didn't want them. However, Haji Ismail insisted. It was obvious to him, from our previous behavior, that we were only being polite. Back and forth we went, Haji Ismail refusing to believe that we were turning down such a choice delicacy, and we, on the other hand, having no desire to pluck and gut these tiny bodies for the sake of a little bird meat.

At last Jared said, "Giving these partridges to us is like throwing them into the garbage. We wouldn't eat them."

Haji Ismail looked stunned, but he soon recovered. We were foreigners, and he accepted that. Before he drove away he wished us a good evening and a speedy return to his village. The glow from his warm goodbye and the goodbyes from the rest of the people in the car, the fond farewells from Nasreen and Maryam as we left the village, and all the hospitality we had enjoyed in Dustan stayed with us until we reached our front door. Then we discovered we were locked out.

We had keys only to the courtyard gate and to our apartment door upstairs. Never, in all the months we had lived in Rezaiyeh, had we found the front door to the building locked. But never before had Houshang and Shehrzad been away. In their place, watching over the apartment and the two children, was Houshang's elder sister. She had, on more than one occasion, alluded darkly to all the crime in the city. No longer were the courtyard and apartment doors left permanently ajar as they were when Shehrzad was at home. Now this aunt had locked the front door to the whole building with a key we didn't know existed. Since her house was unlit, we assumed she had gone off somewhere, perhaps for a long time.

At first we wandered about the kucheh looking for her; then we simply waited, exhausted in the dark courtyard, for her return. At last she came back with the children in tow, offering no apology when we explained to her that she had locked us out. The exchange between us was just short of openly hostile, and Jared went straight upstairs to avoid further conversation. As she opened the door to the Jaffari apartment, the aunt said to me for the tenth time or so since we'd met, "*Befarmayeed*, Khanim. Please come in and have some tea."

Before, when she had issued this invitation, I had steered clear of accepting, not knowing whether she really meant it. But tonight I was in need of tea. Besides, I did not want to turn down her invitation and seem even more unfriendly after the edgy conversation about the lock. Without reflecting on the fact that the woman had been out of the house and her samovar might not be heated up, I accepted. As I walked into the foyer with her, she stood looking at me without inviting me to sit down.

Finally she said, "Please sit down." Then she went into the kitchen.

When she came back she handed me a large mushy apple. "This is from my uncle's orchard," she told me. "I must give the boy his bath."

There was an awkward pause as I slowly realized that she was dismissing me. The apple was a substitute for the proffered tea which she had never intended me to accept in the first place. I stood up quickly, holding the apple, my face burning.

"Excuse me. I must go now. Goodnight," I managed to say.

"Goodnight, Khanim," she called after me.

As I walked back up the stairs, holding the apple, at first I couldn't understand how I had made such a mistake. When was the last time I had accepted an invitation at face value and forgotten to give the person inviting me a chance to accede gracefully to my refusal? Then I realized what the problem was.

I had spent the last two days with Kurds in Kurdistan, another country, another culture. There, every offer, every meal, had been extended with strong pressure to accept. On the way home we had puzzled and perhaps even hurt Haji Ismail with our *ta'arof*-like refusals. He didn't realize how confused we were. On the one hand we made the mistake of practicing *ta'arof* with Kurds, and on the other we forgot to use it with Persians and Turks.

Now, more than ever, it was time for us to commit ourselves. Where did we belong in Iran? We had been offered a place in Kurdistan.

"This is *your* village," Haji Ismail had said.

Yet, we continued to live in Rezaiyeh. Our work was there. Our household was there. Despite our early efforts to avoid it, we were being sucked into declaring our allegiance. Once, we were total outsiders, going around in innocence and ignorance—occasionally spending time with Kurds if we could find them, occasionally socializing with other Iranians if they really invited us or accepted our invitations. That period of innocence and friendlessness was ending.

"Do you have any *ajam* friends?" Khadija had inquired, eyes narrowed, on more than one occasion.

"Why do you go to Kurdish villages? Disgusting, filthy places!" Shehrzad's mother commented.

It made no sense to urbanized Turks that we, sophisticated Americans, would choose the company of dirty, backward villagers. Yet we were forming the opinion that Kurds, or at least Haji Ismail and his family, acted far less foreign than other Iranians. The absence of *ta'arof*, the emphasis on personal honesty, and, above all, ethnic pride distinguished Kurds from most Iranians that I met. Perhaps it was the pride that counted the most. Kurds—real village Kurds—did not yet feel the need to ape the West, and thus they met us as equals, without resentment. But I cannot dismiss this conflict so lightly with a trio of neat generalizations. I was about to discover Kurdish villages where I could never feel anything but "other." And there were still Turks and Persians I wanted as my friends.

The hatred and fear had been there centuries before my arrival on the scene. The Turks couldn't understand my affinity for Kurds, and the Kurds couldn't understand why, if I was their friend, I would have anything to do with *ajam*. Christian Armenians and Assyrians as well as Rezaiyeh's Jews were astounded by my interest in what they saw as the wildest Muslim group in the area. Then there were the Persians, who felt that Rezaiyeh was a remote outpost, unbearably far from their beloved Tehran or Meshed or Shiraz.

It was too late to change course, even if I had wanted to which I didn't. Kurdistan had been my destination from the beginning. All the uneasiness I felt at my neighbors' spying on my Kurdish guests, the anger and fear inspired by the dean's edicts and veiled threats, even my worries about SAVAK faded.

"This is Kurdistan," Nasreen had said.

In the coming months I would feel less and less as if I were living in Iran.

CHAPTER 15

A TALE OF TWO VILLAGES

Just as in Mawana, a good part of the strangeness of Haji Ismail's village, Dustan, lay in its dirt. In Kurdistan, villages, unless they were once Assyrian, tended to be constructed primarily of soil. Houses were made of adobe with dried mud walls and dried mud courtyards. A main source of fuel for the winter came from dried cakes of manure, and those too were stored in mud shelters.

Since Haji Ismail was a rich man, his house had been put together with yellow city-made bricks, and Maryam's house was newly constructed of fitted stones, without mortar. Haji Ismail, with his wheat crop, his combine, and his Land Rover, could have afforded to build a castle. He could have had two stories to his house instead of one and run a refrigerator or a television on his generator. He could have bought expensive Western furniture. If he had commanded, his house could have been clean and flyless.

Instead, he did not live so differently from his vastly poorer neighbors. His house, like theirs, was infested with fleas and sheep bugs. His babies, like theirs, had fly-covered faces. Haji Ismail's sister told us that her brother had once put screens on the windows of his *diwankhaneh* and harem. He soon determined that this only increased the problem because the flies became trapped inside. So he had ordered the screens removed.

Now there were iron bars to keep out thieves and marauders, but no screens. The beaten mud courtyard of his house was usually littered with garbage. Since relatively few disposable wrappings or products were available in the village, there seemed to be no fear that trash would pile up. If paper wrappings were brought from the city or if vegetables were peeled by the large concrete tub of water, they were simply left where they dropped.

For some reason that I never understood, Haji Ismail wasted gallons of water. As the khan of the village he had proprietorship of a spring at the base of the mountain where water was collected and carried down through a pipe to an open spigot which poured into a tub in his *diwankhaneh* courtyard. The pipe was also connected to an open spigot over another tub in the harem courtyard and then ran down the hill to a spigot in Maryam's yard. These three spigots were left open day and night.

The beaten dirt of the surrounding courtyards turned to slithery mud, But this didn't bother the chickens or the raggedly dressed little children who ran around in the filth. The water just helped the trash to stick to the ground better. There were no trees and no plants to absorb the water. Trees were grown in stands away from the house and cut down as soon as the wood was salable. Ornamental plantings were nonexistent.

One day when we were visiting for the afternoon, Haji Ismail took Jared into the *diwankhaneh* and amused himself by having target practice on the slightly soiled dark-green plaster wall. Jared was horrified.

"But what about your wall?" he asked the haji.

"Oh, I am planning to re-plaster and paint it," said the haji, looking nonchalantly at the ugly holes made by the bullets.

The haji's idea was to have dark-blue walls and a black ceiling, but somehow Jared managed to talk him out of it, suggesting shades of light green instead.

"I will do whatever you tell me," promised the haji, giving Jared sole choice over the colors.

Haji Ismail was as good as his word, and the harem, the *diwankhaneh*, and even his house in the city were considerably brightened by the pale green that was applied in less than a week by a couple of diligent workers.

Still, the dirt remained, ground into the carpets where flies cleaned up after a thousand meals. Vegetable refuse was scattered on the tile floor of the hall of the harem. In the harem each woman's room was her castle. The bedrooms, which were far from spotless, seemed like models of cleanliness compared with the common ground of utter filth that reigned in the hall and the outdoor courtyard. These were areas that all the women were theoretically responsible for but which in fact did not seem to be acknowledged by anyone. Even when Haji Ismail constructed an indoor toilet the effect was merely to move the old outhouse inside. The color and smell were virtually the same despite the porcelain.

To us there was something perversely charming about Haji Ismail's disregard for comfort. While the Turks and Persians in Rezaiyeh were buying Western conveniences as fast as they could be imported into Iran, Haji Ismail lived in his house pretty much the same way his great-great-

great-grandfather had lived in his. We had become so jaded by civilization and comfort that we admired people who weren't bothered by dirt. Sheikh Avdila, one of the few Kurds we knew who'd been exposed to Western ways, thought we were crazy for spending time with Haji Ismail. If he had known how we romanticized his cousin's style of living, he would have been quite disgusted.

"What do you see in him?" Sheikh Avdila asked us on more than one occasion.

Jared tried to explain the mutual attraction between the educated foreigners used to impersonal antisepsis and the tribal landlord with his predilection for traditional life.

"He is right out of the fifteenth century," Sheikh Avdila said contemptuously. We agreed. But, unlike Sheikh Avdila, we were fascinated.

Sheikh Avdila too had been born in the fifteenth century. But he had been educated in the twentieth, and now he was living, like many urban Iranians, in a nether-century while the shah futilely attempted to undo years of neglect by wildly disbursing huge oil profits in the space of less than a decade. Sheikh Avdila had seen and read and learned things that Haji Ismail could not fathom and did not want to fathom. But Haji Ismail was all of one piece, while Sheikh Avdila, the modernized son of an old-time Sufi sheikh, was a mass of contradictions.

I was dying to have a look at Aisha and Avdila's village, Khoshkan, but at the same time I dreaded Aisha's departure from the city. That would spell the end of her proximity and availability for conversation, conversation that had become a lifeline for me as the situation at the college grew progressively worse.

In the spring semester, after Newroz, there were small strikes and boycotts of individual teachers. Gradually these snowballed into one large strike which coincided with the announcement that all students who wanted to be in good standing with the government were required to join the shah's new party, *Restakheez*, "Resurrection."

The students didn't dare to denounce Restakheez openly—that would have been too dangerous. They merely demanded the resignation of the dean and various unpopular teachers as well as the postponement or, better yet, the abandonment of all examinations for the year. This was a time-honored tactic, as we learned, where it was acceptable to reject exams and criticize your teachers as long as you didn't attack the shah or his government.

When the strike began in earnest, one hundred percent of the students stayed away from class. Most simply went on extended vacation, glad to be relieved of the bother of having to study. Only a very small number of students actively struck, remaining on campus, where they sat peaceably on the ground chanting while soldiers with machine guns waited a few yards away. These brave few were left by the other students to state their case and suffer the consequences.

The whole town was buzzing with the news of the strike. All of a sudden Shehrzad, who had previously expressed interest in little besides clothes and parties, was stopping me and inquiring about the situation every day.

"Is it true the army came on campus yesterday and beat up all the students—girls as well as boys?" she asked breathlessly.

To Shehrzad and to other middle-class urban Iranians who paid lip service to the shah, these university strikes were fascinating. To almost everyone in town, the student strike was *the* news event, but without the media coverage, since, of course, all meaningful news was routinely censored.

The idea of the students standing against the shah was extremely exciting. Even people who tried to look loyal to the shah by condemning the students betrayed their ambivalence by endless discussion of the strike. The Kurds were not nearly as fascinated. *They* had no connection with these colleges.

As far as I was concerned there was one worthwhile by-product of the strike—I didn't have to go to the college anymore. Classes didn't meet, and we were naturally not invited to the higher-level faculty meetings on how to force the students back into form.

"You must come to the village," Aisha told me. "We are going to go there as soon as the snow has left the mountains."

I nodded politely, thinking how much I didn't want her leave town. I was still curious to learn more about Sheikh Avdila. He had remained a larger-than-life historical figure whom I was sometimes privileged to see in the halls of his house. The flow of refugees had fallen off, since most of Aisha's and Avidila's friends seemed to have gone back to Iraq. But the refugee presence in Iran remained. Thousands of refugees still filled the camps, and many more were coming over the border daily.

The former headmistress of the Rezaiyeh Kurdish refugee school had left her dachshund in Rezaiyeh with Aisha and Avdila, making this already anomalous couple less like their neighbors than ever. Iranians, especially urban ones, seemed to have no use for pets. The only dogs I saw people keep and feed were out in the villages, strictly to herd sheep. More than once I had caught boys pelting a litter of stray puppies with stones on the building site across from my house. A serious slur in both Persian and Kurdish was "dog father." But for the sake of her departed friends Aisha worried about the happiness of a displaced, homesick dachshund that hovered near the edges of her long skirts.

On the day of my friend's departure for the village I walked over to her house and found her sunk rather dejectedly in one of Avdila's huge stuffed chairs that had been placed in the middle of the downstairs hall. The house was a jumble of furniture in the latter stages of being moved out the front door. Aisha and Avdila were taking most of their possessions from the city to their new house in the village.

Aisha, usually so attentive, listened to my tales from the college with only half an ear. Watching her try to cope with the accumulation of a ten-year stay in the city made me realize that nomadism was not in her blood even if her ancestors had been tent dwellers, following the seasons with their flocks. Aisha was as anxious as I would have been. Since she insisted there was no way to help her, I left.

Now that we were free of our teaching duties I was eager to go to more villages, but, as always, I waited for specific invitations. Both Haji Ismail and Aisha had said to come any time, but I did not yet feel comfortable enough to do that. At last my patience was rewarded when Aisha's roly-poly woman servant arrived at my door one warm spring day with a huge caldron of sheep's milk yogurt sent from the village. Along with the yogurt was an invitation—"Come." The roly-poly woman gave us the directions to Khoshkan., the village the sheikh's father had bought back from the shah's government.

In Dustan there had been a hot discussion about which village was prettier— Dustan or Khoshkan. Aisha's mother and sister had held out for Khoshkan while everyone else went for Dustan. But Susin Khanim said flatly that Khoshkan was obviously more beautiful because it had more water. To Kurds, the green *kesk o sheen* of spring is the most exquisite color in the world and only water can produce it.

The region in which Khoshkan lies is the best-irrigated part of Kurdistan that we saw during our stay. A river running down from the mountains of Iraq cut a gorge through the mountains, watering the whole plain and making it possible for Sheikh Avdila even to grow a few fields of short-grain rice. But it was not water that was so remarkable about Khoshkan. Other villages had water, but nowhere in Iranian Kurdistan was there a house like the sheikh's.

From a distance, as our car was struggling through the mud of the plain, we saw a large red brick building standing on the highest point of land overlooking the river. I assumed it belonged to the government. Perhaps it was a gendarme post or one of the government summer camps built to keep the high school and university students quiet when school was out.

As we came steadily nearer, driving past a small dusty village, we wondered that we saw no building midway between that official-looking edifice and a mud hut. Where was Avdila's house? Surely he didn't live like a common villager. When we stopped to ask a shepherd standing near the road, he pointed to the red brick building. *That* was Sheikh Avdila's house.

The fact that I had arrived in Khoshkan with mistaken preconceptions was evident from the way Sheikh Avdila regarded my attire when we got out of the car.

"What are you doing in that?" he asked, giggling slightly.

I looked down at my brocaded gold-and-white *fistan* covering a bright-red-and-pink voile *kiras* and suddenly felt quite ridiculous. After the weekend in Dustan I had thought that I would feel much more comfortable wearing Kurdish clothing in a village. Most of my time in Dustan had been spent sitting on the floor of the harem, where the voluminous skirts of a Kurdish *kiras* made a much greater variety of positions modest than did tight-fitting jeans. But there was little at Sheikh Avdila's village that resembled the routine of Haji Ismail's harem. For one thing, there was no harem.

Aisha came down the steps leading out of the bedroom, past all of her potted plants, which were now massed out of doors around a patio. She welcomed us and then went away, to do some work, she said. I stared after her in dismay.

Sheikh Avdila then led us to his porch, which overlooked the gorge and the river. On the side of the slope was a terraced garden, and all around the house, which was still not quite finished, petunias and roses, phlox and snapdragons had been planted in freshly dug beds.

After the garbage-strewn chaos of Haji Ismail's courtyards, Sheikh Avdila's domain looked like part of Switzerland. At one side of the huge circular drive was a sunken rabbit hutch. Below the drive were an almond and apple orchards, a vineyard, and a manufactured beehive. On the porch near the bedroom stood an unused incubator, and on the porch overlooking the gorge an uninstalled porcelain sink was propped near the door.

When it was finished Sheikh Avdila's house would have not one but two indoor toilets, both with porcelain fixtures. Beneath the house was the kitchen, windowless and dark with a mud floor like the kitchens in other villages. But this kitchen did not have an open hole with a fire for an oven and stove. There was a fancy gas range with a brand-new pressure cooker from Germany sitting on top of it. Most fantastic of all was the formal dining room upstairs complete with buffet, table, and chairs, This was the only village dwelling where we ever sat down to a meal at a table.

Although I was dazzled by the physical luxury and cleanliness of her house, I was disconcerted by the way Aisha had disappeared. With all the servants she had, I couldn't figure out why she was working so hard. I began following her around to try to find out what she was up to. I found her downstairs in the kitchen where she was preparing an enormous pot of stuffed vegetables to serve to the men laboring on the house and in the fields.

As I stood and watched she continually urged me to leave and wait upstairs. Finally, tired of looking on and not knowing how to force my help on her, I went away. Later, when I heard that Aisha had gone from the kitchen to see about a field of eggplant, I decided to go after her. This time, a servant named Mohammed who wore his fringed turban went drooping over one eye went running after me with the clear intent of heading me off. But I just kept going despite his efforts to stop me.

I was getting bored sitting on the porch, where a couple of mullahs were studiously ignoring me while Jared played a losing game of chess with the sheikh. I wanted to find Aisha and catch up on the close friendship we had enjoyed in Rezaiyeh. That was what I had looked forward to in Khoshkan. I had not expected to be relegated to the men's porch with a couple of misogynist mullahs.

Aisha did not appear at all pleased to see me. She was standing in the middle of a large irrigated field, where I soon started to feel faint from the glare of the sun. I had slipped in one of the irrigation ditches that were hidden under the growing vegetation, and the hems of my Kurdish dresses were all muddied.

"What's she doing here?" Aisha asked Mohammed as she frowned.

"I'm sorry, Khanim, I tried to stop her."

I was then led away like a naughty child, reflecting on how I might have offended her. Given all the resources she had at her disposal I couldn't believe she needed to work this hard.

At lunch the sexes ate separately. Jared sat on chairs with the sheikh while I stayed with Aisha, eating off a tray placed on the rug next to her Western-style raised double bed.

Just as we were starting to actually talk to one another the sheikh appeared at the bedroom window and announced it was time for everyone to take a nap. Jared and I were offered no choice in the matter but simply led over to the guest room inside the door leading off the sheikh's porch. A couple of mattresses were spread out with sheets laid over them, and we were then left to doze in the heat as the flies buzzed at the window screens.

That afternoon after we awoke from our naps and were served tea. I did not try to find Aisha again but sat quietly on the porch along with the men. In the evening toward sundown Aisha returned to the house, and I noticed freckles on her normally pale skin. I commented as the servant set down not one but two glasses of tea and Aisha told me she now drank tea rather than hot water in order to stay awake during the long day of chores.

"Did you work when you were a girl in Dustan?" I asked her as we sat drinking the tea.

"Oh no," she replied, laughing. "Never."

Then she told me she enjoyed working hard on the farm, that it was important to her.

I have to work hard," she added. "We need the money."

I was surprised at first. But then when I thought about it, I began to understand. This was the place they expected to inhabit in their old age. Aisha was still young, but the sheikh was not. I thought too that Aisha had discovered she liked to work. It filled her days.

She had no females close to her in status in Khoshkan to socialize with, and no babies to care for. I noticed that she spent a lot of time fussing over the child recently born to the wife of one of the sheikh's bodyguard-drivers. I once suggested to Aisha that perhaps she and the sheikh could adopt a child, and she looked at me as if she didn't know what I was talking about.

"Aren't there any orphans?" I asked, knowing that the government operated an orphanage in downtown Rezaiyeh. "What about the war in Iraq? Surely there must be children without parents or family."

"No," replied Aisha, looking shocked.

That evening in Khoshkan Aisha and I went for a walk among the wildflowers near the mountains. Then we returned to her bedroom, where the electricity had been switched on. There were lights and television—*Ironsides* dubbed in Persian. As soon as the show ended, bedtime was announced and Jared and I were again led over to the guest room. Because there had recently been several murders in the neighborhood a man was posted outside our door with a rifle. Even if we were guests at a deluxe country manor, this was still Kurdistan.

Every time we came to Sheikh Avdila and Aisha's house, it was more complete, more equipped with luxuries that were unheard-of in a village. Yet the village remained the same. It was much smaller than Dustan and looked even poorer. Perhaps this was only due to the contrast between the sheikh's house and the rest of the houses. Unlike Haji Ismail's village, it included no other prosperous farmers. No one except Sheikh Avdila owned a car or a tractor or even a decent dwelling.

In Khoshkan I felt more hostility directed at me from the villagers. Here I never saw any of the hand-kissing that was so common in Dustan. Sheikh Avdila made a point of telling us that he did not exercise his prerogative of requiring villagers to work for him without wages a certain number of days in the year, while Haji Ismail still enforced this feudal practice. But, despite all of Sheikh Avdila's advanced thinking, the village was there to be seen like an ugly sore on an otherwise comely face.

The villagers labored to build his house, to plant his fields. These ordinary people of Khoshkan lived their lives in dust. Their children could not attend school, as even the literacy corps had not reached this village, and the nearest medical care was miles away. Aisha showed some interest in the sufferings of various families, but it was the concern of a lady dispensing charity to those far beneath her. Sheikh Avdila had often alluded to his contempt for Haji Ismail and the way he ran his village. I wondered if the people of Khoshkan were better off for Sheikh Avdila's socialist education? This village was far from being democratic, let alone socialist.

Khoshkan and Dustan are only about two hours apart by car. But once when we wanted to go directly from Khoshkan to Dustan and Avdila was going to Rezaiyeh he flatly refused to drive to the city via Haji Ismail's village. This meant that we would travel three quarters of a circle to avoid passing Dustan.

"If you insist on going there, then I will drop you in Rezaiyeh and you can take the bus," he said.

I never again made the mistake of wearing Kurdish clothes to Avdila's village. I also did not try to photograph anyone or anything in the village proper after my first visit when I had aroused a great deal of hostile curiosity by taking pictures of the various storks that were nesting on the straw roofs of some of the houses and manure fuel sheds. Storks, or *haji laklaks,* as they are called, were a sign of good luck.

The last time we went to Khoshkan, Sheikh Avdila showed us the home movies he had taken during the celebration of his wedding to Aisha. Unfortunately there were no pictures of the bride. Sheikh Avdila, being properly aware of custom, had been too shy to photograph his bride himself, and the servant he had entrusted the camera with had ruined that whole portion of the film.

I was still able to see hundreds of guests who had converged on the sheikh's father's village, the thousands of loaves of bread spread out on the ground to cool, the tents that had been specially set up for the guests. There was a younger Haji Ismail grinning into the camera, and pictures of Dustan where they fetched the bride. Sheikh Avdila had given a physician friend from the Persian-speaking part of Iran Kurdish clothes to dress up in and a horse to ride in front of the camera. I got the impression that Sheikh Avdila had been an observer, a tourist, at his own wedding.

However, my perception of Sheikh Avdila as a sophisticated man who was capable of looking at his own culture with the detached eyes of an outsider was not always on the mark. Once, as Aisha and Avdila were inspecting a series of slides I had shot in Khoshkan, I heard them remark in amused tones to each other how I had actually taken pictures of their servants. Sheikh Avdila had numerous cameras, but he never used them to photograph servants. Of all the Kurds I had met, Sheikh Avdila was the only one who had heard of the feminist movement in the West.

He listened to the BBC regularly. When he and Aisha came to dinner at our house he thanked me numerous times for the meal, so I pointedly remarked that Jared had been the chef. At this reminder, the sheikh giggled nervously and mumbled something about the "feminine revolution" in the West. I didn't say anything, but I wondered if he had talked this way in the USSR, if women there had made him uncomfortable. What would his first wife have to say about Aisha, who couldn't stand to eat in the same room with men?

How did Sheikh Avdila manage to integrate the disparate parts of his life? It was easy to buy a dining-room table, but not so easy to make your guests feel comfortable sitting on straight-backed chairs. It was the most natural thing in Kurdistan to marry your cousin who is thirty years younger, but not so natural to expect her to be an intellectual companion for your old age.

For a long time I thought Avdila and Aisha managed amazingly well. I knew, from Aisha's comments about her upbringing, that she was bitter about her father and ambivalent about her mother and that she was glad to have escaped from Dustan. But there was another side to her that she revealed only after we had known each other awhile—migraine headaches and insomnia, an inchoate longing for children and romance.

It was astonishing to hear such wishes even hinted at by a Kurdish woman. Fate in Iran and in Islam is *ser nivisht*, "written above." Aisha's fate was in the sky before she was born. Yet she must have been surprised to find herself in England at the age of eighteen and entertaining a stream of Iraqi refugees at twenty-eight.

Both Aisha and Sheikh Avdila himself told me he desperately wanted to travel again. It had been over ten years since his post-wedding trip to Europe with Aisha. But the Iranian government said they would seize his land and all of the possessions he left behind as soon as he crossed the border. I wondered how Aisha would feel about going with him. She still had not learned English or any other European language.

More than anyone else Aisha made me feel what the Iraqi Kurds had suffered. When we returned to Iran shortly before the shah fell from power, she told me of the time that spring when the Iraqi government had begun systematically setting fire to all Kurdish villages within twenty-five kilometers of the Iraqi border. This was not far from Khoshkan where hundreds of Iraqi Kurds fled to a nearby mountain within the Iranian border. This time the Iranian army helped the Iraqi Arabs and not the Kurds. Together Iranians and Iraqis surrounded the desperate refugees, bombing those they could see and trying to isolate and starve any remaining.

"They say that some of the *muhajireen* came to people's doors around here and crammed flour into their mouths they were so hungry," Aisha said with a look of horror on her face. Over five hundred people were reported to have died.

I had a strange dream about Aisha two years before I came back to see her. I dreamt she was being tortured and I heard her cry out in Kurdish, "I am afraid." I awoke from the dream sure that something dreadful had happened to my friend. I wanted to call her, but of course I did not. There were no telephones in the village, and besides, if she had been seized and imprisoned I could do nothing about it.

Two years later when I saw Aisha again I didn't mention my dream. She seemed fine, if a little older and a little more cynical. No one was about to torture this richly dressed Kurdish lady, wife of the illustrious Sheikh Avdila. Yet, in my unconscious, I had sensed Aisha's vulnerability. There was nothing to stop the shah's government from torturing such a woman, nothing to stop the Turks if they decided to go after her. A blood feud with her family would result, but who were *they* against the Iranian army?

This was the terrible precariousness that underlay all life in Iran and particularly the lives of Kurds. They were strangers and enemies in their own land. One by one the government picked off people believed to be leaders, nonconformists. Aisha told me of an uncle who had been jailed for twenty years, accused of writing a letter to someone in Russia. Khadija introduced me to the proprietor of the city *hammam* where all the Kurds went. "He is a good man, Margaret," she mentioned later. "Do you know he just got out of prison? They hanged his father."

These people were hardly full-time revolutionaries, but in Iran all Kurds were assumed, perhaps for good reason, to be against the government in Tehran. The Iranian government had not just been willing but eager to send fighter-bombers against unarmed Iraqi villagers. If the bombs happened to fall on Iranian villagers as well, so much the better. They were all Kurds.

Fawzia and Nasreen making dolmas in the village

CHAPTER 16

A WOMAN-RUN HOUSEHOLD

No one intimidated Dara Ahmedi—not his elder nephew, not the dean of the college, and least of all me. As far as I could see there was no obvious reason why a poor village-born Kurdish boy should exhibit so much pride, especially not in Iran, where hierarchy and *ta'arof* make obsequiousness a necessity. One exchange at the Iranian Ministry of Education in Tehran between Jared and a Persian-speaking worker brought home the absolute normality of cringing:

"How are you?" Jared asked this large, poorly dressed man.

Jared was expecting to be told, "Thank you," the usual Persian response. Instead the huge workman answered, "I am small."

Iranian friends later assured us that it was quite proper for this tall man to suggest that his status vis Jared was as a small man.

All the evidence pointed to an unequal status relationship between Mr. Ahmedi and me. I was an educated foreign woman with money and a university post. He was a sophomore on a scholarship at a local technical high school. He had been as far as Tehran once in his life, and to Tabriz perhaps half a dozen times. Despite these limitations, his manner, his carriage, and his expression were self-assured beyond his years.

Toward the end of the school year I got a little tired of Mr. Ahmedi. Every time I vaguely hinted at visiting his village he put me off. I wondered if he wanted to make sure there would be no repeat of my embarrassing visit to his sister's house.

As my Kurdish got better and I spent more and more time with Khadija and Aisha and the rest of the women I began to wonder whether I still needed his help. His standoffishness offended me. Surely he understood that I had put my own reputation in doubt in order to work with him. Why did he have to be so tight-lipped about his family?

I was on the verge of cutting back his hours when I asked him to transcribe a recording I had made. Before he could do this he had to master the modified phonetic script that would capture all the sounds used by Kurmanji speakers. He performed this difficult task with such accuracy and speed that I realized that his help was critical. Without it I might not accomplish the task I had set myself – namely to amass the largest corpus of words, phrases, and sentences I could in order to properly analyze the sounds of the language when I returned to America.

One day Nana, our once-a-week cleaning woman, showed up with her daughter as Mr. Ahmedi and I were working on a tape together. As I sat trying to concentrate on Kurdish phonetics I noticed the eighteen-year-old daughter inspecting all of my possessions, snickering at my photographs, and, worst of all, swinging around the long wooden box where I kept about 1,500 slips of paper which were the beginning of my Kurdish-English dictionary. This box represented hours and hours of work. As the daughter continued to fool with it, I became more and more distracted and what might have been a small, insignificant annoyance grew all out of proportion.

Nana and I could not communicate in any language, so I turned to Mr. Ahmedi for aid. Was it right for Nana to have brought the daughter without asking permission? My assistant was noncommittal. How should he know? I asked him to convey my unhappiness in Azeri Turkish. But the daughter continued to run around disarranging my possessions as Nana explained through Mr. Ahmedi's translation that her daughter's husband had allowed his wife out just this once, as a special favor. She was really enjoying herself running around my apartment with her chador draped around the bodice of her low-cut blouse. Was I going to be the party-pooper and squelch this poor girl's one outing away from her husband and master?

For months I had put up with rude behavior directed at me by veiled Iranian women in the streets. Now, here was one in my own home, commenting loudly on my photographs, calling her mother over to look at the ones she considered particularly interesting, inspecting every artifact of my life, from my living-room furnishings to my underwear. But still I restrained myself.

I had not lived in Iran all this time for nothing. I again tried to get Mr. Ahmedi's advice on the proper course of action. Could I, should I, ask Nana to ask her daughter to leave? My assistant shrugged. A feeling of helpless frustration washed over me. Why couldn't I ever get the information I needed to function successfully in this society? Why, when a taxi driver from the airport tried to cheat us, did Shehrzad tell us to pay whatever he asked? *She* wouldn't have. Why did Mr. Ahmedi act as if it were perfectly normal to have your house vandalized in front of your eyes by your servant's daughter?

I instructed Mr. Ahmedi to ask Nana in the politest manner possible to send her daughter away. In a second, the small birdlike mother and the large-boned, greasy-haired daughter were in front of me, accusingly gesturing, squinting, and wagging their heads.

"She says that you have nothing to worry about. Her daughter will not go after your husband," Mr. Ahmedi translated for Nana.

I glanced in the direction of the spare bedroom, where Jared had removed himself. I hesitated for one more minute, hardly having believed my ears. Had Nana's daughter really suggested that I wanted her to leave because I was afraid she might seduce my husband? I told her to get out. This much Turkish I could handle.

Several weeks later I accepted an invitation that meant I would be out of town over an appointment I had scheduled with Mr. Ahmedi. That evening Jared and I drove to Kucheh Sunniha— the Street of the Sunnis—where I remembered his sister's house as being. When we got there nothing looked familiar to me in the murky glow of the streetlamp. Although I didn't want to stand by myself on this alien street we agreed that it would be better for Jared to go alone into a nearby teahouse to ask directions. Never, during all of my time in Iran, did I see a woman in a teahouse.

I waited uneasily until Jared came out, looking disconcerted.

"Did you ask them which kucheh this is?" I wanted to know.

"Yes. They said they were workers."

"What?"

"I asked them if this was Kucheh Sunniha and they replied, We are workers. We are workers."

As we stood in the middle of the dark shadowy kucheh pondering this reply I began to feel as if we were being watched. Before long a man appeared at my elbow, asking if he could help us. At his directions we got back into our car and drove up the paved main street a bit. But as soon as we had gone several blocks I was sure he was deliberately misleading us.

We turned around, went back to the teahouse, and parked in the same cul-de-sac. Then I led Jared through the winding mud kucheh past blank courtyard walls until we came to a door that somehow looked familiar. I rang and a tall thin man in baggy Kurdish trousers and eyeglasses answered.

"Is Dara Ahmedi here?" I asked in Kurdish.

The man looked at me with a blank expression on his face, as if I were a Martian speaking gibberish. I repeated Mr. Ahmedi's full name several times and the man jerked his head upward. No, there was no Dara—what a curious name—here. At this I gave up.

Just as Jared and I were turning the car around, Mr. Ahmedi came running up, out of breath.

"My brother said some people came and I thought it might be you."

"Your brother?" I repeated. "Was that your brother? He said he didn't know anyone named Dara Ahmedi."

"He couldn't understand what you were saying."

"He understood perfectly well. Margaret repeated your name at least four or five times," Jared said.

"What did you want?" my assistant asked.

I actually had to think for a moment. Suddenly our mission seemed ridiculous and trivial. Had we really come all this way, past all of these people who obviously thought two well-dressed foreigners had no business being in their neighborhood, just to save Mr. Ahmedi a walk to our house? I told him. Dara looked nonplussed. He too thought we had come where we did not belong. We exchanged cold goodbyes.

Even if I now knew better than to try to force my way into Mr. Ahmedi's life, there was still my dissertation research to worry about. I was beginning to realize that there were almost as many different Kurdish dialects as there were Kurds. Different tribes had different ways of speaking. Kurds who spent time in the city did not pronounce words the same as Kurds who stayed only in the village. Men spoke differently from women. Most of these differences were subtle, but I could not afford to ignore them.

I still did not know any ordinary Kurds. Haji Ismail, Aisha, Avdila, and the rest of their family were aristocrats. I had not been to a single village where I spent time with poor people who were neither tribal leaders nor schoolteachers like Mr. Sheikhzadeh. When Mr. Ahmedi told me his mother spoke no language but Kurdish I wanted to meet her. Every other Kurd I had met knew some Persian and, usually, some Turkish. In the villages the vast majority of the women were monolingual. They didn't go to school and they didn't go traveling or get drafted into the army.

When I told Mr. Ahmedi that I wanted to meet his mother just because she spoke only Kurdish, he heard me out, but he did not respond. When I proposed that we might all drive to his village for the day, he said, awkwardly, "But then you would have to eat there."

I wondered if the problem was that they didn't have enough food to entertain guests.

"We can bring our own sandwiches," I offered.

"Maybe it would be better, because you might not like what we have to eat there," he said thoughtfully.

It occurred to me that Dara had no idea how we might behave ourselves as guests. He had never seen me with Khadija and her friends. He didn't know of our trips to Dustan and Khoshkan. As far he was concerned we would no doubt behave as gauchely as he had seen me act with Nana's daughter or when we were trying to find his house, Although I had first thought maybe his reluctance was from shame at his poverty, I now realized that he was afraid of being shamed by us, the foreigners, in front of his family and neighbors. Who knew what embarrassing scene we might stage if we came to his village?

At last an opportunity presented itself. I had more and more work for Mr. Ahmedi, and, as the weeks went by, I did not know how long I would remain in Iran. I was anxious for him to finish. Mr. Ahmedi too seemed anxious to put in the time, because then he could earn more money. One day, in the middle of a large assignment, he announced regretfully that he couldn't go on because he had promised his mother that he would spend the next day, Friday, in her village. If he didn't catch the bus leaving downtown Rezaiyeh in an hour he would not be able to get there.

When I offered to take him in our car early the next morning he didn't reply right away, so I asked, "Will it be all right with your mother if we come?"

"Of course, if you bring me there, she will be happy," he said.

I took this grudging invitation for what it was worth. At last I would see this village and meet the source of all those folk tales I had been hearing and analyzing for so many months.

Mr. Ahmedi's village was peculiarly situated. It was not far from the city in miles, and most of the route lay over asphalt. But the last six kilometers could be reached only by traveling through a riverbed and winding up a steep grade to a high plateau. No bus went off the asphalt road toward the village, so, in relation to the city, it was, in fact, rather remote. In winter and spring the eroded dirt road was difficult even on foot because the river was full of water.

When at last we reached Bazdo, Mr. Ahmedi's mother, his two younger sisters, and a host of neighborhood children were waiting for us. Sulheya kissed her son and then led us to her dried-mud house after advising that we park our car inside the walls of her almond orchard to make sure the children didn't pry anything off it.

The house was small and crudely built, but scrupulously neat, much cleaner than Haji Ismail's far more lavish dwellings. Mr. Ahmedi immediately began preparing tea in a way that I had never seen before. At Haji Ismail's, tea had always been brought to us from some unseen part of the house by servants. But in Sulheya's house there were no unseen parts —just the one room with its stack of pillows and mattresses, its wooden trunk of clothes in the corner, its sewing machine, and some crudely penciled sketches which adorned the straw-flecked mud wall.

The tea was already made and waiting, kept hot in an antique Thermos which Mr. Ahmedi extracted from a shelf in the wall. Before he diluted it he filled one glass with boiling water from the samovar, poured the water into a concave saucer, and rolled the glass in it. Then he poured the still-steaming water out of the saucer and into the next glass on the tray. Working deftly, he managed to clean all of the glasses on the tray before the one glassful of water had cooled. Next he poured a bit of tea solution from the Thermos into each glass and filled the rest with water from the samovar. As tea was served Sulheya asked me why I was collecting Kurdish stories.

"To take to America. To put in a book," I said.

Sulheya nodded. As she sat she held a flat silver box of acrid Azerbaijani tobacco and cigarette papers in her hand, rolling cigarettes which she smoked nonstop. Occasionally she gave out great hacking coughs. Her voice was lower than any other Kurdish female voice I had heard. Dara had not lied when he said she knew not a word of Persian, because Jared soon gave up trying to communicate with her.

I knew that Sulheya was sizing us up. Her whole manner was radically different from Khadija's or Nasreen's or even Maryam's. Here was no effusiveness, no giggles, and not a hint of *ta'arof*. She was extremely polite, making sure we had cushions at our backs, serving us tea first and setting out huge piles of *qand* so we would not be in danger of having to taste anything bitter, but she was quite reserved, even laconic. As she watched me, she spoke at first almost in riddles. There was no doubt that this was Mr. Ahmedi's mother.

Very gradually, as the day wore on, the atmosphere in the room eased. Sulheya announced that she would recount the story "Tears of Gold." The room filled with listeners—her daughters, her daughter-in-law, who was breast-feeding her baby in the corner, and some neighbors. No one uttered a word as Sulheya's cracked voice began with the formula "When there was and there wasn't, there was nothing but God." Then she plunged into a long complex narrative about a girl named Monavar. "When Monavar cried, gold came out of her eyes, and when she laughed, she laughed flowers."

The story begins, "There once was a poor man with a wife who had a daughter," but Monavar's father soon fades out of the picture when his first wife dies and he remarries. With the arrival of a stepmother and stepsister, Monavar's luck disappears. The local prince had wanted to marry her because of her beauty, but the stepmother puts out Monavar's eyes, locks her up, and substitutes her own daughter in the wedding ceremony.

After years and years of imprisonment Monavar manages to escape with a peddler who walks over the root cellar where she is held. Because the stepmother needs Monavar's flowers and gold to keep up the stepdaughter's disguise she hires a witch to fly around on a cheese crock until she finds the girl in the peddler's house. The peddler, who has become "like a father" to Monavar, wanders for seven years before he finds her again—this time in a cave where the stepmother has hidden her. But Monavar is not reunited with her prince until their son arrives after many more years. This is the same son that was born to Monavar nine months after her stepmother locked her in the root cellar.

Monavar's son came as a shock to me, since premarital sex is forbidden among Kurds. But perhaps the vast class difference between Monavar and the prince can explain her acquiescence to his "impatience," as the storyteller put it. Premarital sex is not the only surprise in "Tears of Gold." When Monavar's long-lost son unknowingly finds his mother living in a hut in the middle of the forest with her "peddler-father," he falls for this lovely blind "girl" and decides to marry her.

Monavar is aware of his identity but goes along with the wedding as a way of approaching the prince to tell him what has happened to her. At the wedding Monavar recounts her story to the assembled guests. The prince, who admits to having had a vague suspicion that his consort was not Monavar, is overjoyed to find his long-lost fiancée. God smiles on them by restoring sight to Monavar (a difficult miracle, since her eyes were plucked right out of her head by the stepmother). Then the stepmother and her daughter are hitched up to a pair of horses, which drag them out of town smashing their bodies and scattering the parts over the countryside. Monavar "stays at home and lives very well, never again falling into the hands of oppressors."

At the end, Sulheya dedicated her telling of the story to me with the words "For the health and well-being of Khanim." The room stayed silent. I didn't know what the other listeners were thinking. They had undoubtedly heard the story many times before, but "Tears of Gold" was a revelation to me. For one thing the story had come from Sulheya's memory. Yet she had told of Monavar's adventures—really the adventures of her tormentors and saviors, since Monavar is essentially passive—as if she had been reading off the page.

At first some of the story seemed unbelievable to me. How had Monavar's ugly stepsister managed to impersonate her for several decades of marriage? But when I thought of how little Haji Ismail sees of some of his spouses it seemed conceivable. And how did the prince not recognize Monavar, his former lover, when he visited her in the forest during negotiations for her marriage to their son? Simple—she wore a veil.

The cruelty in the story was as matter-of-fact as Grimm's tales before they were edited for generations of protected American children, but I still cringed when the stepmother put out Monavar's eyes without a second thought. Cruelty was hardly unknown in modern-day Iran. When the stepdaughter has an ugly son at the same time as Monavar miraculously bears a golden-haired baby after nine months of cramped captivity, the stepmother just lets her own daughter's son go without food until he dies. Monavar's son lives because he is necessary for keeping up the pretense that the prince is married to the real Monavar. In the end the stepmother and stepdaughter get only what they deserve.

It was a long way back from "Tears of Gold" to Sulheya's little mud room. The smell of food was in the air as lunch was served by Sulheya's daughter-in-law. It was a meatless but elegant meal of stuffed grape leaves along with eggs and stewed tomatoes. Here, for the first time, we ate from a common tray with no dishes or silverware but bread to pick up the food. I ate very little, having suffered a bout with dysentery the night before. At this, Sulheya suddenly became solicitous.

"You don't like the food, Khanim," she said. "Tell me what you like so I can fix it for you the next time you come."

I protested that the food was delicious but I had been sick. She then turned to Dara, asking *him* what I liked. Back and forth we went as I assured her I loved *dolmas* when my stomach was feeling good. But she was convinced I was just being polite. I saw that the more Sulheya heard how I spoke Kurdish and that I knew how to express myself politely, the more her respect for me grew. Dara's eyes widened when he saw me turn over my tea glass on its side to signal I had had enough. He had never guessed that we had the vaguest idea about Kurdish etiquette.

Sulheya was at least as serious as her son. She treated him not as if he were a fifteen-year-old boy, but as her equal. A neighbor dropped by to ask him to help her settle up accounts at the tiny village store she ran, and Sulheya also took her son aside to ask his advice about something I couldn't hear.

"Your son is very, very smart," I remarked to Sulheya.

"Yes, I know. He was always smart, from the time that he was a baby," she said proudly. "All my children walked and talked by the time they were a year old. Kurds are very smart."

Sulheya ran her household and her life by herself, independently of any man. She was not like Maryam with Haji Ismail up the hill. Sulheya had six children, three of them grown. The elder girl was married off and living in another village. One son was in the army and the other worked in the city. Her tidy orchard and house, the tray of food she served, and the well-swept courtyard she kept all attested to that. She alone had raised the bride price for her son's wife. Her two younger daughters attended the village school. And there was Dara—her jewel. He had a scholarship to a high school in Rezaiyeh. He would go to college. He would care for her in old age.

In the course of the afternoon we discussed the source of all the stories Sulheya knew.

"My mother taught them to me and my brothers. They know many, many stories," she said. "My brothers are famous for their stories."

I was fascinated. "Tears of Gold" had whetted my appetite for more. Could we go to the village of her brothers? Sulheya looked excited by the thought.

"I have not been there in many years," she told me.

I pictured a protracted family reunion. "You know we will not be able to stay there a long time," I warned her. "Perhaps only a day or two."

"That will be very good for me," she replied. "If you have to go, then I will have to go. My mother will not expect me to stay."

I studied the flat tanned cheeks and the dark serious eyes. How, exactly, had Sulheya managed to keep from going back to her village to live with her brothers and mother when her husband had died? How had she managed to live? I was curious to see her in the context of her home village. Would she seem as forthright and independent there as she seemed here?

I decided we should return to Bazdo in a few days with Dara, pick up Sulheya, and continue on to Zhillah, the village of Sulheya's girlhood. On the way back to Rezaiyeh, Jared, Dara, and I all talked of the coming expedition. Without remarking on it, I felt Dara's attitude toward us had completely changed. We had not behaved in a ridiculous fashion. Sulheya had accepted us. In fact, Dara's mother had become almost loquacious as we were leaving.

"Please come and stay with me any time," she said, giving me a firm shake with her thin leathery hand.

Afterward Dara came to my house as punctually as before, working as hard and as conscientiously as ever. It wasn't as if we suddenly started having long heart-to-heart conversations. But, for the first time, there was understanding between us. I realized that his guardedness did not necessarily signal unfriendliness or contempt. He realized that foreigners could adapt to Kurdish ways and that my blunders did not necessarily mean I was a hopelessly insensitive person. I began to like him as much as I had first wanted to. He was an amazing boy, different from anyone else I ever met in Iran. Without mentioning it, without asking his permission, from that day in Bazdo, he ceased to be Mr. Ahmedi and became simply Dara.

Sulheyya

CHAPTER 17

JOURNEY TO THE SOURCE AND FINALLY A WEDDING

Zhillah was the first Kurdish village I located on my new map. Up until then I had not been aware that there were such maps. All the maps we had been able to buy made Iran look like a nation of far-flung cities with nothing in between. But this map, drawn by the British army in the 1940s, was covered with names of villages and mountains and small seasonal rivers. Not only was it not for sale to the general public, we were told by the weapons experts from the American Army that it was illegal except for military use.

After Dara got over his surprise that we had this map, the three of us pored over it, trying to find the fastest, shortest route to Zhillah. We saw a thin line running due west over the mountains from Bazdo. The only problem was that Dara had never been on this route. Perhaps the line on the map was some defunct mule track. Dara made inquiries but could find out nothing definite. No one who wanted to go from Bazdo to Zhillah owned a car. They were obliged to take the bus, which ran only on the asphalt route going north toward the city of Shapur, where they could get another bus that led south and west along the graded road into the plain of Soma.

By the morning of our expedition I had convinced Jared we should try the route across the mountains. To me a line on a map signaled a road, and the road over the mountains was less than a third the distance of the asphalted and graded gravel route. But two hours after we had picked up Sulheya in Bazdo I was forced to admit that the line was not a road.

We had covered only four kilometers, and that was with all of the passengers—Sulheya, Dara, Dara's small sister, and me—walking as Jared tried to take the Citroen over the bumps and gashes in what was left of a road. Although I had been the one to press for taking this shortcut, I was the first one who wanted to quit. The Kurds were up for anything—it was not their car—and Jared was enjoying the challenge of driving over a mule track. When he disappeared around one blind turn the car tipped so far to the drop-off side of the track that I was sure I was going to find him at the bottom of the ravine on the other side. But just around the corner, the road simply stopped, so I didn't have to argue anymore. We had to turn back.

What had begun as an early start grew into an all-morning expedition as the sun rose high and hot in the sky. Because the road was so narrow and tilted there was no room to drive the car around. We had to turn it by hand, lifting the rear end off the ground and pointing the front end in the opposite direction. We made much better time downhill to the road to Shapur, although everyone but Jared still had to walk most of the way back to Bazdo.

The turnoff to the graded road that crossed the plateau to the west of the lake came just before the asphalt road reached Shapur. This dirt road took us over the barest, poorest land we had yet seen in Azerbaijan, although by this time our eyes were so accustomed to the unremitting dust of the Kurdish landscape that when we came to the merest trickle of a waterfall we thought we had reached Niagara. I got out and took half a dozen pictures. Not until I was back in the United States did these pictures strike me as excessive.

Past the waterfall was a dried-up riverbed and gray-green scrub growing where it could on the eroded land. A surprising number of sheep were out nibbling this dry vegetation. We passed village after village on land which which made Mergawar and Tergawar look like gardens of Eden. But to Sulheya, the whole place was bathed in a golden glow of memory.

Excitedly she pointed out first one village and then another by name. Here lived a friend, there lived a cousin, and in another was a grown daughter she had not seen in years. I could hardly believe that we were only ten miles, over the mountains, from her present home. The dividing line between Sulheya's present and past was so final that the villages of her childhood and wifehood might have been in two different countries.

At last we left the road and climbed up a gradual slope to a village set on a loaf-shaped mound. Here we disembarked under the windows of a large two-story mud house. When I got out of the car I realized again that green was only relative. The plain we had traversed was lush compared with this village. Here there was no gray-green scrub, just bare, bare dirt with not one blade of vegetation.

Sulheya and Dara led us eagerly up the stairs of the two-story house, past the animals stabled on the ground floor to the large room above where we met Musa, Sulheya's eldest brother, the owner of the house and our host.

As soon as we entered, the room quickly filled to capacity, adult males and females together lining the walls, with children massed at the doorway, everyone craning and peering to see the foreigners. Sulheya was being greeted by her mother, who, with her toothless jaw and leathery skin, looked ancient. The uncles, Sulheya's brothers, were smiling and trying to talk to us, while everyone else was simply staring. At last the commotion at the door became too much for our hosts. Someone went up to the crowd of ragged children and shooed them away. They went much faster than I expected, and one of the uncles came back and reported that he had told them that I was a new doctor, come to give them all shots.

A group of the most enterprising children who had been kicked out of the doorway went down and around to the roof of a neighboring house that faced toward one of the two windows of the room we were in and boldly resumed staring at us. They were standing stock-still, perfect for a photograph. So I grabbed my camera and aimed it at them. They fled in terror.

All the people in the room laughed.

"If you had only told them it was a camera and not a gun, they wouldn't have run away," explained one woman.

I sat back, feeling strange. What kind of village was this, where doctors were bogeymen and children expected strangers to aim guns at them?

One thing was sure; this was not Dustan. Almost as many women as men sat in this long reception room. Jared's presence did not seem to make the slightest difference. No one put her scarf over her mouth, and all of the women talked as loudly and as unselfconsciously as the men. Tea was made not by a servant, but by a younger boy of the family. I wondered uneasily about our car. Just as we were leaving it I had noticed a horde of village children and goats descending on it, the children no doubt trying to remove all interesting appurtenances that had not been welded on, the goats seeking shade.

Jared went over to the window to check and communicated in alarm that it looked as if our car might be stripped in an hour or so. We asked our hosts to tell the children to go away, but they looked at us doubtfully. What did we expect? Since there were no cars in Zhillah, the courtyard door was not wide enough for us to drive through, Our car had to remain in the public domain. To placate us, our hosts yelled down at the children, but there was really no way to keep them away. This time we were in the middle of a village among ordinary people instead of high on a hill with the khans.

But Sulheya had my interests at heart, and as soon as she had caught up with the news and gossip she began mentioning over and over how I had come to collect stories to take to America. After a lunch of rice pilaf with a few bits of gristly meat scattered in for flavor, Sulheya organized a storytelling session, and my microphone passed from one tanned hand to another as the tape filled with long fairy tales like "Tears of Gold."

A spell fell over the room. Everyone was listening intently to the stories, forgetting about us, the foreigners, perhaps even about the bare land and hot sun outside. For the time being there were only princesses, dragons, witches, and knights. I couldn't believe how easily my tape was filling up, and I looked over at Sulheya gratefully. She smiled. But the tape and the stories could not go on forever, and soon someone was asking, "Is it true Americans make a lot of money?"

We liked this question better than "How much money do you make?" Perhaps this way of asking was more appropriate in Zhillah, where there wasn't much of a money economy. Our current hosts locked up their tiny supply of rice in a closet as if it were jewelry. They obviously didn't eat meat. Yogurt from sheep's milk and bread made from government wheat formed their staple dict. There was not a fat person in the room.

"You know workers in America can make more than university professors," Jared volunteered in answer to their question. A hush fell. Now the foreigners were about to tell some stories of their own.

"How is that possible?" asked one bold man.

"Well," replied Jared. "No one *gave* them more. The workers in factories just demanded more. They went on *strike*."

At this our audience looked at each other uneasily. "Some workers in Rezaiyeh have gone on strike," said someone else.

"For how long?" asked Jared.

"Maybe a day, two days."

"That's not long enough."

"But it's dangerous. It's too dangerous," they said, looking hard at Jared as if he might have the answer they lacked.

"It was dangerous in America too. People were killed," Jared commented.

Then no one said anything. They looked at each other and us. I raised my eyebrows at Jared. Just a report of this one conversation would be enough to get us thrown out of Iran. But the discussion went no further. It was obvious that these villagers with their dirt-streaked faces wanted to hear more, but they were afraid.

Now the room, which had been dark when we arrived in the shadowless sun of noon, was growing darker. I began to wonder again about the state of our car. One woman named Khiyal had taken up my microphone and was telling about how she was bringing a bride for her son. My ears pricked up at the mention of a wedding, but then I forgot about it. It was time to go. The drive that morning had been exhausting, and the road would be impossible in the dark.

Downstairs, near our car, a strange thing happened. It seemed as if the entire village had gathered to say goodbye. It was as if we had spent the last five months in Zhillah instead of the last five hours. The crowd clamored for a photograph, so I took one which showed young boys lined up in front, saluting at the camera. In the background was the sun setting over the barren hills, outlining the pointed roofs of the manure-storage huts.

With such a crowd it was impossible to get into the car at once. While Sulheya was saying goodbye to her relatives, everyone started asking us why we didn't stay.

I heard Khiyal's voice. "Don't you want to come to my wedding?"

I turned to her, indecision and eagerness, written on my face. Several people sensed that the wedding had caught my interest.

"Yes, the wedding, the wedding," they repeated. Surely the foreign woman didn't want to miss the wedding. They were right. But I looked around at the bareness and the strange sunburned faces surrounding me and I hesitated.

"Stay, stay. You must stay," said Shero, one of Sulheya's brothers. My brain whirled with excitement and dread. If the truth were known, all I wanted to do was get out of Zhillah. But a Kurdish wedding? If only it had been in Haji Ismail's village, where both we and our car could be assured of safety.

Even now as I stood, trying to make up my mind, there were two women at my elbow fingering my hair.

"Can she really be a woman?" I heard the one woman ask the other.

"See her hair and her skin. She must be a girl."

I began talking to Jared over the heads of the crowd. Should we turn around and go upstairs again to await this wedding?

"You keep saying you want to see a Kurdish wedding," Jared said, putting the decision off on me.

I turned to Sulheya. "When will the wedding begin?"

She turned to her brothers. "Perhaps tonight. Perhaps the day after. Maybe even the day after that," she relayed back.

The uncertainty made me uneasy. Why didn't they know when the wedding would happen? Maybe they were making the whole thing up just to lure me into staying. I knew this was not Turkey, yet the feelings I had about Zhillah reminded me of Yuksekova. To these remote villagers I was irrevocably "other." I wanted to go, but I didn't want to miss a chance to see a Kurdish wedding.

"We can come back," Sulheya told me. "I don't think the wedding is going to start right away."

With the thought of a respite away from the village, I made my decision. We would return. But it would be in a couple of days, after I had had some good food and some sleep and a chance to don my Kurdish clothes. Perhaps if I dressed like a Kurd the people of Zhillah wouldn't stare at me so much.

When we met two days later near the bazaar in Rezaiyeh. Sulheya and Dara's little sister Finaz were in high spirits. They had enjoyed their vacation away from Bazdo, spending most of their time soaking in the salt and sulfur mud flats near the lake. That morning Khadija had plaited my hair into fourteen tiny braids and woven a ribbon through them. Dara and Sulheya seemed awed by the transformation effected by Kurdish clothes and hairstyle. Dara, especially, looked at me as if he had never seen me before. We took yet another route to Zhillah, which got us there in less than two hours, and when we arrived a large crowd gathered again.

We were welcomed as old friends, but the answer to my immediate question was: No, the wedding had not started yet. When would it start? Soon, right away, coming up, they assured me. I still could not understand why they didn't know when their own wedding would be.

Throughout the afternoon, no matter how much I tried to relax I kept wondering when the wedding would begin. There was tea and an afternoon dinner and a walk to Shero's storage pond next to the grove of trees he had planted in a gully at a distance from the village proper. Since Musa owned the pond and grove of birches out past the other side of the village, I realized that Sulheya's two brothers must be among the richest men in town. But their clothes were threadbare, their teeth sparse, their bodies so thin. If these were the khans, how did the rest live?

Toward the evening I was still wondering about the wedding when Jared looked out the window of the large second-story room and saw a group of four men dancing arm in arm through the mud streets of Zhillah. Our hosts told us that this was the ritual invitation for the villagers to come to the festivities. A little while later two odd-looking men appeared in the doorway of the long reception room where we had been spending the day. Musa, our host, immediately set up metal folding chairs for them. Both men were wearing pale-green Western-style suits. From the time they entered the room until the time that they left, neither man would take his eyes off me.

I felt their eyes burning into the shadowy corner where I sat next to Sulheya. For some reason, Sulheya seized this opportunity to rearrange my headdress. Without consulting me, she simply took off my orange scarf so that my hair was entirely uncovered. This display fascinated the men, and I heard one remark to the other across the room, "Why doesn't she take off all her clothes?"

Sulheya continued fussing with my scarf, adding a black scarf of her own so that now I had two. She acted as if she hadn't heard the man's remark, but I could not get it out of my mind. At night Zhillah was even spookier than in the day, and I didn't like these men sitting there ogling me. If these were our hosts for the wedding I wondered if I really wanted to go after all. I could only hope that because they lived in the city of Shapur, not in the village, their behavior would not be typical of male behavior in Zhillah.

At ten o'clock everyone finally stood up and walked over to the courtyard of Khiyal's house. As we came through the opening in the mud wall, we saw a row of folding chairs set up toward one end of a dense knot of about forty excited wedding guests sitting on the bare ground. As we were shown to the chairs, the crowd of people sitting on the ground stared up at us. It was as if we were on stage. There were no spotlights, but two flickering, buzzing lanterns added to the light from the moon to make us and everyone around us eerily visible.

Up in front of the crowd two *deng bezhes*, both wearing heavy wool winter hats, were taking turns singing, their hands cupped over one cheek and ear. The beat was heavy and unvarying. A few men and women stood up to dance, and my eye was caught by three magnificently dressed girls— probably the groom's sisters— clothed in brocade with broad metallic belts and gold nose studs.

I wanted to just sit and slowly take in this fantastic scene—the moon, the dried mud, the gold nose studs, the singers. But that was not possible. The attention should have been on the dancers and singers and especially on the groom's family. Instead it was on us. Little children could not keep their hands off us. One man with a big stick kept coming over and banging the heads of the worst offenders. But as soon as they were kicked out, others took their places.

Shero and Dara pulled Jared up to join the line dance, but I stayed where I was next to Sulheya. I didn't want to get up and dance in front of this crowd, nor did I want to get close to the two men in pale-green suits. They were also dancing, hand-rolled cigarettes held loosely in their mouths, blissful expressions on their faces.

When Jared came back from dancing he informed me that they were smoking hashish. That seemed to explain their weird behavior, but I could hardly believe they were smoking dope. In Rezaiyeh, Kurds had assured us that no Kurd ever touched drugs even if they did occasionally smuggle them. "Only for *ajam*," Mr. Khalili had remarked contemptuously. I wondered if the two green-suited men were the only ones getting high in Zhillah that night. We had already heard that many people in this village had spent time in prison for smuggling. The proximity to the border and poverty made it likely.

The staring and the dancing seemed to go on for hours. I blinked and squinted with fatigue. "This is very *ajeeb*," I commented to Dara, who had sat down again. Ajeeb can mean "strange" with the added sense of "wonderful" or it can mean just plain strange. Dara selected the first meaning.

He smiled. "You mean the dancers are very beautiful." I frowned. Why were Dara and I always on different planets?

I tried to explain. "Everyone is staring at me so much. That's why it's *ajeeb*."

"Of course. The people here are not used to seeing a foreign woman," he said. "Especially not a foreign woman in Kurdish dress."

I looked at Dara, exasperated. It might be unusual to him that I was in Kurdish clothes, but suppose I had been sitting there in jeans where anyone could see the outline of my thighs and crotch or in a dress which exposed my legs? Maybe Dara had lived in Rezaiyeh so long that Kurdish dress no longer looked normal to him.

Sulheya, who was a lot more tuned in to my discomfort than her son was, suggested that I was tired and we should leave. I nodded gratefully, and we soon filed slowly out of the courtyard after thanking our hosts. We were invited to return for the next day's activities, when the bride would actually be brought to the house.

Back in Musa's courtyard, the immediate problem was where we should sleep. Jared and I had discussed this at length before setting out for Zhillah. Our idea had been to sleep on the roof, using the sleeping bag we had brought with us in the car. But Sulheya had spotted the bedding earlier that morning as soon as she got into our car.

"My mother's house is very clean," she said pointedly. "As clean as mine. There are no bedbugs."

Bedbugs were precisely what I was worried about, although I would not have mentioned them by name. When Sulheya said that her mother's house was as clean as her own I was impressed, because Sulheya was the most meticulous housekeeper that we ever met in Kurdistan. But Zhillah was not up to Sulheya's standards.

Shero's little daughter, who was about the age of her cousin Finaz, had a jumble of snarled hair that looked gray from the accumulation of dust and dirt. Finaz had her long bangs and two thick braids combed out daily. She always wore clean clothes. It was not a matter of money, but of pride. Both Dara and Sulheya were long on pride. But even if the women of Zhillah had been scrupulous housekeepers it would have been difficult for them to get rid of bedbugs. Zhillah had more sheep than Bazdo. The floorboards of the big sitting room where Musa and his family wanted us to sleep had more than ample space between them for thousands of sheep bugs to crawl through from the stable below.

We tried to insist on sleeping on the roof, but our hosts were adamant. We had to take the best room. This room ordinarily slept at least a dozen people at night, but our hosts emphasized that we would be alone.

"Just like a bride and groom," Sulheya pointed out.

After we were led back up the stairs by Sulheya and her sister-in-law, brightly colored bedding was unrolled and spread invitingly on the floor. The women handed us one of the kerosene lamps, and we were left alone to enjoy the luxury of this huge space all to ourselves. As soon as the lights went out the bugs started biting. I was sleeping in my entire Kurdish outfit, long pointed sleeve endings wrapped tightly around my wrists and the elastic at the end of my bloomers pulled down over my socks. I had even kept my scarf tied around my head. But the bugs managed to burrow in, and after fifteen minutes I was sure I wouldn't sleep five minutes that night.

"We have to get the sleeping bag," I whispered to Jared, who was dropping off to sleep. For some reason, the bugs seemed to ignore him.

I turned on the flashlight we had brought with us and showed Jared the little black bugs. Reluctantly he agreed to go out. But when he came back he was empty-handed.

"They are all sleeping in the courtyard because we took their room," he explained.

Hours later in a chill gray dawn I awoke from a sleep permeated with the feeling of insects crawling over my body. About an hour after that a breakfast of strong tea and flat whole-wheat bread was served. Toward midmorning we went for another walk, this time to Shero's pond.

Shero was unlike other Kurds we met in Zhillah or anywhere else in Kurdistan. He was Sulheya's favorite brother. Like Sulheya he had a long face with high color. But where Sulheya had black eyes, Shero's were green. While Sulheya was serious, Shero acted lighthearted. Life for Kurds was a struggle. For some it was the fight for human rights. For others, like the inhabitants of Zhillah, it was the battle to survive. But Shero did not have an air of struggle about him. He seemed to enjoy life.

In Kurdistan people do not ordinarily sing and dance. I constantly asked people to teach me songs, and almost everyone refused. Songs, they made me understand, were the province of professionals—the *deng bezhes*—who sing at weddings. Shero, with his gravelly cigarette-scorched voice, was hardly a *deng bezh*. Yet he loved to sing and sang many songs for me while I was in Zhillah. He also enjoyed dancing. Shero delighted in the fact that I wanted to learn new words in Kurdish. As we followed in his jaunty steps along the way to his tree grove he picked the most unlikely thistles and puffballs off the ground and told me their names.

When we arrived in the wood, Shero and the young boy who had served the tea took turns singing the traditional series of wedding songs for my tape recorder. Sulheya held the microphone for her brother until one verse when her eyes filled with tears and she got up and went off by herself. The recording went on, and eventually Sulheya came back.

Later she explained, "The part where they come to take the bride from her village reminded me of my own wedding. It was a sad time."

It was disconcerting to see Sulheya cry. She wasn't exactly tough; she was too sympathetic for that. But I imagined that she had put most of her feelings behind her. How else could she have survived the luck that made her an old man's wife and left her a widow with six children? I wondered that she had cried leaving Zhillah. Bazdo was far pleasanter. But, of course, she could not have known that. Like a proper bride, she had seen neither her future husband nor her future home.

After the singing, Shero decided to teach Jared to dance. The men lined up in the hot sun away from the trees, held hands, swung their arms, and strutted, skipped, and squatted in the fast dance that is done by Kurdish men. Shero waved a handkerchief and the boy sang. When this was exhausted as a diversion we returned to the village.

Back in the large crowded room, lack of sleep, bug bites, and general apprehension started to catch up with me. Again we were sitting, sitting, sitting. Endless rounds of tea were served. Periodically I asked about the remainder of the wedding celebration. When was the bride going to be fetched? It was a while before 1 understood that she was already in the village. This bride had run away from her father two months ago and come to Zhillah alone with her husband-to-be because her father wanted a higher bride price than anyone was willing to pay.

"Does that mean there will be no bride price?" I asked Sulheya.

"No," she answered. "The groom must pay something or else there would be a war between the two families."

Trying to get the show on the road, I asked if the bride would be brought by horse from the house where she was staying in the village. Horses were the traditional means of bringing a bride, although rural taxis had generally replaced them,

The villagers looked at each other. Then someone asked if they could use our shiny pale-violet Citroen. Before I could answer, Dara suggested that they use a horse. He knew I wanted to take photographs. And understood right away that a horse would be more picturesque. But Dara's plea was ignored. In Zhillah everyone except Sulheya treated Dara exactly as if he were a fifteen-year-old boy.

The conversation drifted away from the wedding. The room had darkened. I glanced toward the window. The sky had clouded over, and it was starting to rain. The huge drops of water seemed to presage a summer cloudburst. I could just imagine what would happen if it didn't let up soon. All the gulches we had crossed would turn into rushing rivers.

I began questioning our hosts about the after effects of a downpour. Yes, the road sometimes became impassable, they confirmed.

At this news I stood up, walked over to Jared, and said, in English, "I'm sick of waiting for this wedding. We're going to be stuck here when the roads wash out."

Jared gazed back with a horrified expression. I almost never spoke English to him in front of Kurds, but used Persian so we could be understood.

"What are you doing?" he whispered. "Go back and sit down."

At this unsympathetic response I panicked. Every square inch of my skin itched. Rain was coming down harder and faster. The synthetic materials of my voluminous clothing were sticky with sweat, and the rest of the people in the room were looking at me more curiously than ever as I stood near Jared speaking frantically in a foreign language.

I didn't think I could stand another moment in Zhillah. If Jared wouldn't leave, *I* would leave. I wasn't going to be trapped waiting for a wedding that would never take place. With these thoughts I stalked out of the room, down the stairs, and outside into the pouring rain. There I unlocked the car door, swung it open over the horns of a goat, and locked myself in. Then I began to sob. It was my first solitary moment in thirty-six hours. I had not even been able to urinate alone in Zhillah. Because there were no outhouses in the village Sulheya had accompanied me each time and stood guard.

A minute later Jared appeared at the window of the car, yelling in at me through the rain. I stared at him angrily, and then, suddenly, Sulheya was standing there getting drenched, her face full of concern. I opened the door for her.

"What's the matter?" she asked.

With my tear-stained face I felt ridiculous. "Jared and I are having an argument," I explained lamely.

"Come back inside, Margaret," she said gently. "You can't drive in this rain."

Slowly I got out of the car and back into the rain. Sulheya took my hand and led me into the house and up the stairs. I felt better for my cry and moment of solitude, but I was afraid to face the people upstairs. What would they think? Everyone would know that I had been crying.

But when I looked at the people in the room—Musa and his wife, Shero, Dara, all the uncles and cousins—they seemed different. Instead of acting shocked or annoyed, as I had expected, they looked worried and a lot less alien than they had seemed to me before. Perhaps I too looked less alien to them. We smiled at one another.

Then Musa spoke. "You have to wait until the rain is over before you drive anywhere. When it's like this, driving is dangerous."

A half hour later the rain stopped and the wedding commenced. First Sulheya and I went into a tiny windowless hut where all the women had gathered, their skirts rustling and smashing against one another as one by one they threw presents onto a flat basket set on the floor in the center of the room. Most of the gifts were bars of soap and scarves, but there were also dresses and shoes from the groom's kinswomen.

Then the women filed out of the little room. The villagers formed a circle and began the ritual dance in step with the rhythm of the *deng bezh*. Jared and I, along with Sulheya, Shero, and two of the groom's sisters, squeezed into our car for the 200-meter trip to the house where the bride was staying. The rest of the guests climbed aboard a flat trailer pulled by the only tractor in town.

A few minutes later we arrived at a house where Jared and I were ushered in to drink tea. The wedding guests formed a circle and danced around our car until the bride was led by her mother-in-law out of a room at the side of the courtyard. An orange scarf was draped all around her face so that all we could see of her was her red satin dress and two stylish black-and-white high-button shoes peeping out from under the ruffle at her hem.

At this point ten people tried to climb into our tiny Citroen. There was a slight scuffle as Sulheya and Shero refused to give up their places to the groom's party. Only the bride rode with us. Sulheya pulled up her veil to show me her face, but all I glimpsed were two black eyes before the bride shrank back and the veil dropped into place again.

We drove around for a little while, at Shero's instruction, in order to make believe we were really fetching the bride from somewhere far away. Then we returned to the groom's house, where the groom and his friends were waiting on the roof to drop a large cone of sugar on the bride's head before she crossed the threshold. The sugar hit her head with a thud, ensuring that she would be a sweet wife and, no doubt, giving her a terrific headache. She would spend the remainder of the evening sitting in the little windowless room with her presents while the party went on without her.

Although the bride had been fetched and the sun would soon set, I was no longer desperate to leave Zhillah. There was another reason for going

that had nothing to do with my former fears. As long as we stayed this would not be a wedding, but the spectacle of two foreigners watching a wedding.

While Shero and Sulheya had provided a running commentary on Kurdish customs, the rest of the villagers could not take their eyes off us. The groom's sisters had not worn their finery so that everyone could stare at a couple of outsiders. It was time to give the wedding back to Khiyal's in-laws.

When we turned to our hosts to say goodbye, the wedding stopped completely and didn't start up again until we drove away. As we drove back over the plain, Finaz fell asleep and everyone seemed to be off in some private space. At Bazdo, Finaz, Sulheya, and Dara got out. Jared and I drove back to Rezaiyeh.

As we headed east toward the lake, the setting sun turned the wheat fields around us to burnished gold. In the near distance was the turquoise of the lake, several shades more intense than the pale blue of the sky. Behind us the village lay in shadow. As we came into the city at dusk the shops were just turning on their lights. We sped past the cinema and the chrome-framed plate-glass windows of the boutiques, past the trees lining the boulevards and the fountains next to the statues set in lush green circles of grass. I took it all in with the eyes of a villager. How modern and colorful it seemed after the brown uniformity of Zhillah. Was it possible we were still in the same year, the same day?

What did the people of Zhillah feel when they left their village and came to cities like Shapur and Rezaiyeh? Did they hate the Turks for getting control of these oases? Did they accept the difference as a difference that was God-given? Or did it jolt them as it did me?

I spent a lot of time thinking about Zhillah, about how the people there had acted. I could not decide if there had been anything real to fear. Few Tehranis or even Rezaiyeh urbanites would be comfortable in Zhillah. It wasn't that we were non-Iranian but that we were from the city and the middle class. The words of the workers on the street of the Sunnis echoed in my mind. "We are workers. We are workers."

Zhillah was my taste of deeper Kurdistan. Although Dustan, Khoshkan, and Mawana are on far richer land than Zhillah, most people in these villages do not live like the khans we visited there. They do not have tractors, Land Rovers, and electric generators like Haji Ismail's. They do not own the land on which they work or control the water supply needed for growing crops. Most Kurdish villagers are even poorer than Shero or

Musa. In Dustan, Khoshkan, or Mawana as in Zhillah they would have enjoyed dismantling our car, but our hosts effectively prevented them.

Zhillah represented Kurdistan stripped of its illusions. There I saw nothing but awful bare land, decrepit mud dwellings, and the kind of desperation that takes horses over the border to Turkey for anything to sell in Iran's inflated marketplace. Back in comfortable Rezaiyeh, listening to the stories I had collected, I realized that if the people in Zhillah were dirt-poor in the harshest sense, they were rich in another.

In the evening by the light of the kerosene lamp or in the long dark days of winter the villagers had spun these tales, traded and embroidered them like the richest tapestries. It took several weeks of working with Dara before I understood all the complicated plots and dialogue, but when I did, I wished I could go back to Zhillah and look again. I wanted to see better where those dragons and bold princesses and witches came from. For ribaldry, exaggeration, and golden fancy the stories I collected are amazing. They forced me to see those half-starved men in a new light—as human beings triumphing over a hostile environment, not with the fertilizer or farm equipment they couldn't afford, but with their imaginations.

CHAPTER 18

AN INLAND SEA

SAVAK evidently spent some time poring over a mysterious photograph which a friend in the United States sent us. When we received the already opened package several weeks after its arrival in town, we studied it carefully, trying to figure out what it was that the secret police had been so interested in. Then Jared spotted the dark-blue sea-horse shape in the upper right corner. After that the blotches of white in the dark creases that looked like veins made sense as we recognized the snow-covered foothills and peaks of the Zagros in winter. It was a satellite photograph of Kurdistan. The dark-blue sea horse was the great inland sea of Rezaiyeh (now Urmia), which floats mysteriously in the northwest corner of the landmass known as Iran.

Once upon a time Iran had more than one inland salt sea, but now these

seas are deserts and Lake Rezaiyeh itself, although still vast, is slowly drying up. Despite its deadly high salt content, in a place as water-starved as Iran, the lake was considered a bountiful sea. Kurds called the area between the city and the lake *ajamistan*, land of the *ajam*, and over the centuries, they have made more than one attempt to seize it.

Some of the most fertile land in West Azerbaijan lies near the lake. It was planted in fruit orchards and vineyards. Now as then the land remained in the hands of non-Kurds—Turks as well as some Armenians and Assyrians. The Kurds, living in their mountains, were limited to a yearly pilgrimage, if they could afford it. They loved soaking in the salty water and sulfurous mud, both of which were considered to have health benefits

In the hot summer months the lake turned into a tourist destination: Turks and Kurds, Christians and Muslims, all bathed in close proximity. The only other place with this degree of mingling was the bazaar. But in the bazaar everyone was veiled or otherwise well covered. In all of West Azerbaijan there was no place like the lake. Here was Iran at its most naked.

We loved driving out to the shore and walking on the hills to pick poppies or going out on the pier to watch the arrival of the ancient ferry, the *Noah*, on its voyage from Tabriz. In the Iranian month of Teer the road from the city to the lake—about ten kilometers—became thronged with buses, taxis, and private cars. Corpses of unlucky dogs and sheep littered the asphalt highway that passed the milk and wine factories and the Rezaiyeh prison.

We still managed to swim in peace by going farther away. We would drive past the town public beach, the Boy Scouts' beach, and the exclusive officers' club until we were out next to the rocks where there was no sand and no other bathers. Several times when I came here with Khadija, she had complained that it was no fun to wade in over the rocks.

Since the Kurds were not real swimmers, the surface of the shore was more important to them than it was to me. But the real reason for Khadija's and later Nasreen's objections lay elsewhere. I did not learn where until I finally spent an unforgettable day on the town beach.

The expedition began at the house where Aisha and Avdila were storing some of their furniture in the city. It was now late July, high season at the lake, and the Kurds who could afford it were coming down from the mountains for some serious bathing. Aisha and Avdila, who visited the city more often than most Kurds, traveled in style.

When we reached the place of our rendezvous we found no less than half a dozen servants assisting in loading up the big Land Rover. There were several huge metal pots wrapped in towels, a samovar, a china teapot, and tiny tea glasses and saucers as well as bags of other unknown foodstuffs and utensils. Besides the servants there were six people—Aisha, Avdila, Khadija, Jared, myself, and Nasreen, who had been allowed by Haji Ismail to leave Dustan for this special occasion.

When we reached the lake there was a polite pause as Jared and I were asked where we would like to swim. Having a premonition of what the public beach would be like, I suggested the secluded spot where we usually went. This seemed to appeal to Sheikh Avdila, but there were expressions of dismay from my friends.

"That place Margaret wants to go to is terrible," said Nasreen.

Khadija agreed. So we drove through the gates of the public beach as some seedy-looking Turks approached. Sheikh Avdila negotiated with them for three cabanas, if they could be called that. They were the crudest sort of shelters, constructed from sticks and burlap with dirty cardboard floors. After we settled down in our "cabanas"—the servants in one, the other women in the second, and Jared and the sheikh in the third—the decision was made to proceed toward the water. The women went in one direction and Jared and the sheikh went off in another. Most of the servants stayed where they were to prepare lunch.

When we reached a spot deemed appropriate by Aisha, the women all disrobed down to the thin cotton or nylon slips they wore under the *fistan* and *kiras*. Since I had worn my tank suit under a long dress I was finished undressing before they were. As I stood waiting I noticed that there was a considerable flow of fully dressed male traffic strolling up and down the beach even though it was still morning and the offices in town were not yet closed for the day.

At last the women walked into the water at a stately pace, gradually submerging themselves. I could see that the slips, once wet, were much more revealing than my tank suit. However, this did not seem incongruous to anyone but me. None of these Kurdish women would have considered wearing a bathing suit, called *may-oh* in Persian, from the French *maillot*. As the name indicated it was not a native item. The majority of women I saw at the lake did not wear them.

As we were all floating and soaking in the shallow water, a couple of young dark-haired Turkish-speaking men in black trunks swam near us. I looked at them worriedly, wondering how the women would react to their presence.

To my shock, Nasreen began laughing and talking with them, seemingly encouraging the men to stay near us. Khadija also acted very friendly. Even prim Aisha, who had to be forced to eat in the same room as my husband, did not seem bothered by the proximity. It was hard for me to believe that these women who ordinarily went veiled on the streets of Rezaiyeh were now lounging about the lake in revealing slips as Turkish men—total strangers—swam near them.

I turned and began swimming farther out. The women stayed where they were, calling me to come back. The water was dangerous; I would surely drown. Despite the salt content of the lake, which floats the human body like a cork, my friends were terrified of drowning. They walked easily alongside mountain ravines that made me shudder, but water was not their element. The men began swimming after me. I was quite sure that their motive was not fear for my safety. It was all very well to flirt with a bevy of Kurdish women, but I was the real thing—a Westerner in her sexy *maillot*.

I looked across the water for Jared and swam hurriedly in his direction. Gradually the men were left behind. When I reached Jared I voiced my complaints. Not only was this beach filled with men whose sole purpose seemed to be to get an eyeful of female flesh—an understandable goal, perhaps, after the chadors of the street—but the water was also filthy. It was necessary to swim quite far out to get away from the garbage that had been dumped near the shore. The rocks where we usually went had no trash on them.

When I came out of the water I raced down the beach to the place where I had left my dress. I knew that running made me more conspicuous, but I was willing to do anything to shorten the time that my body was visible in the tank suit. The male eyes on my skin made me so nervous that I barely noticed all the exposed flesh of the women along the shore. Only later when I had relaxed more and accepted the staring as inevitable did I get a chance to really take in the bare breasts hanging out of chadors and the soaked slips that clearly revealed the surfaces and contours of these normally hidden female bodies.

Laughing excitedly, the Kurdish women walked slowly back to the cabanas. When we arrived at the burlap-and-cardboard shelters they hurried inside, away from Jared's eyes. But the proximity of men on the beach and Nasreen's flirting had made a mockery of this chaste separation. It was hard for me, as a Westerner, to understand how Haji Ismail's daughters and daughter-in-law could justify behaving like this after the fuss they made over being in the company of men anywhere else.

After a huge heavy dinner followed by steaming glasses of tea, we drowsed, and then it was time to brave the shore again. By now, in the middle of the afternoon, the activity on the beach was peaking. Crowds of men were milling back and forth to stare blatantly, while old and young women alike, some with menfolk, some alone, hung out on the edges of the shore and in the shallow water.

Hardly any swimmers went out over their heads, and the few who did were male. To my chagrin, when I joined Jared, thinking to get away from the creepy crowd on shore, a group of men began swimming near us, trying to get a better view of me and addressing us in pidgin English.

As soon as we came out of the water again, caked with salt, Khadija complained to me that her period had started. That was all I needed. I suggested that we drive her home immediately. Any excuse to leave. Khadija gratefully accepted my offer, but Nasreen made vague noises of disapproval. I got the impression that she thought Khadija shouldn't travel alone with a foreign woman and her dangerously male husband. Or perhaps Nasreen just wanted an excuse to go with us. In any case, she announced that she too was leaving. Sheikh Avdila looked at us disappointedly. Why were we going so soon? It was impossible to explain truthfully.

Here we were, Westerners who loved to swim, who had expressed over and over how delightful this lake was. And here was the lake, or, rather, the town beach, with the Iranian social scene at its crudest.

It was as if someone had turned the streets of Rezaiyeh inside out. On the streets of the city, women were covered and men wore what they pleased. Here the men were fully dressed while the women were half-naked. Back in the village it was important to Nasreen that no one should say she had ridden alone with Jared and me. But no one would worry about how she had come across to a couple of swimming Turks.

"Let's walk for a few minutes," Khadija and Nasreen suggested to me just before we left. Since Jared and Sheikh Avdila seemed to be deep in conversation I had no excuse to refuse. Reluctantly, I strolled along with them, arm in arm, seeing and being seen.

Here was the only real meeting of Kurds and *ajam* that I ever witnessed during my time in Rezaiyeh. It was an impersonal sort of thing, like a college mixer, a social scene born of desperation, of sheltered Kurdish virgins and wives let out of their villages and of men who lived in a society where many cannot afford to marry until they were in their thirties or forties.

It was all very interesting and enlightening except for one thing. I could not be an aloof observer. As always, my actual behavior and attire were irrelevant. My long dress, my businesslike tank suit, signaled nothing except exotic foreignness. If Kurdish women went so far on a public beach, how much farther might an American woman go? I preferred the waters of Dermanawa, unsullied by garbage or gawking Turks. But to Nasreen and Khadija, Dermanawa, although fun in comparison to their daily routine, offered no surprises. Lake Rezaiyeh was a fantasy come alive.

From my first months in Rezaiyeh I had sensed the sexual contradictions of Iranian society. Because sex is so strongly prohibited it seemed to be constantly on everyone's mind. Some Iranian men struck me as adolescent in their predisposition to hear double entendres. Once Houshang and Shehrzad were teaching me a card game and Houshang invited me to be his partner. Then he began snickering and added, "Only for the game."

My students at the college could be counted on to giggle hysterically at anything remotely sexual or scatological. But there was also a romantic side to this obsession—a kind of longing reflected in the national love of poetry and songs. Even the Rezaiyeh chief of police had a verse from the great Persian poet Saadi hung on his wall.

The Kurds would say proudly that they had no native word for "prostitute." The usual term is a loan from Arabic. Villages were not large enough to tolerate working whores. But in Kurdistan, a smaller, in some ways more puritanical society than urban Iran, I felt sex to be less of an obsession with the men I met. Perhaps this was the result of earlier marriages or the acceptance of polygamy. Although Haji Ismail was always eager to talk to me, I never felt the kind of lascivious attention from him that was focused on me by other Iranian men. But how did Haji Ismail's wives feel about him? Were they frustrated and resentful? I wondered about that.

One day I had the following conversation with Taha:

"Is it true that it is against the law for a man to have more than two wives in Iran and that the first wife must agree to the second?" I began my line of questioning.

Taha nodded, a faint smile on his face. We both knew I had asked a rhetorical question, since Taha was as aware as I was of the shah's Family Protection Act. This was a piece of legislation designed to give women rights which they did not enjoy under Islamic law. The Quran allowed a man four wives and instantaneous divorce. In the past, there had been almost no way for a woman to obtain a divorce if her husband didn't want to let her go. Theoretically the shah had changed all that.

"What would you do if the gendarmes came to Dustan and questioned your father about all of his wives?" I asked Taha seriously.

He grinned. "We would invite them up to the *diwankhaneh* and serve them tea."

"And then?"

"And then they would go away."

After so many months in Iran, Taha's words hardly came as a revelation. The Family Protection Act and the rights of women were surely the last priority on the list of laws that the government wanted to enforce in Kurdistan. Still, I had heard from so many Iranians about the so-called liberation of women, a government "event" that was celebrated each year on "Women's Liberation Day," that I could not resist asking. According to Khadija, Taha's bride of less than a year, her husband was already looking around to take another wife, an *ajam* girl.

Kurdish men seemed to regard national marriage laws rather as they regarded national borders—as something to get around. Both Iraq and Turkey passed legislation to limit polygamy, and in both countries it was in Kurdish villages that the law was most often broken.

In the beginning of the summer I came to Dustan one day with my tape recorder, planning to use marriage as a subject for interviews. Susin Khanim, the haji's first wife, said she had been thirteen years old when her father had promised her to an old man. But unlike poor Parweneh of Mawana, Susin had not allowed herself to be thrown into the fire.

To avoid that awful fate, she ran away with Haji Ismail, whom she had met at a local wedding. Because their tribes were enemies, Susin's father would not speak to her for a long time afterward. I tried to picture the ailing, overweight Susin as a thirteen-year-old running away with a young Haji Ismail, but my imagination failed me. I wondered if the haji, with all his subsequent wives, ever thought of Susin, sitting immobile hour after hour in her room. Did he have any affection for her, any memories of the past, or was he totally engrossed in his newer, younger brides?

Since Maryam, the haji's second wife, was not in the room, I could not ask about her marriage, but the third wife, Zeinab, usually so reticent, spoke up.

"*I* didn't want to marry the haji," she said, shaking her head and laughing. "I was very unhappy." But she would not say more.

As usual, neither of the two most recent wives were in the room. I wondered where they spent their time. Evidently the first three wives, all of whom were from aristocratic families, considered the two latest wives too inferior to socialize with.

Just before I left Iran the first time and then when I returned I had a couple of glimpses of Shareefa, the fifth wife. Both times she was hugely pregnant and slightly unkempt. She regarded me with a mocking air as the other women made sure we had little to do with one another.

On the day that I brought my tape recorder I asked Haji Ismail to tell me about running away with Susin Khanim. He looked at me in consternation and flatly refused to discuss it, saying it would be "shameful." He then proceeded to give me a long rambling discourse on how religious his family was.

Even if Susin and Zeinab didn't want to elaborate about the past or their feelings toward Haji Ismail, something happened that day at Dustan to make me realize the extent to which the village woman is outside the protection of any law enacted 600 miles away in Tehran.

As we were sitting around after dinner in Maryam's bedroom, the microphone leisurely went from hand to hand, everyone adding some joke or anecdote. Then suddenly the sharp-featured woman with the blue tattoo on her chin began to speak. This was Fatma, the same woman Khadija had identified many months earlier as the mother of one of the haji's latter two wives—the woman that no one liked.

Fatma was speaking in a hard-edged voice about having no roof over her head, about traveling around looking for a place, about being "finished." For some reason I couldn't follow, she seemed to be without a home. At last, when she came to a break in her impassioned recital, I asked what she was talking about. The room fell silent.

Finally Nasreen answered, "Her husband has taken a new wife."

The women in the room watched my face as I silently pieced together Fatma's grievances. Obviously she had not given her permission for a second wife, and her husband had not been rich enough or sensitive enough to afford separate houses for the two wives. Fatma felt driven from her home. I looked at her sympathetically, but the room seemed to crackle with Maryam's disapproval.

I sensed that our hostess would have liked to shut this woman up, to prevent her from airing her troubles on my recording. But I was a guest, and Maryam said nothing. Was it because Fatma was the mother of one of the despised wives, or was there some other reason for her unpopularity?

Not long after Fatma's recital, Jared and I were saying our goodbyes for the day when Fatma came over to me and asked, in a whisper, if she could ride with us into the city.

"Of course," I answered, but from the way Fatma's eyes darted back to Maryam, who was not close enough to hear, it seemed that she was trying to keep her request a secret. As she was going back into Maryam's house to fetch something, Khadija and Taha came over to the car window. Khadija spoke to me.

"Margaret, you aren't going to take that woman with you, are you?"

"Yes, why not?"

"Because she is feuding with her husband. He doesn't want her to go into Rezaiyeh. You shouldn't do what she says," Khadija explained, looking worried.

"It's no trouble to us. We have enough room in the car," I said, refusing to get Khadija's meaning. "If she is fighting with her husband, it is not our affair."

"But, Margaret," said Khadija, looking anxiously up the hill toward her father-in-law's residence. "It *is* the haji's affair. This woman's husband is a member of the haji's tribe. You are the haji's guest. If you take this woman into the city, her husband will blame the haji. There will be trouble."

Out of the corner of my eye I saw the tattooed woman creeping toward the car, but when she noticed Khadija talking to me, she backed off.

I never had to refuse her directly. All I had to do was acquiesce to Khadija's plea. On the way home in the car I wondered guiltily what I should have done. Made a scene? Set up a feud for Haji Ismail, who had shown us every kindness, every courtesy?

I couldn't get the tattooed woman out of my mind. Had she truly been so desperate that she needed to approach two foreigners for help in getting out of her village? Or was she deliberately trying to embarrass Haji Ismail? Why did Maryam feel such animosity toward her? Was it because Maryam herself had had to live through her husband's bringing another wife into her house? Maybe Maryam had no sympathy for women who couldn't tolerate what she'd endured.

In Maryam, the politest of hostesses, the most loving of mothers, I sensed a hardness that showed itself most in her dealings with her daughters-in-law. Like Haji Ismail, Maryam considered herself to be very religious. She prayed five times a day and regularly read the Quran. Despite her proud independent spirit, I was sure that she accepted the Islamic laws regarding women. Very likely Maryam viewed Fatma as a weak complainer who was only making trouble for herself and the rest of the village.

But it wasn't only wives who were imprisoned in Dustan. Unmarried girls had even less freedom. Just when Jared and I were beginning to take it for granted that Kurdish women were less hidebound than their urban Persian and Turkish counterparts, an incident occurred which showed us how much we still did not understand.

Of course, Dustan was not every village and Haji Ismail was not every father. Khadija had not been raised as Haji Ismail's daughters had. Her village was too remote and her father's way of life still semi-nomadic. Unlike her sequestered sisters-in-law, she had spent plenty of time on the back of a horse. Her family had evidently not been concerned with protecting her hymen to that extent. The girls of Zhillah too were obviously not being raised as were Amina and Alal. But Haji Ismail was making no mistakes as far as his women were concerned.

It was the end of July and huge pyramids of straw appeared at the entrance to the village as we drove up to Haji Ismail's courtyard. We parked, got out, and walked to the front of the harem, where we saw no one —not the usual crowd of raggedy children, not the servant men or women, not even a dog. Haji Ismail's green Land Rover was gone, and the deserted courtyard was eerie in the burning sun.

Just as we were regretting our spontaneous decision to make this unannounced trip, Amina and Alal appeared in the doorway. "Margaret, hello, how are you, welcome!" they called to me.

"*Selam*, Alal, *selam*, Amina," I answered. Then, awkwardly, I asked where Haji Ismail was.

"He is out with the harvest," Amina replied. "Do you need to see him?"

I was feeling more and more uncomfortable. We certainly didn't *need* to see Haji Ismail. In fact we had no good reason for being in Dustan, no reason to call Haji Ismail away from his harvest.

"How can we find him?" I asked, not knowing what else to say.

"Maybe he's over there," replied Amina, pointing her finger. I saw no signs of human beings, only the broad golden plain below.

"Why don't you come in and sit down where it is cool?" suggested Amina. Alal said nothing. She stood staring at me out of large, blank eyes.

I glanced at Jared, who was standing at a slight distance. The girls had not addressed one word to him or acknowledged his presence. In this strange situation with only Amina and Alal at home and no one in Haji Ismail's *diwankhaneh* it suddenly occurred to me that Jared had never been inside the harem.

"Why don't you wait out here until I see what is happening?" I suggested to him.

Jared nodded, squinting in the bright sunlight. It was extremely hot in the unshaded courtyard. I followed the girls into the cool stillness of the thick-walled women's sitting room, where we settled on the floor.

"Where are your mothers?" I asked the two girls, marveling that Susin Khanim was not sitting in her accustomed place, her cane at her side.

"They are out under the trees, trying to stay cool," answered Alal, opening her mouth to speak for once. "They didn't know you were coming," she added.

"Maybe we should leave, then. I think this was not a good time to have come," I said, starting to rise.

"No, no. You cannot leave. You have just arrived," said Amina, who had more social grace than her cousin.

Amina spoke to one of her little half sisters. "Go to the grove and tell my mother that Margaret and her husband are here."

At this reference to Jared's presence, I glanced through the window bars and saw him standing in the hot sun. Moving closer to the window, I called out, "Jared, how are you doing?"

Jared glared at me. "It's really hot out here. What are you doing in there? You think I could come inside? Or would it be too threatening to their highnesses?"

Amina and Alal at the other end of the room couldn't understand the English, but they sensed my discomfort and started whispering to each other.

"Why don't you invite your husband to come in?" Amina ventured.

"They are inviting you to come inside," I said to Jared through the bars. A second later he was standing in the doorway of the sitting room, At his arrival Amina and Alal backed off into a corner, drew their scarves over their faces, and began whispering frantically to each other.

I sat between the girls and my offending husband. Amina and Alal kept talking excitedly to each other. Occasionally, trying to be polite, they would address a remark or two to me. But they studiously ignored Jared. I was aware that although Jared was being outwardly polite, he was getting more and more annoyed.

I thought I understood where Amina and Alal's nervousness came from. As virgins, they could not afford to have the slightest shadow cast on them. The situation presented an impossible dilemma: on the one hand, hospitality to guests was mandatory; but on the other hand, girls were never supposed to be in the presence of a man unchaperoned by some member of their family.

Fortunately Alal's mother soon returned from the woods and escorted us over to the house her brother, Haji Ismail, had built for her off to one side of the harem courtyard. Gelawezh Khanim was in her late forties. Many years ago she had been married to an Iraqi Kurd who had been predisposed to polygamy. But when he took one wife too many, he and Gelawezh were divorced and she came to live with her brother in Dustan. Evidently Jared posed no threat to her reputation. Maryam too did not fear being left alone with the foreign man.

Being married made some difference, as did being older and relatively independent with grown sons. Both Maryam and Gelawezh seemed far more relaxed around Jared than did Haji Ismail's third wife Zeinab. But outside of Kurdistan, even educated married women would not risk being alone with my husband.

One day he dropped by our neighbors to give a message to Mr. Aminzadeh, a teacher at the college. His wife, Nazi, the same Nazi who had ditched me on the way to the bazaar many months before, answered over the intercom that her husband was not at home but would return soon. "*Befermayeed bala*," she told him, meaning "Please come up."

Jared waited, thinking she would buzz the door open and he would come and deliver the message in person. When nothing happened he rang again and the woman repeated, "*Befermayeed bala*."

Again he waited. Still nothing happened as he stood there, trying to understand what she was up to. At last he figured out that she had no intention of buzzing him in. Her invitation was merely *ta'arof*. Nazi worked outside of her home; she was a college graduate married to a mathematician. But it was unthinkable that her husband's colleague should pass through her outer door when her husband was not at home, even if he was scheduled to return in a few minutes.

A similar thing happened on another day when Jared went to speak to the husband of a woman I had spent time with, a thirty-eight-year-old matron with two grown sons. Even though the woman, Mrs. Jam, was not inside her house, but supervising the servants out in the courtyard, Jared was not allowed in the front gate in order to leave a message.

"Come back when my husband is at home," Mrs. Jam said flatly, shutting the gate.

It was no joke when the workmen on our street stopped laying bricks in order to stare in our windows when Dara came to our house. Evidently no other respectable woman in town took such chances with her chastity.

Our study of the behavior of women in the village and in the town came full circle when we noticed Haji Ismail observing us. One afternoon we were visiting Dustan when I decided I wanted to go home. After hours of sitting in the harem, listening to desultory gossip, I was not only bored but suffocating in the summer heat. The layers and layers of synthetic materials in my Kurdish dress absorbed no sweat at all.

Knowing full well I was committing a *faux pas*, I abruptly stood up and announced I was going over to the *diwankhaneh*, where Jared had been eating lunch with the haji. The women stared at me, puzzled, as I marched out of the harem, and Haji Ismail's very tall male servant gave me a look as I arrived in the entrance hall of the men's quarters.

From the doorway I explained in English why I had come. Haji Ismail watched attentively as Jared replied that he wanted to stay because Haji Ismail had asked him to go hunting. I said, in no uncertain terms, that I wanted to go. There was no way for *me* to politely join a male hunting expedition, and I had had enough of the harem for the day. All I wanted to do was go home, strip off my dresses, and take a shower.

"What are you saying?" the haji asked us curiously.

Jared explained that I wanted to leave, and the haji, crestfallen, urged Jared to stay. In the end I prevailed. The haji looked at us as if he were figuring a math sum and then he said, "*She* is the one who decides, isn't she?"

It was not an indictment, but an observation, and it gave me pause to realize that Haji Ismail was trying to figure us out as much as we were trying to figure him out. Back in the harem the women did not want to see me leave, but they assumed it was my husband's will. I did not undeceive them.

Although it was natural for me to generalize from my experiences in Dustan, I had to remind myself once again that Haji Ismail was not all Kurdish men and Dustan not all Kurdish villages. Some places in Kurdistan seemed more like Rezaiyeh, both in the men's treatment of me and in their treatment of their women. One village where Jared never sat talking to Kurdish girls or women was Mawana, where the men had tried to convince Jared to take a second wife.

As Dustan came more and more sharply into focus for me, my memories of Mawana had grown hazy. It felt as if several years rather than months had passed since I had traveled to distant Tergawar in the company of Mr. Khalili and his driver at a time when I could barely speak Kurdish, knew nothing of Kurdish customs, and did not understand that all the adult women of the village were away planning the wedding of poor Parweneh, the girl who "threw herself into the fire."

For a while I had wondered about Parweneh's fate, but gradually she had faded from my mind. Shireen and Parweneh had been friendly on that long-ago day in Mawana, but they hadn't urged me to return to their village. Nor had Mr. Khalili ever asked me to come with him again. If it had not been for coincidence I would never have seen Mawana again. At one time I had regarded the different groups of Kurds I met as totally separate—the Iraqi refugees, Haji Ismail's family, the Mawana crowd, and Turkish Kurds. But gradually I realized that they were all part of a greater whole and that many of them knew each other.

The war had ended and it was now summer, but the Kurdish refugee school in Rezaiyeh continued. The shah's authorities had moved the Kurds to another building, and I got the impression that they were trying to make it as inconvenient as possible for the refugees to continue to run their school. It was a precarious situation.

At best the Iraqi Kurds whom Iran had once helped were an embarrassment; at worst they were regarded as a dangerous influence on Iran's own Kurds. The Iranian authorities were well aware that the Iraqi Kurds who remained in Iran were vulnerable. Many were hoping to emigrate to America or Europe or somewhere, but, for the moment, Iran was refusing to let them leave the country. America was not showing any interest in taking them either. Vietnam had just fallen, and although these Kurds would have been a tiny trickle in contrast to the flow of Vietnamese refugees to the United States, someone in Washington had made the decision—no Kurds.

The faculty at the refugee school had almost completely changed. Instead of college graduates and experienced teachers, there was a much younger crowd, many of whom had been at university when the Kurdish War broke out. These people—mostly men—were the most qualified teachers available now. Refugee leaders were determined to have the children taught in Kurdish until the Iranians forcibly stopped them. Because of the time lost when the school had closed after the cease-fire, the students were asked to continue through the summer,

I volunteered to teach English to the upper-level students. But I felt more and more uncomfortable in the school. The new group of teachers had been working in Naqadeh, a town near Mahabad to the south of Rezaiyeh where Barzani had his headquarters. No one except the Assyrian gym teacher had ever seen me before, and they made it clear that they did not for a minute believe that I was who I said I was.

One day Massoud, the second-grade teacher, a very tall nineteen-year-old, mentioned in the teachers' room that he was going to Mawana that weekend.

"What is in Mawana?" I asked curiously.

His glance fell suspiciously on me. "What do *you* know about Mawana?"

"I visited there last fall," I answered.

"Who took you there?"

"No one you know," I snapped, not liking his inquisitorial tone.

He gave me a look, and I reconsidered. If I wanted to go back to

Mawana—and I did—I could not afford to alienate Massoud, who might prove to be my ticket there.

"Mr. Khalili, who works at the radio station, took me when he was doing reportage," I volunteered.

Massoud nodded impatiently as if he had not really been at all interested in the information.

"And why are *you* going there?" I asked.

"My family lives there," he said.

"So you are Herki?"

"Yes, I am Herki."

I studied Massoud's fleshy face with its pale skin and gray eyes. Someone, I couldn't remember who, had suggested to me that the Herkis had not been a hundred percent behind Barzani. Maybe it was just gossip left over from the collapse of the Mahabad Republic. But I had not realized before that there were Herkis among the people in the school. In fact many of these Kurds were so urbanized they did not consider themselves currently affiliated with any tribe. Massoud was the first instance I had heard of where there was a connection between a refugee and Kurds in an Iranian village.

I had long wondered how the Iranian government was managing to control these sorts of associations. It was obvious that they wanted as little contact as possible between local Kurds and refugees. For several months since the cease-fire there had been rumors that the government would move all the Iraqi refugees away from the western border where they could be in contact with Iranian Kurds, But as yet this had not happened.

"Do you think I could go to Mawana with you?" I asked now. Sensing he was about to refuse, I quickly added, "We have a car, so we can give you a ride."

That did the trick.

The next Friday, Jared, Massoud, and I set out for for the first Kurdish village I had ever visited. When we arrived, the men came over to greet us. Massoud pointed his finger in the direction of the harem and said to me, "You go there with the women."

I briefly considered staying with the men just to annoy him. Massoud always wore a well-cut gray suit. He spoke a little English and had evidently made it to junior year in the Iraqi university system before he had been forced to flee. His dress and his education suggested nothing of the village. But his behavior toward me as a woman was far more uncomfortable and sexist than that of any tribal Kurd I ever met.

When I arrived inside one of the rooms of the harem, a slim girl with honey-colored hair approached, and I looked at her, startled. She was the image of Parweneh. Perhaps the wedding had not taken place after all. But no. This was Parweneh's half sister. They were almost exactly the same age, and they looked like twins. I wondered how their father had picked one over the other to throw into the fire.

"Where is Parweneh now?" I asked her sister.

"In Iraq."

"Iraq?"

"Yes, she had to follow her husband there after the war ended. She cried and cried, but they made her go."

I had not known that in addition to his other liabilities, Parweneh's ancient bridegroom had been Iraqi. I thought of the gentle, shy Parweneh denying that she was about to be married. Now she had been forced to leave her native land. Perhaps she would never see her family again. With the new joint Iran-Iraq crackdown on Kurds, it was possible that the annual Herki migration would never take place again.

Parweneh's sister pulled out the photograph album and showed me Parweneh's wedding pictures. The one that stayed in my mind was of Parweneh leaning out of a small upper-story window in Amir Khan's city residence. The tiny girl seemed hopelessly imprisoned inside the huge house like a princess in a fairy tale. But this story had no happy ending.

The rest of the day proceeded, on the surface, very much like a day in Dustan. Jared stayed with the men, while I stayed in the harem with the women, venturing out on one walk chaperoned by Parweneh's look-alike sister. Amir Khan himself was not in Mawana that day.

Before we left in the late afternoon I came outside and asked Jared if he would use his complicated Chinese camera to take pictures of the women inside, since the light there was not good enough for my camera. Jared pointed out that I shouldn't ask *him*, but the khans he was visiting with. When I redirected my request, the men looked at each other, amused.

"Why not? Why not?" the eldest one said heartily. They were all ready for some fresh entertainment. The group trooped up the stairway of the harem with Jared at the head, but the women shrank back when everyone appeared in the doorway.

"You see," said the man who had given permission, "it is all right with us, but the women don't like it."

Jared took a few photographs and then beat a hasty retreat, the men laughing behind him.

When it was time to leave, the women invited me to spend the night. I was tempted, but the Iraqis had to go back to teach the next day.

We made one more trip to Mawana, partly because Massoud vastly preferred our car to the rural bus and partly because the women had begged me to return, But when I came back on the date we had set, they were not there. Such a thing would have been unthinkable in Dustan. If anything, Haji Ismail and his son Taha were more punctual than we were.

Again Massoud betrayed his nervousness at bringing us to his family's village. This time he did not order me to the harem, but instead his horrified attention fastened on the tape recorder I had brought.

"What are you doing with *that*?" he asked.

"I am going to record stories."

"You should not have brought it. You must leave it in the car."

Jared opened his mouth, and I could tell we were about to have an all-out confrontation. Jared was as tired of Massoud's touchy arrogance as I was. I told Massoud that recording stories was part of my work and I planned to carry on with it regardless of his suspicions. But, not wanting to make a scene, I decided to leave the machine under the car seat for the time being and retrieve it later when Massoud was not around.

Up in the women's quarters I found things much as they had been the first time I visited. Most of the women were away. This time the girls, Shireen and her sisters, were gone as well, to the lake. I became the charge of one of Amir Khan's wives, a tall, silly-acting black-haired woman.

I sat with her in a large room where a number of servants were eating the last bits of breakfast bread and yogurt. A couple of women sat before clay pedestals, using small hammers to break cones of beet sugar into the bite-sized lumps needed for tea. One of the women said she knew a story to narrate for my collection, and I started to leave the room to fetch my tape recorder. My hostess asked me where I was going.

"To my car."

"Khanim, your car is not here."

Sure she was mistaken, I went over to the window and looked down into the courtyard. Where our ear had stood was bare dust.

"Where is it?" I asked.

"The men have taken it to go fishing," said the dark-haired woman.

I couldn't believe Jared had gone off with my tape recorder without saying a word. He knew very well I had been planning to use it that morning.

I looked around at the roomful of women I had never seen before and felt trapped. I was beyond the stage of sitting and talking, especially with these women. I had come to Mawana expecting to work. How long would it be before the men came back? Suppose fish and water got on my tape recorder?

The story I had planned to tape was already lost, because the woman who had volunteered to tell it had to go outside and bake bread in the *tendoor*. But I knew I could get other stories if only I had my tape recorder. What disturbed me was the way Jared had simply taken off without getting my machine back to me. Was he ashamed to cooperate with me in front of Massoud?

I tried to explain to these women why I was upset, but they only looked at me. How could a wife question her husband's decision? My hostess, anxious to put me in a better mood, walked me over into the village for a visit with the wife of the mullah,

Later that afternoon when the men had returned and I was sitting with my hostess in her bedroom, my tape recorder safely at my side, I suggested to her that we could take a trip to the creek where the men had gone fishing.

"But how, Khanim?" she asked, giggling.

"I can drive us there," I answered.

"Without your husband?" she asked, wide-eyed.

"Yes," I said.

But as soon as I'd suggested this little excursion I realized that I didn't want to go. I just wanted to demonstrate that I too could take the car. Unfortunately, with this woman there would not have been any point or fun in such a demonstration. She had already told me that she didn't swim or fish and that she was afraid of turtles. I was sure she'd want to take five other people with her to guarantee her chastity. Pretending I needed my husband's permission but having little intention of going to the creek, I said I was leaving for the *diwankhaneh*. The woman nodded, and I set off down the steps and across the courtyard.

Over in the men's sitting room I met Amir Khan for the first time. As Jared had said, he looked very much like a midwestern insurance executive with his pale-blue eyes, smooth face, and well-fed body. There was nothing of Haji Ismail's nervous excitement in his demeanor. The man exuded confidence and coolness. He looked at me carefully without smiling.

In my purse were prints of the pictures I had taken of Shireen and Parweneh during my first visit to Mawana the previous fall. I had long ago given Mr. Khalili a set of these pictures to give to someone who was going out to Tergawar, but not surprisingly they had disappeared. On my last visit, Shireen said she had never seen them. Now I had another set to give Shireen, who was not in the village as she had said she would be. Not knowing which of the women in the harem were related to Shireen, I hesitated to hand them over.

Face-to-face with Amir Khan, I realized that this was my last chance. But, as I handed him the pictures, asking him to give them to Shireen, I doubted she would ever see them. Why would a man who had married off a fifteen-year-old daughter to an old man with two other wives worry about whether another daughter got some photographs that somebody had left for her?

Just as we were about to leave, Amir Khan suddenly began acting the solicitous host, serving us huge slices of watermelon. We ate these standing up outside and then got into the car. As we drove away I wondered what Amir Khan made of us. Was he convinced, like Massoud, that we were spies? It was far more likely that he thought we were nonentities, of no use whatsoever to him or to anyone else he considered important. Amir Khan was a very political man. As he told us himself, he had just flown to Tehran for the first congress of Restakheez, the shah's new political party.

Haji Ismail paid lip service to the shah's government, but he had not gone so far as to become an enthusiastic supporter of Restakheez. Although Haji Ismail did not treat his daughters all that well, I had not heard of any marriages like Parweneh's in *his* family. Every photograph that I later sent from America for Khadija, Nasreen, or Maryam care of the haji had been duly delivered. Obviously Amir Khan was the clever businessman, recognizable in any culture, while Haji Ismail was a hotheaded dreamer, a tyrant at times, but a lover as well. Amir Khan only made us more aware than ever of how fortunate we were to have met Haji Ismail.

CHAPTER 19

SER CHAVA

The first time I heard the expression *ser chava*, I was a little overcome. The women intoned the words in such a serious way. As I came and went from Kurdish households to the tune of hundreds of repetitions of the phrase, I understood better. *Ser chava* was not spoken lightly. Literally it meant "on my eyes" and was used for promises as well as for marking arrivals and departures. Persian has a cognate expression, *chashm*, which has been debased, like many of the old Persian formulas. While *chashm* in the jargon of taxi drivers or servants just means "okay" or "I gotcha, boss," *ser chava* is something quite different. To Kurds, *ser cha*va is not just a couple of words; it is an oath. And oaths are not easily broken in Kurdistan.

Whatever *ser chava* meant to my hostesses, I began to hear it internally as I felt my time in Kurdistan hurrying by. I wondered what *ser cha*va would feel like when the time came to hear it from Khadija and Aisha and Haji Ismail and the rest in final farewell.

On my eyes forever would be the sight of Nasreen and Khadija on the rocks by the lake, their dresses billowing out like giant poppies, their braids encrusted with salt; of Khadija squatting next to a pile of mangled apricot flesh as she cracked one pit after another, popping the almond-like seeds into her mouth and discarding the fruit. On my eyes would be Haji Ismail as he squinted at us in the sunlight outside his *diwankhaneh*, straining to understand our English and thereby understand Jared and me, our relationship to each other and to him, The emaciated Mr. Khalili would also be engraved on my memory sitting next to me on the metal chairs of the radio station as I followed his impassioned reading of the great Kurdish epic *Mam 0 Zeen*. Rainbow dresses in the desert, ice-cold springs trickling out of mountainsides, the blue waters of the lake, the blue of the cloudless Kurdish sky, the blue of Haji Ismail's and Maryam's eyes—I would never forget them.

I knew that I would not always be in Kurdistan; yet the rest of the world, as much as I missed it at times, had receded. No longer did I think of leaving for America every week the way I had during the dark days of winter after the light-bulb incident. No longer did I await the mail with the desperation of having no one nearby to call my friend.

Kurdistan had opened up to me, and I had even begun to take Rezaiyeh and the rest of Iran for granted. The behavior of people around me was beginning to seem more normal. Life was made up of a thousand inconveniences that had somehow come to have meaning—drinking tea and waiting for the customs officials to give me my packages, bargaining at the bazaar, going in to speak to the dean and sitting in the anteroom for an hour with his secretary. Kurdish villages no longer seemed so dirty, and the rows of formally posed faces in photograph albums made some sense now. I knew what the appropriate answer was when someone said *ser chava*.

But even as we had become used to our surroundings we knew they did not belong to us nor we to them. As long as we stayed in Iran we would only be part of the larger American presence here – a presence resented by many of the locals.

Jared and I decided to leave at the end of the summer. We scheduled an appointment to tell the dean so that he could begin to arrange replacements for us—evidently no simple task, since our own hiring had been so fraught with delays and broken promises that anyone less determined would never have come to Rezaiyeh at all.

The dean reacted to our news with cold fury and instantly fired us, cutting us off from the summer pay we had been counting on receiving. We were stunned. The dean rationalized his decision by saying that we had committed ourselves to at least a two-year stay. But our contract specified only a year and hadn't even required us to give notice as long as we were planning to stay out that year.

There was no legal redress for the manner in which the dean terminated our contracts. He came from the same northeastern Iranian town as the prime minister, and people said that made him more powerful than the governor of West Azerbaijan. It was not the first time we had been made to feel helpless in Iran.

Our colleagues and neighbors shrugged when we told them. Hadn't we known better than to deal with this dean in a straightforward manner? As usual, the reaction of the Kurds was different. They, like us, were "other" in Iran. They understood the maddening ways of the *ajam* and they had been fed up with the shah long before we were born.

Our friends in Dustan heard the story of our firing with sympathy. Only later did I realize that they had misunderstood. They thought the dean had fired us before we told him we were leaving.

"But why?" asked Sheikh Avdila. He had understood the real chain of events and the fact that we had actually quit. He also knew there was a serious unemployment problem in the United States.

"What will you do when you go back there?" he asked in his adult way. "Wouldn't it be better to stay here?"

Haji Ismail too questioned our departure, but not on the basis of what was good for us. As a feudal landlord he accepted the superiority of the West. Naturally we wanted to go back to our own country. But did we have to go so soon? Because there were so few days to spend with each other, he took time away from his harvest to see us before we left.

One day we went out to the place where his Land Rover was parked alongside a pile of grain sacks and a scale. Under the blinding sun of the wheat field we found Haji Ismail maneuvering his gigantic combine.

"You come up here, Jared, and sit with me," he said. "Margaret Khanim, will you please take our picture?"

This was the first and only time Haji Ismail asked me to take his picture. He had tolerated my photographing him in the village in front of his *diwankhaneh*, but this was the way he wanted us to remember him in America, as a modern farmer.

Khadija constantly urged me to come and spend every day with her in the haji's town house, but I could not come as often as I liked, since I was busy selling off the possessions we had acquired. It was hard to separate the potential buyers from the gawkers. I soon discovered that it was as time-consuming and frustrating to be on the selling end as on the buying end of a sale in Iran. One woman came and purported to cast a spell on a set of dishes we wouldn't sell dirt-cheap, saying they would break after she left.

Khadija wanted me to spend time with her now because she would not be in Rezaiyeh or Dustan to say goodbye when we left. For at least a month now she had been planning to return to her childhood village, her first visit since her marriage the previous summer. Haji Ismail's Land Rover would be taking her back there along with Taha's brother, the midwife Gulbehar, and several other people.

Taha himself was forbidden by custom to go, but he and Maryam were sending Khadija home with a mountain of gifts, boxes of candy and bolts of fabric, to let each of Khadija's ten paternal uncles know how much her new family valued their bride.

When I arrived at Haji Ismail's house on Khadija's day of departure, she was trying to act solemn. Not only was this a serious occasion, a bride's first return home after her marriage, but one of Khadija's relatives had recently died, which explained the uncharacteristically dark shade of green in her *fistan* and the lack of her usual gold bib. There was also my departure to be sad about. Khadija and I sat together holding hands and watching the bustle around us as still more candy and fabric were fetched from the bazaar along with a rural taxi to carry all these presents. As hard as we tried, neither of us could summon the sadness that the occasion demanded. Khadija's upcoming trip was just too exciting and my departure was still several weeks away. I don't think either of us believed in the finality of it.

"Margaret, I'm so sad that you are leaving. Don't leave, stay," she said, smiling and squeezing my hand.

"I'll come back and visit," I said blithely, not wanting to focus on the fact that even if I did come back, it would never be the same as living here.

Everyone in the house, including Taha and Jared, followed Khadija down the stairs and out the front door, where boxes of presents were being loaded into a blue-and-white Volga. Taha's brother climbed into the driver's seat of the Land Rover with Khadija on his right, her black lace chador in place over her head. The rest of the retinue sat in the back.

We all waved as they drove off, and then Taha, Jared, and I stood on the dusty street staring at Haji Ismail's house. It was completely empty now. Zeinab, the boys, the servants, and the villagers were all in Dustan for the summer. Taha would wake up alone each morning as he went to his job in the city and return each afternoon alone to find his own dinner.

"Do you think I did the right thing, letting her go back?" Taha asked us, half joking, half serious. "It's a long time, three weeks."

"Of course you did," I said reassuringly, wanting to congratulate him on being a more considerate husband than he had to be.

Now it was time to pay our last visit to Dustan, to say goodbye to Haji Ismail and his harem and Nasreen and her mother. We went by bus, since our car was already sold. The ride was an experience in itself. It was our first time on the inside of one of the dilapidated buses we had seen careening out to Mergawar past the college several times a day, tilting dangerously to one side from overloading and disrepair. After arriving at the Mergawar bus stop we had to walk several hundred yards through the thistles and scrub to reach Maryam's house.

My hostesses reproached me for not having told them we were carless so that someone could have come into town to pick us up. As I sat with Nasreen and Maryam they continually urged me to reconsider my decision to leave.

"If you stay just one more year, Margaret," said Maryam, "you will learn our language perfectly. You will really become a Kurd."

"How will you keep from forgetting Kurdish in America?" Nasreen wanted to know.

"I probably *will* forget some," I admitted.

"Then teach our language to your mother and father," said Amina, who had come down to Maryam's to see me. "Then you can practice with them."

"Yes, and wear your Kurdish clothes so that Americans can see how beautiful they are," suggested Nasreen.

Talking about what I would do in America made me feel strange. The Kurds and Dustan had seemed so separate from the rest of my life. I had not thought of what I would do with the Kurdish language back in America beyond using it as a subject for a dissertation. Now it struck me that Kurdish would no longer be of much use in everyday conversation. What would I do with my Kurdish clothes? Lock them up in a trunk, I supposed, to show my grandchildren. I would never wear them as clothes again; they would just be an exotic costume.

I did not expect to see Iraqi refugees that day. Only after they had appeared on the horizon did Amina and Nasreen casually mention that groups of *mohajir* had been walking into Dustan for the past several weeks. These desperate tribal people from the northernmost part of Iraq were being driven out of their villages by the Iraqi government.

Although they had promised amnesty to all Kurds at the end of the war, the Arabs continued their policy, begun before the war, of forcibly moving Kurds off their land in the northern mountains and resettling them in camps in the desert of southern Iraq. The good Kurdish land was then given to Arabs. All this was supposed to ensure that one day there would be no concentration of Kurds anywhere near Iraqi oil, so that Kurds would never be able to claim any of the benefits Iraq reaps from the resource under Kurdistan.

The arrival of the refugees generated little excitement in Dustan. They had been walking in the mountains for twelve days, somehow avoiding the soldiers and land mines along the borders of Iraq, Turkey, and Iran. Maryam's servants offered them tea and cigarettes, and Haji Ismail immediately sent his truck down to carry them to the refugee camp.

Nasreen, who initially acted quite excited by their arrival, never spoke to them but stood at a distance, as they sat under the trees of the apricot orchard. Their exhausted faces were blackened by dirt and sun; the ragged clothes on their backs and the babes in their arms looked to be their only possessions in the world.

I stood a little uncertainly, watching the scene. Maryam, her scarf wrapped tightly around her head, was kneeling on her prayer rug spread out in front of her house. Nasreen and Amina were standing off to one side staring while the refugees milled around, looking uneasily at the Dustanis. I checked my watch, worried about missing the bus. It was time to go up to the harem to say goodbye. The handshakes there were curiously flat. I couldn't believe I was really going.

Down at Maryam's, things were a little different. Nasreen kissed my face and began to cry while Maryam also kissed me and then turned to comfort her daughter. Haji Ismail came to drive us back into town, and he too looked sad. Feeling numb, I climbed into the Land Rover.

As we drove this last time through the pass from Mergawar to the plain of Rezaiyeh I studied the shadowy curve of the mountains at twilight, the flow of the river, the way the shepherds walked alongside. It was possible I would never return to this remote place, never see these mountains again, never ride with Haji Ismail. Possibly I had seen my last of Nasreen, the emotional village girl who dreamed of eloping with a Barzani tribesman and looked forward to my every visit. I had been a contact with the city and the wide world where she wanted to spend her life.

I took in everything, trying to mark it indelibly in my memory, "on my eyes." Somehow I did not believe that Iran would always be here for me to come back to, even though the American government seemed to think the shah's reign would last a hundred years. Although Dustan itself had been built less than a century ago, the Kurds had been wandering the area for millennia. There was no real reason to think that *they* would not be here. Yet my own impermanent way of life led me to believe that nothing would remain the way it was.

In spirit and style, the Rezaiyeh Airport was a million miles from Kurdistan. It sat a few miles to the northeast of the city and thus was geographically as well as culturally and economically a part of *ajamistan*.

When Taha, Jared, and I pushed open the glass doors to the marble-walled waiting room of one of the shah's provincial masterpieces, we had to weave through a crowd that was already too large for the facility. There were no actual lines in front of the check-in counters, merely a shoving mass which the clerk was attempting to wait on all at once.

My mind was far away from this place even before I sat down, sharing a corner of a black plastic seat with Jared as the crowd surged around us. It was already past the time for takeoff and people were still coming in through the doors. Some went directly to the airport restaurant for the requisite Coke and chicken or hamburger. Others checked in, while those who were meeting people or seeing them off stood around talking loudly to each other. The scene in front of me resembled nothing so much as a large dry cocktail party.

Jared and Taha were deep in conversation, which I couldn't hear over the din of voices. I was thinking of all the things we had to do in Tehran and then in England, where we were going to attend an academic conference. It was as if I had already left Rezaiyeh, although there continued to be announcements that our plane was arriving momentarily, At last, I had become Iranized enough to believe that eventually it would come.

As I was waiting I looked around me and felt the shock of recognition, I *knew* many of these people. They were not the strangers I had seen when I had arrived in Rezaiyeh at the beginning of the year. These were my neighbors and colleagues. Depressed, yet fascinated, I kept watching them glancing at me, waiting for me to notice them.

At one point Shehrzad came over, her painted lips pouting in that disdainful smile I had seen all too often on her recently. I scrambled to my feet as Jared and Taha sat, oblivious in their handholding and conversation.

"I hope you have a safe trip," simpered Shehrzad, refusing to look me in the eyes as her tone dripped *ta'arof*. I thanked her and she sashayed away.

Looking around some more I counted two officers from the U.S. Army, the jeweler from the bazaar who had spoiled Jared's Christmas surprise, the father of the see-no-evil boy who had witnessed the light-bulb incident, the dean of the college, several faculty members, and a host of other people that I knew.

When the flight was finally called, Jared and Taha stood up. Taha had waited through most of the afternoon even though he was supposed to be in his office for the whole day. Instead of focusing on his unwavering loyalty, I had allowed myself to be transfixed by this crowd.

"Goodbye, Taha. Thank you," I said, looking into his blue-green eyes. I wanted to say more, to express the feeling that was welling up in me, the realization that this man and his family had asked nothing of us but to be their friends. We shook hands, and Jared and I walked toward the plane. For a second, as I was boarding, I looked back and saw Taha still there waiting, amid the crowd of *ajam*, to see us safely off.

The author and Taha in her living room

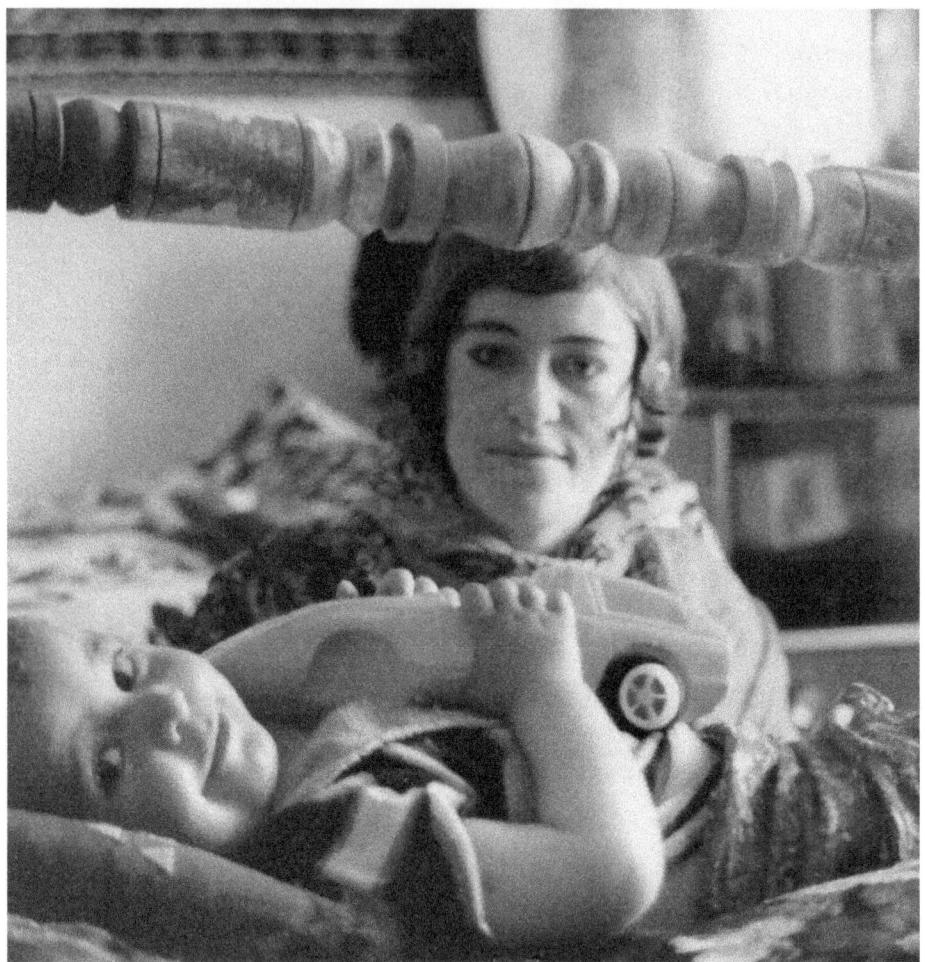

Khadija and her son in a Kurdish cradle

CHAPTER 20

KURDISTAN REVISITED

Back in America analyzing the language data I'd collected made my Kurdish friends seem less, rather than more, real. All the experience and emotion had to be cleared away so I could focus on the sounds I had recorded and transcribed on paper with the help of Dara. Sometimes I even asked myself if there had been any Haji Ismail or Dara or Khadija. Their voices were on the tape, but where were *they*? Only in my mind, which was having a hard time reconciling the sterile university atmosphere with the intensity of Kurdistan.

There *were* Kurds in the United States. In previous decades a handful of Kurds had come to the United States to study. A few had stayed on. As for the thousands of refugees from this latest revolution, there had been a small trickle let into America. The doctor who had cooperated with SAVAK was here, as well as several others who had managed to get past U.S. immigration.

One man I had met in Iran got caught at Kennedy Airport using a false passport, his pale frightened wife beside him with a six-month-old child in her arms. I got a call from them in their New York hotel room as they waited, terrified, for their case to be decided. Would the U.S. government allow them to stay? No one had ever officially declared the Kurds to be refugees, and when this man tried to contact the CIA people he had met in Iraq, they insisted they didn't know him. Mysterious pressure came down from obscure places in Washington not to let this man into the United States.

No one in America seemed to know about the role of the CIA in a place no one had ever heard of called Kurdistan. Letters, one by one, began to arrive from Haji Ismail, from Dara, and from Sheikh Avdila, sending me warm greetings and asking when I would return.

I heard on NPR about the report from the Pike Committee in Congress. They were investigating the role of the CIA in covert action, not only in well-known places like Angola and Italy, but among an "ethnic insurgent group" called the Kurds. Finally the Pike Report was published.

The portion that dealt with the Kurds consisted of only a couple of cryptic columns. They described how the United States, acting under the direction of the shah, encouraged the Kurds to begin their 1974 revolution because Iran wanted to harass Iraq. Henry Kissinger guided Kurdish leadership to act against the interests of the Kurdish people for the benefit of the shah. The two columns went on to tell how, when Iraq gave Iran a couple of slight concessions, the United States simply turned its back on three million Kurds who were trapped in Iraq and two hundred thousand refugees inside Iran. In the words of the congressional committee, "Even in the context of covert action, ours was a cynical enterprise."

I was still not ready to believe the worst, and neither was a Kurdish friend who had emigrated to America over a decade ago. Together we took a copy of the Pike Report and went to a lecture given by an official high in the Middle Fast section of the State Department. We waited patiently until the lecture was finished and repetitive speculations about an Arab-Israeli war had been thoroughly gone over. Then the Kurd, Asad, raised his hand.

"What about American involvement with the Kurds?" he asked in his accented English.

The State Department official stared at us as the rest of the academic crowd turned to see who was posing this unwelcome question.

"The Kurds?" the official said blankly. I was reminded of the time I had gone to see the dean about Dara. "What about them?"

"What do you have to say about the way America treated them, using them and then leaving them to a terrible fate?"

The exhalation of the official's breath into the microphone was audible. "I don't know what you are referring to. America has had no direct dealings with the Kurds."

Asad held up the copy of the Pike Report for the State Department man to see. The audience turned their heads away. I knew what they were thinking. Just another Middle Eastern crazy. Asad was no fashionable Palestinian.

"What about the Pike Report?" yelled Asad, his face dark with anger.

"The Pike Report is full of inaccuracies. It was never finalized or properly released for publication. Nothing in it can be taken with certainty to be factual."

The man took someone else's question, and Asad slowly sat down. Someone in the audience, one of the university's budding young experts on

Middle Eastern affairs, whispered over in our direction, "What happened to the Kurds is entirely their own fault. They *allowed* themselves to be used."

I tried to put Kurds out of my mind and concentrate on my dissertation, but it was difficult. The refugee in New York called me again and said that he had been granted asylum. There was another piece of limited good news. Seven hundred Kurdish refugees were to be allowed to come from Iran to America. Seven hundred out of two hundred thousand. Close to a hundred thousand Vietnamese refugees and seven hundred Kurds. If only the story of the Kurds had been fully reported on CBS News.

One bleak winter day I went to visit the man who had come on a false passport and nearly been expelled since the Kurds were not "official" refugees. His wife had managed to find all the ingredients to cook a complete Kurdish meal of stew, rice with noodles, bread, tea, and fruit. We ate on the floor of their hotel room, sitting in the cramped space at the end of the beds with the food placed on old issues of *The New York Times*. The man told me he had been anxiously scanning the papers for news of the Kurds.

The man's face was drawn and unshaven. He and his wife seemed delighted to see someone who had known them from their previous and more auspicious existence.

"What will you do now?" I asked them.

"We do not know." The man smiled ruefully. I felt they were waiting for me to make a helpful suggestion or offer. But I had a tiny apartment and no contacts to help this man get a job. I tried to explain these facts to him. He smiled even more.

"Yes," he replied. "I understand. It is all right."

* * * * *

It was three years before I returned to Kurdistan. The summer of 1978 was a time of reckoning for Iran, of settling up accounts with a shah and his father who had been plundering the nation of its riches for as long as most people could remember. Jared and I heard friends in Tehran speak out more openly against their government than they had ever dared before, even in the United States.

As the orange city taxi turned into Haji Ismail's village, my head was still buzzing from the long bus trip to Rezaiyeh. The first change I noticed was the concrete poles. They ran out on a diagonal from the line of electric wires along the road leading to the Iraqi border. Although there were as yet no wires on those poles coming into Dustan, the day of electricity seemed near. The second change we found in Dustan was Taha and Khadija's son. He had been conceived shortly after we left Kurdistan and was now a very spoiled two-year-old, his grandmother's darling.

Taha had finally quit high school. We guessed that he had resolved the choice between being a twenty-five-year-old high school junior or taking his place as prospective landlord of one of the richest villages in Iranian Kurdistan. Because her husband had moved to the village, Khadija was now under the close supervision of her mother-in-law. Between her duties around the house and her baby, she was not the old carefree Khadija that I remembered. She was cranky and often complained of headaches.

But, of course, that was all beneath the surface, and I did not notice it at first. The whirlwind of hospitality obscured everything but our hosts' seeming delight in our arrival. As the Iranian proverb goes, "Guests are the beloved of God," and the Kurds made us feel more beloved than any hosts we ever met.

Haji Ismail escorted us to Dermanawa in his new Toyota Land Cruiser. There were magnificent meals up in the *diwankhaneh*, where Haji Ismail brought out his new Kodak Instant camera and presented me with several slightly out-of-focus photographs to mark the occasion. Perhaps because this was my second trip and I was more sure of myself and the Kurds, I did more of what I wanted to do in Dustan. I felt freer to joke with my hostesses when they kidded me, and I decided, to Haji Ismail's and Maryam's shock, to climb the mountain that rises behind Dustan all the way to the Turkish border.

I was the sole female in a party of eight of Haji Ismail's sons and nephews along with my husband The Kurds could not have been more courtly. I never even had to carry my camera myself. When two old men appeared along the narrow path leading horses in the direction we were heading, our hosts requisitioned the animals for Jared and me.

Thanks to their solicitude, when we reached the snow and the summer camp of a village that spends winters on the Mergawar plain near Dustan, I was only exhausted instead of dead. Now I knew why Haji Ismail did not regard this climb as a sport and had vigorously tried to dissuade us from it. Climbing is a job required of the shepherds and their families, who must take the sheep to higher pastures away from the parched grass of the plain. It is not something most people would do for fun. Yet, as usual, our hosts had obliged our whims.

The climb was made considerably more interesting by the company of Mohammed. I had been hearing about Mohammed ever since my first visit to Dustan when his mother, Haji Ismail's sister, had told me she had a son who spoke perfect English and studied science at one of the Iranian universities. In the context of Dustan, that seemed so unlikely that I wondered if she wasn't exaggerating a little. After all, hadn't Khadija thought that Sheikh Avdila's Russia and my America were the same place?

But Mohammed turned out to be real. His English was phenomenal for someone who had never been out of Iran. Although he was surely no smarter than Haji Ismail, it was interesting to see the intellect of a village-born Kurd directed toward biology and formal language study instead of toward farming, hunting deer, and tribal politics. Having Mohammed in the village made a big difference in our stay. Never before had there been a person in Dustan with whom we could converse in English. But the language was not really the main thing, as we were getting along quite well in Kurdish and Persian and did not need his help in translation. It was the cultural aspect that made the difference— the comments he made, the informed answers about a village and a family he had lived in for ten years and then left miles behind. In some ways it was a great relief and in others a jarring note to have Mohammed around. But, in the end, his presence raised more questions than it answered.

During our return stay in Iran only two people spoke to me about American involvement in the last Kurdish war. One was Sheikh Avdila, who obliquely referred to the CIA. It is obvious to me now that Sheikh Avdila knew everything that was going on despite his forced official retirement. The other person who knew about the CIA did not let me off so lightly. This was Mr. Khalili, my friend from the radio station who had originally introduced me to the family of Haji Ismail.

According to Mr. Khalili, the CIA was responsible for the deaths not only of the Iraqi Kurds who took part in the fighting but of all the Kurds who had ever been rounded up by the governments in Iran and Turkey. In fact, there seemed to be no limit to America's power and culpability, in Mr. Khalili's eyes. Mr. Khalili, Jared, and I met one night to sit on a park bench. The park, like so many nice places in Iran, seemed to be turning into a parking lot as cars drove right by our bench on a narrow paved lane meant for walking.

When I complained of this to Mr. Khalili, he implied that the ruin of this park was as much the fault of the United States as was the ruin of Iran's agriculture. Some of what Mr. Khalili said was absolutely true, but, in general, his complaints were very similar to the uncontrolled blame that many Iranians like to heap on America. Even now, many liberal Iranians thought the United States put the Ayatollah Khomeini in power. Whatever happened that was bad in Iran, even in its parks, could be laid at America's doorstep.

I turned away from Mr. Khalili's intense face and looked up at the full moon. What did Mr. Khalili want from us? What did we want from him? More than any Kurd I had met in Iran, Mr. Khalili worried me. At the end of our year's stay in Rezaiyeh his health and psyche had appeared fragile. He seemed to carry the weight of all the disappointments the Kurds had experienced in his heart. Now that I had spent time with refugees in America I saw how much Mr. Khalili resembled them, the way they thought and talked. He was a refugee in his own land. Unlike Sheikh Avdila, Mr. Khalili could never be sure that we were not really CIA agents.

Mr. Khalili's criticism was a lot harder to take than that of another voluble Kurdish nationalist, Haji Ismail's nephew, Mohammed. I had spent much of my time in Dustan in Mohammed's company, talking about almost everything. Nothing seemed taboo to him.

In the new free spirit of Iran and the traditional free spirit of the Kurds I did not think it more than a little strange that we had such long discussions about his plan to travel to Turkey and all around Kurdistan politically educating and organizing his fellow Kurds. No one had spoken quite that freely to me before, but then there had been no one like Mohammed.

One day after Mohammed had gone back to his job in Tehran, Sheikh Avdila ruined it all.

"You talk to Mohammed a lot, don't you?" he asked me. I studied his face, wondering if he was worried, like Khadija, about the propriety of my spending so much time with a man who was not my husband.

"You know, some people say that Mohammed writes reports for SAVAK," said the sheikh, smiling slightly.

My stomach dropped. Other people in Iran made these sorts of accusations easily, but not Sheikh Avdila and not about his own family.

"Who says that?" I asked in a ragged voice, trying to hang on to a rapidly fading trust in this promising new friendship.

"I don't know," said the sheikh, shrugging. "But I thought I should tell you."

When we returned to Tehran from our visit in Kurdistan I hesitated but then called Mohammed at work as he had requested. He said he was eager to show us around the city or help us in any way possible. Hearing his voice again, I was disarmed. In some ways Mohammed reminded me of Haji Ismail. Indeed, Mohammed had told me at length how much he loved and respected his uncle despite all of the haji's conservative ways.

We met Mohammed at the Iranian Museum of Modern Art, an institution that reflected the Empress Farah's interest in French painting. Mohammed was with a co-worker, a woman, and I wondered if they both worked for SAVAK. Later, after staring politely at the art collection, Mohammed took us to the house of his in-laws in northern Tehran. I was very impressed that Mohammed had married a classmate from his university. No Kurdish bride had been "brought" for him.

As we were being ushered in through the courtyard and then into the usual stiffly furnished Iranian guest parlor, I began to feel doubtful again. His wife's family all referred to Mohammed as "Mohammed Khan," which seemed extremely odd since they were not Kurds. Why were they being so deferential to this village-born son of a Kurdish tribal leader? During the course of the evening Mohammed brought out a pair of Baluchi sandals made of dried date-palm fiber. Back in Dustan he had told me how his paramedical work had taken him all over Iran.

Mohammed had been to unbelievably poor and backward places—places that made Kurdish villages seem like Westchester suburbs. The plight of the Baluchis in southeastern Iran had impressed Mohammed the most, perhaps because Baluchistan, like Kurdistan, was split between countries, with both Iran and Pakistan doing everything they could to thwart Baluchi nationalism.

"Here, take these sandals," said Mohammed, handing them to me. He had told me back in Dustan that he meant to give me this souvenir from Baluchistan. Yet in Tehran I suddenly decided that he was merely offering them as *ta'arof*, so when I went home I left them sitting on the coffee table.

We saw Mohammed again on a weekday, and I wondered how he

managed to come and go from his work so easily. But Mohammed was as enthusiastic as ever. He followed us to the Russian bookstore across from Tehran University, where we browsed, looking for Russian books on Kurdish. Of course, there were none. (We had been there several times before; there never were any.)

Mohammed met us one more time, to say goodbye. In his hand were the date-palm sandals.

"You did not take them," he said, puzzled. "I gave them to you. Don't you want them?"

I was confused. Why had I been so sure that he had not really meant to give them? There had not been a hint of *ta'arof* in his manner. Perhaps I wished that there was. At least *ta'arof* would have given me an excuse to dislike him.

I wondered then, as I wonder now, if Mohammed sensed our strange coolness. More than once I opened my mouth to speak, to clear the air, but I could not. Sheikh Avdila had spoken.

As we stood on the street in Tehran shaking hands, Mohammed reminded me that his plan was to come to America and get citizenship.

"It is the only way I will be free to help my people," he said.

"But you will forget the Kurds," I suggested. "Once you are in America you will not think of returning to Kurdistan."

He regarded me earnestly. "My father and his father and his father dedicated their lives to the cause of Kurdistan."

Could these be the words of a SAVAK agent? I wondered.

We finished shaking hands and he strode quickly down the street.

"Wait," I almost cried out. "Wait, Mohammed."

But instead I said nothing as I stood unhappily watching him depart.

The Story Continues....

When I was writing *Children of the Jinn* I had a fantasy. If I could just accurately describe the mysterious, and sometimes vexing encounters I had, then someone I had written about would read my book, get in touch with me and explain what had "really" been going on. The fallacies behind this kind of thinking are numerous. But the bottom line was that I was still trying to understand the events that I experienced and witnessed during what remains one of the most vivid years of my life.

The publication of my book coincided with the taking and keeping of hostages at the American embassy and the Iranian Revolution. Interest in all things Iranian other than how to free the hostages waned in America. The ability to post letters to and from residents in this now-enemy country became problematic. As a result my knowledge of what happened to my friends in subsequent years has been limited.

When Kurds fought the repression of the central government once more the Iranian government chose to crack down with public executions – this time rebroadcast on American television. The friend from Mahabad I called "Hassan" and his wife left their comfortable existence in America and went to Kurdistan to fight alongside their fellows. They were lucky to escape with their lives.

The student I called "Ameer" got in touch after receiving a doctorate in animal husbandry. He seemed bemused to have found himself in my book and not really concerned about how he was portrayed. Nor did he have an explanation for all the misconceptions and missed communications, but instead hoped I would come to Europe and visit with him.

The nephew of Haji Ismail, the man I called "Mohammed," telephoned me one Christmas Day from his home in Texas. He expressed hurt and disbelief at the doubts his family member Sheikh Avdilah had shared with me. Mohammed further told me that he had recently gone back to his country to help with relief efforts in the aftermath of the earthquake in Bam. He traveled north to Kurdistan to see his family in Kurdistan where my dear friend "Khadija" wanted to know why he hadn't brought me with him. A Kurdish acquaintance in California told me that "Aisha" was living in Baghdad and was thrilled to have born a son.

Despite all the setbacks, the culture and language of the Kurds not only survive, but thrive. The internet is full of their wonderful music, some of it collected in remote villages not very different from the ones I visited. Kurdish film directors like Bahman Ghobadi have shown the world the marvelous spirit and culture of village Kurds. In Turkey too there is more freedom culturally than there was although this waxes and wanes depending on who is in power in Ankara. In Iraq, the Kurds have their own regional government. In social media and on the internet the Kurds have seized the opportunity to showcase their culture and their dreams.

For the Kurds and their friends, the dream of a united Kurdistan never dies. The saying that the Kurds have no friends re-surfaces in every generation, but I would rephrase it now. The Kurds have many friends and admirers, but not enough to change the policies of the governments around them. That too could change....

Glossary

When a foreign word or phrase first appears in the text, I have tried to set it off in italics and give the meaning. If it is used repeatedly, it reverts to regular font. I have listed those words here that are used repeatedly followed by the chapter numbers where they can be found. These glosses are meant only to elucidate the text; for more a complete Kurdish lexicon, check Michael Chyet's excellent Kurmanji-English and Inglizi-Kurmanji Dictionary *Ferhenga Birûskî*. Many thanks to Michael Chyet for his transcriptions into Kurmanji orthography, given in square brackets.

abeya (2) –cloak-like women's veil (from Arabic)

ajam ['ecem] (8, 13,14) – 'non-Arab;' in Arabic, this refers to Iranians; in Kurmanji to Shi'ites

chador [ç'adir] – originally 'tent' in Persian and Kurmanji; extended to refer to 'veil'

chelow kebab (1) –steamed rice with kebab (grilled meat)

deng bezh [dengbêj] (17) – traditional singer or storyteller

diwankhaneh [dîwanxane] (15) –drawing room; reception hall; place to entertain guests

finjan [fîncan] (11) – tea glass

fistan [fîstan] (12, 14) – overdress

harém (15) –separate living quarters for women and children from Arabic, meaning 'forbidden'

kesk o sheen [k'esk û şîn] (14) – dark green

khan [xan], **khanim** [xanim] (1, 9, 15, 16) – male and female titles of respect originally from Mongolian

kheyr hati [xêr hatî] (3, 7) – welcome

khilbileek [xilbilîk] (12) evil spirits that are believed to appear at sundown in the guise of real people, and who wreak havoc on their victims

khoda hafez (11) – 'goodbye' in Persian

kiras (12) – underdress with long pointed sleeve ends

kucheh [kûçe] (2, 8) – alley or lane

mobarak (12) – congratulations (from Persian)

muhajir/muhajireen – (15, 19) – refugees (from Arabic)

Newroz (intro) – the Kurdish version of No Rooz, the old Zoroastrian new year which falls on the vernal equinox

perries and **deevs** (intro) – fairies and demons (from Persian)

peesh kesh (9) -- phrase used in making a polite offer, often part of ta'arof (from Persian)

qand (7, 11, 16) – lump sugar (English 'candy' derived from this word)

shalwar [şalvar/şelwar] (11) – baggy trousers, usually worn as undergarments

Suggested Further Reading

Bird, Christiane; *A Thousand Sighs, A Thousand Revolts,* Ballantine Books, 2004

Chaliand, Gerard, ed.; *People Without a Country: The Kurds and Kurdistan,* 1978

Eagleton, William; *The Kurdish Republic of 1946;* Oxford University Press,1963

Hansen, Henny Harald; *Daughters of Allah*, George Allen and Unwin, Ltd., 1960

Hassanpour, Amir, *Nationalism and language in Kurdistan, 1918-1985*; Mellen Research University Press, 1992

Kemal, Yashar: *Memed My Hawk,* 1961

Kinnane, Derk: *The Kurds and Kurdistan*, Oxford University Press, 1964

Saleem, Hiner; *My Father's Rifle: A Childhood in Kurdistan,* Picador, 2004

Soane, E.B; *To Mesopotamia and Kurdistan in Disguise,* 1912

Acknowledgements

I would like to thank Jeff Grote, Michael Chyet and Mary Hegland for their pivotal roles in my decision to publish this second edition. Jeff's critical teasing out of English text scanned from the original made this project possible. In addition his skillful image editing breathed life back into my ancient photos. Big thanks also to my husband Phil Wasserstein for his encouragement and support in this and all my writing projects.

ABOUT THE AUTHOR

Born in New York City and raised in New Jersey and Maryland, Margaret Kahn is a graduate of Barnard College where she majored linguistics and minored in writing. She pursued graduate work at the University of Michigan where she received her masters and doctoral degrees in theoretical linguistics. Her dissertation *Borrowing and Variation in a Phonological Description of Kurmanji* was published as part of the Michigan Phonetics Laboratory Natural Language Series. She held a post-doctoral research position at the Research Lab of Electronics at MIT. Later she worked in Silicon Valley as a speech engineer. After bailing out of the tech industry, she edited and published t*echnology update* and and helped organize a conference on access to the graphical user interface for blind people. Her plays have been produced at community theaters in Northern California where she enjoys playing her harp, singing, swimming, bicycling and walking next to the ocean with her husband, the neurologist, Phil Wasserstein.

www.ingramcontent.com/pod-product-compliance
Lightning Source LLC
Chambersburg PA
CBHW031818110426
42743CB00057B/652